# Learning to Use
# WordPerfect

## SHELLY AND CASHMAN TITLES FROM BOYD & FRASER

Computer Concepts

Computer Concepts with BASIC

ClassNotes and Study Guide to Accompany Computer Concepts and Computer Concepts with BASIC

Computer Concepts with Microcomputer Applications (Lotus® version)

Computer Concepts with Microcomputer Applications (VP-Planner Plus® version)

ClassNotes and Study Guide to Accompany Computer Concepts with Microcomputer Applications (VP-Planner Plus® and Lotus® versions)

Learning to Use WordPerfect® Lotus 1-2-3® and dBASE III PLUS®

ClassNotes and Study Guide to Accompany Learning to Use WordPerfect® Lotus 1-2-3® and dBASE III PLUS®

Learning to Use WordPerfect® VP-Planner Plus® and dBASE III PLUS®

ClassNotes and Study Guide to Accompany Learning to Use WordPerfect® VP-Planner Plus® and dBASE III PLUS®

Learning to Use WordPerfect®

ClassNotes and Study Guide to Accompany Learning to Use WordPerfect®

Learning to Use VP-Planner Plus®

ClassNotes and Study Guide to Accompany Learning to Use VP-Planner Plus®

Learning to Use Lotus 1-2-3®

ClassNotes and Study Guide to Accompany Learning to Use Lotus 1-2-3®

Learning to Use dBASE III PLUS®

ClassNotes and Study Guide to Accompany Learning to Use dBASE III PLUS®

Computer Fundamentals with Application Software

Workbook and Study Guide to Accompany Computer Fundamentals with Application Software

Learning to Use SuperCalc®3 dBASE III® and WordStar® 3.3: An Introduction

Learning to Use SuperCalc®3: An Introduction

Learning to Use dBASE III®: An Introduction

Learning to Use WordStar® 3.3: An Introduction

BASIC Programming for the IBM Personal Computer

Turbo Pascal Programming


## FORTHCOMING SHELLY AND CASHMAN TITLES

RPG II and III

Systems Analysis and Design

# Learning to Use WordPerfect

**GARY B. SHELLY**

**THOMAS J. CASHMAN**

**RUTH GURGEL**

Boyd & Fraser

The Shelly and Cashman Series
Boyd & Fraser Publishing Company

Boyd & Fraser

© 1990 by Boyd & Fraser Publishing Company

Developed and produced by Solomon & Douglas
Manufactured in the United States of America

WordPerfect® is a registered trademark of WordPerfect Corporation

HyperGraphics® is a registered trademark of HyperGraphics Corporation

Library of Congress Cataloging-in-Publication Data

Shelly, Gary B.
    Learning to use Word Perfect / Gary Shelly, Thomas J. Cashman,
  Ruth Gurgel.
        p.   cm. -- (Shelly and Cashman series)
    Includes index.
    ISBN 0-87835-342-9
    1. WordPerfect (Computer program)  2. Word processing.
  I. Cashman, Thomas J.  II. Gurgel, Ruth, 1944-   .  III. Title.
  IV. Series: Shelly, Gary B.  Shelly and Cashman series.
  Z52.5.W65S46  1989
  652'.5--dc19                                        88-38289
                                                         CIP

10  9  8  7  6  5  4  3  2  1

# CONTENTS IN BRIEF

# CONTENTS

## Introduction to Computers

# Introduction to DOS

# Word Processing Using WordPerfect

## PROJECT 1—TYPING, SAVING, AND PRINTING A SIMPLE LETTER   WP 2

## PROJECT 2—CREATING A DOCUMENT WITH WORD WRAP    WP 28

## PROJECT 3—LEARNING SPECIAL FEATURES    WP 66

## PROJECT 4—MODIFYING A WORDPERFECT DOCUMENT    WP 99

# PREFACE

Today over 20 million microcomputers are in businesses, schools, and homes throughout the world. To use the power of these computers, a new generation of software, commonly called application software, has been developed. One of the most widely used types of application software is called word processing. Word processing skills are essential for students in secondary schools, colleges, universities, and technical schools, as well as for employees in nearly every area of business or government.

This textbook is designed to be used in an introductory course on word processing. It assumes no previous experience with computers and is written with continuity, simplicity, and practicality in mind—characteristics we consider essential for students who are learning about applications software for the first time. This textbook provides an introduction to computer concepts, an introduction to the use of the IBM Personal Computer Disk Operating System (PC-DOS), and detailed instructions on the use of WordPerfect, an industry-leading application software package. After completing this textbook, students will be able to implement a wide variety of applications using WordPerfect.

## ORGANIZATION OF THE TEXTBOOK

*T*his textbook consists of two introductory chapters and six projects using WordPerfect.

### An Introduction to Computers

Many students taking a course in the use of word processing software will have had little previous experience using microcomputers. For this reason this textbook begins with *Introduction to Computers*—coverage of computer hardware and software concepts important to first-time microcomputers users. These concepts include the functions of the computer and the components of a typical microcomputer system—the keyboard, the display, the processor unit, and the printer, as well as discussions of diskettes and hard disks as forms of auxiliary storage.

### An Introduction to DOS

To use a computer effectively, students need a practical knowledge of operating systems. The second chapter in this text, therefore, is *Introduction to DOS*—an introduction to the most commonly used DOS commands—such as loading DOS, formatting a diskette, and copying files.

### Six Problem-Oriented Projects

After presenting the basic microcomputer and DOS concepts, this textbook provides detailed instruction on how to use Word-Perfect. This instruction is divided into six projects. In each of the projects students learn how to use WordPerfect by way of the unique Shelly and Cashman problem-oriented approach, in which various problems are presented and then *thoroughly* explained in a step-by-step manner. Numerous carefully labeled screens and keystroke sequences illustrate the exact sequence of operations necessary to solve the problems presented. Using this approach, students are visually guided as they enter the various commands and can quickly become familiar with important concepts and techniques.

The material instructing students how to use WordPerfect is divided among the six projects as follows:

**Project 1—Typing, Saving, and Printing a Simple Letter**   The first project introduces students to using the keyboard and the WordPerfect template. After loading WordPerfect students move the cursor and view the reveal codes, a practice emphasized throughout the remaining five projects. Students then apply this know-how by creating, saving, and printing a simple letter.

**Project 2—Creating a Document with Word Wrap**   Students learn about word wrap. They then practice more efficient cursor movements. Finally they learn how to delete and restore text.

**Project 3—Learning Special Features**   While creating a memo students arrange text flush right, and learn how to center, boldface, and underline new and existing text. The value of the typeover function is demonstrated next. Finally, students practice using the indent key and right/left indent function.

**Project 4—Modifying a WordPerfect Document**   Most of the major formatting functions are discussed in this project—margin changes, line spacing, justification, and centering a page top to bottom. Clear, simple instruction on tab settings follows. Students learn about the left, center, and right aligned tab settings, as well as how to invoke leader dots while using tab settings.

**Project 5—Formatting Functions, File Management, and Macros**   Project 5 instructs students on file management within WordPerfect, creating headers and footers, using the date function, and macros. Students learn two ways to create macros by way of simple, easy to understand instruction.

**Project 6—Advanced WordPerfect Features**   Students learn search and replace functions as they change a document they created in Project 5. Finally they practice all of the speller and thesaurus functions by using the WordPerfect demonstration example.

# FEATURES

## Companion Software and Template

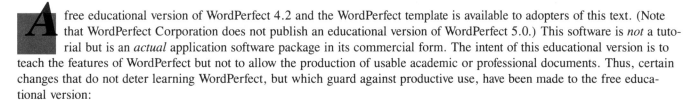A free educational version of WordPerfect 4.2 and the WordPerfect template is available to adopters of this text. (Note that WordPerfect Corporation does not publish an educational version of WordPerfect 5.0.) This software is *not* a tutorial but is an *actual* application software package in its commercial form. The intent of this educational version is to teach the features of WordPerfect but not to allow the production of usable academic or professional documents. Thus, certain changes that do not deter learning WordPerfect, but which guard against productive use, have been made to the free educational version:

- Documents on the screen can be as large as you desire, but saved documents must be 4K (about 4,000 characters).
- Data files created with the educational version can be imported to the commercial version and vice versa.
- Data files of any size can be printed through parallel printer port 1 without defining a printer.
- One font (excluding extended ASCII characters) can be supported.
- The characters *WPC appear randomly throughout printed documents.
- The educational version of the speller and thesaurus permits training on all the functions of these tools; but these tools cannot be used with any of your own documents due to diskette memory limitations.
- The Help function of the educational version presents the function-key template; as with the speller and thesaurus, memory limitations do not allow the complete help menus to be included on the educational version.

Except for these changes this educational version has the same functionality as the commercial version of WordPerfect.

Schools using this textbook may copy the free software as required for classroom use at no charge. This software is available for IBM Personal Computers and PS/2 series, and for IBM compatible computers. For information on how you may receive this free software refer to page xv.

## End-of-Project Summaries

Two helpful learning and review tools are included at the end of each project—the project summary and the keystroke summary. The Project Summary lists the key concepts covered in the project. The Keystroke Summary is an exact listing of each keystroke used to solve the project's problem.

## Student Assignments

An important feature of this textbook is the numerous and wide variety of Student Assignments provided at the end of each project. These assignments include the following: true/false questions; multiple choice questions; assignments that require students to write and/or explain various commands; and a series of realistic problems for students to analyze and solve by applying what they have learned in the project.

# THE SUPPLEMENTS TO ACCOMPANY THIS TEXT

n addition to the educational software six teaching and learning materials supplement this textbook. They are the Instructor's Materials, Data Diskette, ProTest, HyperGraphics, *Instructor's Manual to Accompany HyperGraphics*, and *ClassNotes and Study Guide*.

## Instructor's Materials

This manual includes four items to help improve instruction and learning. These items are Lesson Plans, Answers and Solutions, Test Bank, and Transparency Masters.

**Lesson Plans**—The lesson plans begin with chapter or project behavioral objectives. Next an overview of each chapter or project is included to help the instructor quickly review the purpose and key concepts. Detailed outlines of each chapter and/or project follow. These outlines are annotated with the page number of the textbook, on which the outlined material is covered; notes, teaching tips, and additional activities that the instructor might use to embellish the lesson; and a key for using the Transparency Masters.

**Answers/Solutions**—Complete answers and solutions for the Students Assignments are included to ease course administration.

**Test Bank**—This is a hard copy version of the test questions. It is comprised of three types of questions—true/false, multiple choice, and fill-in. Each project has approximately 50 true/false, 25 multiple choice, and 35 fill-ins. Answers to all of these test questions are included.

**Transparency Masters**—A Transparency Master is included for *every* figure in the textbook.

## Data Diskette

This free supplement contains the letters and memos used to teach WordPerfect in Projects 1 through 6.

## ProTest

This is Boyd & Fraser's computerized test generating system that is available free to adopters of this textbook. It includes all of the questions from the Test Bank included in the Instructor's Materials for this book. ProTest is an easy-to-use menu-driven package that provides instructor's testing flexibility and allows customizing of testing documents. For example, a user of ProTest can enter his or her own questions and can generate review sheets and answers keys. ProTest will run on any IBM PC, IBM PS/2, or IBM compatible systems with two diskette drives or a hard disk.

## HyperGraphics®

How instructors teach has changed very little in the last few decades. After all the flag waving about computer tutorials, CAI, and the like, we have learned that the human instructor is neither replaceable by a machine nor by someone who is untrained. HyperGraphics is a tool that acknowledges these facts.

**What Is HyperGraphics**? HyperGraphics is an instructional delivery system; it is a piece of software that presents all of the Shelly and Cashman textbook content with the use of graphics, color, animation, and interactivity. It is a powerful software tool that enhances classroom instruction. It is a state-of-the-art, computer-based teaching and learning environment that promotes interactive learning and self-study.

**What Hardware Do You Need for HyperGraphics**? You need three pieces of hardware to run HyperGraphics; two additional pieces are optional.

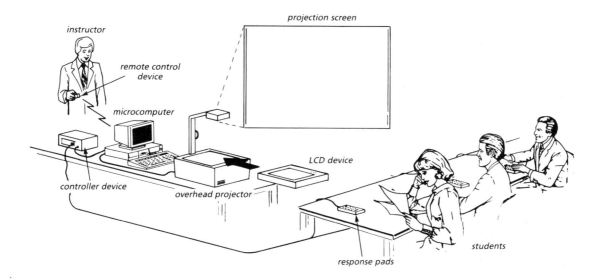

1. An IBM Personal Computer or PS/2 Series computer (or compatible) with a standard CGA graphics card.
2. A standard overhead projector and projection screen.
3. A standard projection device, such as a color projector or a liquid crystal display (LCD), that fits on the projection area of the overhead projector. The projection device is connected to the personal computer, resulting in the projection of the computer's screen.
4. A hand-held remote control device (*optional*), that allows the instructor to navigate throughout the presentation materials and still move freely around the classroom.
5. A set of at least eight response pads (*optional*), small pads consisting of 10 digit keys, that can be pressed to indicate a student's response. (These pads are linked to the microcomputer by a controller device.)

**How Does the Instructor Use HyperGraphics**? HyperGraphics is very easy to use. The instructor presses the appropriate keys on the hand-held remote control device or the keyboard and thereby controls the screen display. This display is projected through the LCD to the overhead projector. The instructor has complete control over the order and pacing of how the lessons are taught. By pushing one or more keys he or she can do such things as:

- View and select from the lesson menu
- Deliver the lesson's instructional materials in sequence
- Repeat any portion of a lesson to reinforce or review material
- Move ahead to specific portions of the lesson
- View the chapter objectives at any time
- View one or more questions about the lesson at any time
- Have students respond to one or more questions via the response pads
- Log students' responses to questions

- Randomly select students to respond to a question
- End a lesson
- Return directly to that point in the lesson where he or she stopped in the previous class meeting

**What Are the Benefits of Using the Student Response Pads**? Instructors have never before had the opportunity to assess student comprehension and retention of class instruction immediately and accurately. They can now do so if they use HyperGraphics with the student response pads.

For example, suppose the instructor presents a multiple choice question on the screen at the end of a segment of a lesson. Students will see an indication light illuminate on their response pads, and they'll have a period of time (controlled by the instructor) to press the button corresponding to the answer of their choice. The answers are tabulated by the microcomputer, and an optional aggregate bar chart of the answers selected is immediately available for viewing by the entire class. Each student's answer is also available on disk for later analysis or review. Thus, the progress of the entire class as well as each student can be tracked throughout the course.

Using these response pads results in substantial and *measurable* benefits to instructors as well as to students. The pads provide a rich teaching and learning experience and actively promote student participation.

**What Does HyperGraphics Cost**? HyperGraphics is *free* to adopters of this textbook. The only cost is for the computer and the projection device and screen, equipment that most educational institutions already possess. (Student response pads and the controller device are available at an extra charge.) HyperGraphics revolutionizes classroom instruction. It brings classroom instruction alive through graphic imagery and interactivity, and it can provide immediate and direct feedback to students and instructors.

## Instructor's Manual to Accompany HyperGraphics

This manual contains teaching tips and guidelines for enhancing your classroom instruction using HyperGraphics. Easy-to-follow installation instructions are also included.

## ClassNotes and Study Guide

The active learning experience of HyperGraphics can also be promoted if students purchase this supplement. As its title suggests, the *ClassNotes and Study Guide* serves three purposes. First, it relieves students from laborious and tedious notetaking responsibilities, freeing them to concentrate on the instruction. Second, if used with HyperGraphics, it provides an active learning experience for students to fill in key terms and key concepts during classroom instruction. Third, used without HyperGraphics this supplement provides a chance for students to review and study independently, as they can with traditional study guides.

## ACKNOWLEDGMENTS

*L*earning to Use WordPerfect would not be the quality textbook it is without the help of many people. We would like to express our appreciation to the following people, who worked diligently to assure a quality publication: Jeanne Huntington, typesetter; Michael Broussard and Ken Russo, artists; Becky Herrington, production and art coordinator; Sheryl Rose, manuscript editor; Scott Alkire and Martha Simmons, production assistants; Mary Douglas, director of production; Susan Solomon, director of development; and Tom Walker, Publisher and Vice President of Boyd & Fraser.

# For More Information about the Shelly and Cashman Series

## 1 ORDER INFORMATION
5101 Madison Road
Cincinnati, OH 45227-1490
General Telephone–513-527-6945
Telephone: 1-800-543-8440
FAX: 513-527-6979
Telex: 214371

### FACULTY SUPPORT INFORMATION
5101 Madison Road
Cincinnati, OH 45227-1490
General Telephone–513-527-6950
Telephone: 1-800-543-8444

| | | |
|---|---|---|
| Alabama | Massachusetts | Pennsylvania |
| Connecticut | Michigan (Lower)** | Rhode Island |
| Delaware | Mississippi | South Carolina |
| Florida | New Hampshire | Tennessee |
| Georgia | New Jersey | Vermont |
| Indiana* | New York | Virginia |
| Kentucky | North Carolina | West Virginia |
| Maine | Ohio | District of Columbia |
| Maryland | | |

*Except for ZIP Code Areas 463, 464. These areas contact Region 2 Office.
**Except for the Upper Peninsula. This area contacts Region 2 Office.

## 2 ORDER INFORMATION and FACULTY SUPPORT INFORMATION
355 Conde Street
West Chicago, IL 60185
General Telephone–312-231-6000
Telephone: 1-800-543-7972

| | | |
|---|---|---|
| Illinois | Minnesota | North Dakota |
| Indiana* | Missouri | South Dakota |
| Iowa | Nebraska | Wisconsin |
| Michigan (Upper)** | | |

*Only for ZIP Code Areas 463, 464. Other areas contact Region 1 office.
**Only for Upper Peninsula. Other areas contact Region 1 office.

## 3 ORDER INFORMATION
13800 Senlac Drive
Suite 100
Dallas, TX 75234
General Telephone–214-241-8541
Telephone: 1-800-543-7972

### FACULTY SUPPORT INFORMATION
5101 Madison Road
Cincinnati, OH 45227-1490
General Telephone–513-527-6950
Telephone: 1-800-543-8444

| | | |
|---|---|---|
| Arkansas | Louisiana | Texas |
| Colorado | New Mexico | Wyoming |
| Kansas | Oklahoma | |

## 4 ORDER INFORMATION and FACULTY SUPPORT INFORMATION
6185 Industrial Way
Livermore, CA 94550
General Telephone–415-449-2280
Telephone: 1-800-543-7972

| | | |
|---|---|---|
| Alaska | Idaho | Oregon |
| Arizona | Montana | Utah |
| California | Nevada | Washington |
| Hawaii | | |

# School Software Direct Order Form

□ Ship to student    □ Ship to reseller (replacement stock)

Qualifying teachers, as well as college, university, and other post-secondary students, can now purchase WordPerfect Corporation (WPCORP) software directly from WPCORP at a reduced price. To qualify, a participant must be a full-time teacher/administrator or currently enrolled as a full-time post-secondary student, and must agree in writing not to resell or transfer any package purchased under this program.

If you satisfy these qualifying conditions and would like to purchase software directly from WPCORP under the School Software Program, complete the following six steps and sign at the bottom of the form.

**Step 1.** From the list below, select the appropriate software and disk size for your computer (please note that you are limited to *one* package of each program) and mark an "x" in the corresponding box(es).

| Product | Price* | Disk Size |
|---|---|---|
| □ WordPerfect 5.0—IBM Personal Computers | $135.00 | □ 3½"  □ 5¼" |
| □ WordPerfect 4.2—IBM PC & Compatibles | 125.00 | □ 3½"  □ 5¼" |
| □ WordPerfect—Apple IIe/IIc | 59.00 | □ 3½" & 5¼" |
| □ WordPerfect—Apple IIGS | 59.00 | □ 3½" |
| □ WordPerfect—Amiga | 99.00 | □ 3½" |
| □ WordPerfect—Atari ST | 99.00 | □ 3½" |
| □ WordPerfect—Macintosh | 99.00 | □ 3½" |
| □ PlanPerfect—IBM PC & Compatibles | 99.00 | □ 3½"  □ 5¼" |
| □ DataPerfect—IBM PC & Compatibles | 150.00 | □ 3½" & 5¼" |
| □ WordPerfect Library—IBM PC & Compatibles | 59.00 | □ 3½" & 5¼" |
| □ WordPerfect Library—Amiga | 59.00 | □ 3½" |
| □ WordPerfect Executive—IBM PC & Compatibles | 79.00 | □ 3½" & 5¼" |
| □ Junior WordPerfect—IBM PC & Compatibles | 35.00 | □ 5¼" |
| □ WordPerfect, Foreign Versions—IBM PC & Compatibles | 175.00 | □ 3½"  □ 5¼" |
| Language _____ | | |
| □ WordPerfect Speller, Foreign Versions—IBM PC & Compatibles | 40.00 | □ 3½"  □ 5¼" |
| Language _____ | | |

*No changes or additions can be made to this list.

**Step 2.** Make a photocopy of your current Student ID or Faculty card *and* a photocopy of some well known form of identification displaying your social security number, such as your Driver License or Social Security Card. (WPCORP will hold this information strictly confidential and use it only to guard against duplicate purchases.) Your school ID must show current enrollment. (If it does not show a date, you must send verification of current enrollment.) If you have serious reservations about providing a social security number, call the Education Division at (801) 227-7131 to establish clearance to purchase any of the above software products at these special prices.

**Step 3.** Enter your social security number:  __ __ __ – __ __ – __ __ __ __ .

**Step 4.** Enclose payment for the total cost of the package(s) ordered with personal check, money order, Visa, or MasterCard.

Account # _____    Expiration Date _____    □ VISA    □ MasterCard

(Make check or money order payable to WordPerfect Corporation.)

**Step 5.** List your shipping address and the address of your local computer store (dealer) in the space provided:

Ship To _____    Designated Dealer  Boyd & Fraser Publishing

_____    20 Park Plaza

_____    Boston, MA 02116

Phone _____    Phone  (617) 426-2292

**Step 6.** Enclose this signed and completed form, the photocopies of your identification cards, and your signed check or money order (or Visa or MasterCard account number and expiration date) in an envelope and mail to School Software Program, WordPerfect Corporation, 1555 N. Technology Way, Orem, UT 84057.

The information provided herein is correct and accurate, and I will abide by the restricting conditions outlined by WPCORP in this document. I understand that at its sole discretion, WPCORP may refuse any order for any reason.

Signature _____    Date _____

*Utah residents add 6.25% sales tax. Prices are quoted in U.S. dollars and apply to U.S. delivery for U.S. customers *only.*

WordPerfect Corporation • 1555 N. Technology Way • Orem, Utah 84057 • (801) 225-5000

# Introduction to Computers

# Introduction to Computers

## OBJECTIVES

- Define computer and discuss the four basic computer operations: input, processing, output and storage.
- Define data and information.
- Explain the principal components of the computer and their use.
- Describe the use and handling of diskettes and hard disks.
- Discuss computer software and explain the difference between application software and system software.

---

*T*he computer is an integral part of the daily lives of most individuals. Small computers, called microcomputers or personal computers (Figure 1), have made computing available to almost everyone. Thus, your ability to understand and use a computer is rapidly becoming an important skill. This book teaches you how to use a computer by teaching you how to use software applications. Before you learn about the application software, however, you must understand what a computer is, the components of a computer, and the types of software used on computers. These topics are explained in this Introduction.

**FIGURE 1**
**Microcomputers: The IBM PS/2 Model 30 (left) and Compaq Deskpro 386S (right) are two examples of popular microcomputer systems.**

# WHAT IS A COMPUTER?

*A* **computer** is an electronic device, operating under the control of instructions stored in its own memory unit, that accepts input or data, processes data arithmetically and logically, produces output from the processing, and stores the results for future use. All computers perform basically the same four operations:

1. **Input operations**, by which data is entered into the computer for processing.
2. **Arithmetic operations**, are addition, subtraction, multiplication, and division. **Logical operations** are those that compare data to determine if one value is less than, equal to, or greater than another value.
3. **Output operations**, which make the information generated from processing available for use.
4. **Storage operations**, which store data electronically for future reference.

These operations occur through the use of electronic circuits contained on small silicon chips inside the computer (Figure 2). Because these electronic circuits rarely fail and the data flows along these circuits at close to the speed of light, processing can be accomplished in millionths of a second. Thus, the computer is a powerful tool because it can perform these four operations reliably and quickly.

**FIGURE 2**
**This microprocessor is shown "packaged" and ready for installation in a microcomputer.**

# WHAT IS DATA AND INFORMATION?

*T*he four operations that can be performed using a computer all require data. **Data** is raw facts, the numbers and words that are suitable for processing in a predetermined manner on a computer to produce information. Examples of data include the hours posted to a payroll time card or the words comprising a memo to the sales staff. A computer accepts data, processes data and, as a result of the processing, produces output in the form of useful information. **Information** can therefore be defined as data that has been processed into a form that has meaning and is useful.

# WHAT ARE THE COMPONENTS OF A COMPUTER?

*T*o understand how computers process data into information, it is necessary to examine the primary components of the computer. The four primary components of a computer are:

    1. input devices    3. output devices
    2. processor unit    4. auxiliary storage units

Figure 3 illustrates the relationship of the various components to one another.

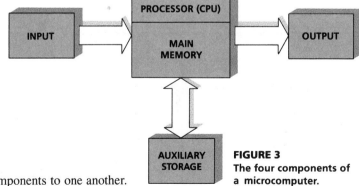

**FIGURE 3**
**The four components of a microcomputer.**

## Input Devices

**Input devices** enter data into main memory. Several input devices exist. The two most commonly used are the keyboard and the mouse.

**The Keyboard.** The input device you will most commonly use on computers is the **keyboard** on which you manually "key in" or type the data (Figures 4a and b). The keyboard on most computers is laid out in much the same manner as a typewriter. Figures 4a and b show two styles of IBM keyboards: the original standard keyboard and a newer enhanced keyboard. Although the layouts are somewhat different, the use of the keys is the same.

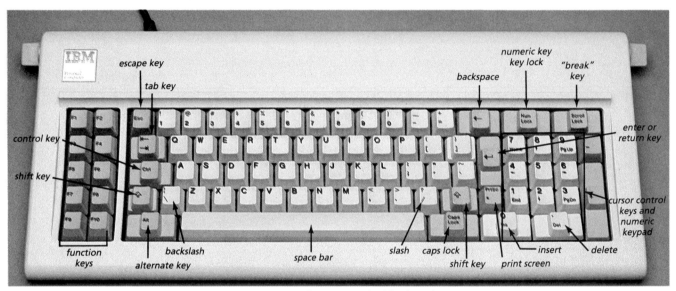

**FIGURE 4a** The IBM standard keyboard

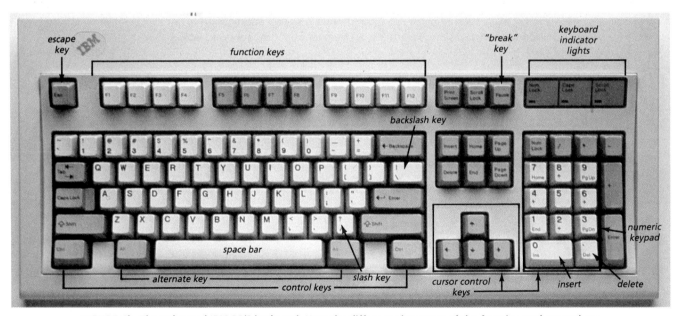

**FIGURE 4b** The enhanced IBM PS/2 keyboard. Note the different placement of the function and cursor keys.

A **numeric keypad** in the 10-key adding machine or calculator key format is located on the right side of both keyboards. This arrangement of keys allows you to enter numeric data rapidly. To activate the numeric pad on the keyboards you press the Num Lock key, located above the numeric keys. On the enhanced keyboard, a light turns on at the top right of the keyboard to indicate that the numeric keys are in use. You may also invoke the number keys by using the shift key together with the number keys located across the top of the typewriter keys.

**Cursor control keys** determine where data is displayed on the screen. The **cursor** is a symbol, such as an underline character, which indicates where on the screen the next character will be entered. On the keyboards in Figures 4a and b the cursor control keys or arrow keys are included as part of the numeric keypad. The enhanced keyboard has a second set of cursor control keys located between the typewriter keys and the numeric keypad. If you press the **Num Lock** key at the top of the numeric keypad, numeric characters appear on the screen when you press the numeric key pad keys. You can still use the cursor control keys by pressing the Shift key together with the desired cursor control key. If the Num Lock key is engaged (indicated by the fact that as you press any numeric key pad key, a number appears on the screen) you can return to the standard mode for cursor control keys by pressing the Num Lock key.

The cursor control keys allow you to move the cursor around the screen. Pressing the **Up Arrow** key ↑ causes the cursor to move upward on the screen. The **Down Arrow** key ↓ causes the cursor to move down; the **Left** ← and **Right** → **Arrow** keys cause the cursor to move left and right on the screen.

The other keys on the keypad—(PgUp), (PgDn), Home, and End—have various uses depending on the microcomputer software you use. Some programs make no use of these keys; others use the (**PgUp**) and (**PgDn**) keys, for example, to display previous or following pages of data on the screen. Some software uses the **Home** key to move the cursor to the upper left corner of the screen. Likewise, the **End** key may be used to move the cursor to the end of a line of text or to the bottom of the screen, depending on the software.

**Function keys** on many keyboards can be programmed to accomplish specific tasks. For example, a function key might be used as a help key. Whenever that key is pressed, messages appear that give instructions to help the user. Another function key might be programmed to cause all data displayed on the CRT screen to be printed on a printer whenever the key is pressed. In Figure 4a, ten function keys are on the left portion of the standard keyboard. In Figure 4b, twelve function keys are located across the top of the enhanced keyboard.

Other keys have special uses in some applications. The **Shift** keys have several functions. They work as they do on a typewriter, allowing you to type capital letters. The Shift key is always used to type the symbol on the upper portion of any key on the keyboard. Also, to use the cursor control keys temporarily as numeric entry keys, you can press the Shift key to switch into numeric mode. If, instead, you have pressed the Num Lock key to use the numeric keys, you can press the Shift key to shift temporarily back to the cursor mode.

The keyboard has a Backspace key, a Tab key, an Insert key and a Delete key that perform the functions their names indicate.

The **Escape (Esc)** key also has many different uses. In some microcomputer software it is used to cancel an instruction but this use is by no means universally true.

As with the Escape key, many keys are assigned special meaning by the microcomputer software. Certain keys may be used more frequently than others by one piece of software but rarely used by another. It is this flexibility that allows the computer to be used in so many different applications.

**The Mouse**    An alternative input device you might encounter is a mouse. A **mouse** (Figure 5) is a pointing device that can be used instead of the cursor control keys. You lay the palm of your hand over the mouse and move it across the surface of a table or desk. The mouse detects the direction of your movement and sends this information to the screen to move the cursor. You push buttons on top of the mouse to indicate your choices of actions from lists displayed on the computer screen.

**FIGURE 5**
A mouse can be used as a cursor control device.

## The Processor

The **processor unit** is composed of the central processing unit (CPU) and main memory (see Figure 3). The **central processing unit** contains the electronic circuits that actually cause processing to occur. The CPU interprets instructions to the computer, performs the logical and arithmetic processing operations, and causes the input and output operations to occur.

**Main memory** consists of electronic components that store numbers, letters of the alphabet, and characters such as decimal points or dollar signs. Any data to be processed must be stored in main memory.

**FIGURE 6**
This dot matrix printer, the IBM Proprinter II, is often used to print documents from an IBM PC and other popular microcomputers.

The amount of main memory in microcomputers is typically measured in **kilobytes** (K or KB), which equal 1,024 memory locations. A memory location, or byte, usually stores one character. Therefore, a computer with 640K can store approximately 640,000 characters. The amount of main memory for microcomputers may range from 64K to several million characters, also called a **megabyte (MB)**, or more.

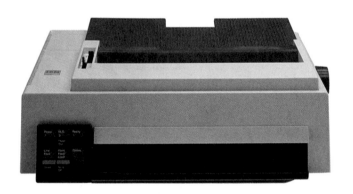

## Output Devices

Output devices make the information resulting from processing available for use. The output from computers can be presented in many forms, such as a printed report or color graphics. When a computer is used for processing tasks, such as word processing, spreadsheets, or database management, the two output devices most commonly used are the **printer** and the televisionlike display device called a **screen**, **monitor**, or **CRT** (cathode ray tube).

**Printers**    Printers used with computers can be either impact printers or nonimpact printers.

An **impact printer** prints by striking an inked ribbon against the paper. One type of impact printer often used with microcomputers is the dot matrix printer (Figure 6). To print a character, a **dot matrix printer** generates a dot pattern representing a particular character. The printer then activates vertical wires in a print head contained on the printer, so that selected wires press against the ribbon and paper, creating a character. As you see in Figure 7, the character consists of a series of dots produced by the print head wires. In the actual size created by the printer, the characters are clear and easy to read.

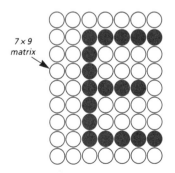

*7 x 9 matrix*

Dot matrix printers vary in the speed with which they can print characters. These speeds range from 50 characters per second to over 300 characters per second. Generally, the higher the speed, the higher the cost of the printer.

Many dot matrix printers also allow you to choose two or more sizes and densities of character. Typical sizes include condensed print, standard print, and enlarged print. In addition, each of the three print sizes can be printed with increased density, or darkness (Figure 8).

**FIGURE 8**
These samples show condensed, standard, and enlarged print. These can all be produced by a dot-matrix printer.

```
This line of type is in CONDENSED Print
AaBbCcDdEeFfGgHhIiJjKkLlMmNnOoPpQqRrSsTtUuVvWwXxYyZz 0123456789

This line of type is in STANDARD Print
AaBbCcDdEeFfGgHhIiJjKkLlMmNnOoPpQqRrSsTtUuVvWwXxYyZz 0123456789

This line of type is in ENLARGED Pr
AaBbCcDdEeFfGgHhIiJjKkLlMmNnOoPpQqR
UuVvWwXxYyZz 0123456789
```

Another useful feature of dot matrix printers is their ability to print graphics. The dots are printed not to form characters, but rather to form graphic images. This feature can be especially useful when working with a spreadsheet program in producing graphs of the numeric values contained on the worksheet.

When users require printed output of high quality, such as for business or legal correspondence, a letter-quality printer is often used. The term **letter quality** refers to the quality of the printed character that is suitable for formal or professional business letters. A letter-quality printed character is a fully formed, solid character like those made by typewriters. It is not made up of a combination of dots, as by a dot matrix printer.

The letter-quality compact printer most often used with microcomputers is the **daisy wheel printer**. It consists of a type element containing raised characters that strike the paper through an inked ribbon.

**Nonimpact** printers, such as ink jet printers and laser printers, form characters by means other than striking a ribbon against paper (Figure 9). An **ink jet printer** forms a character by using a nozzle that sprays drops of ink onto the page. Ink jet printers produce relatively high-quality images and print between 150 and 270 characters per second.

**FIGURE 9**
Two nonimpact printers: a laser printer (left) and inkjet printer (right)

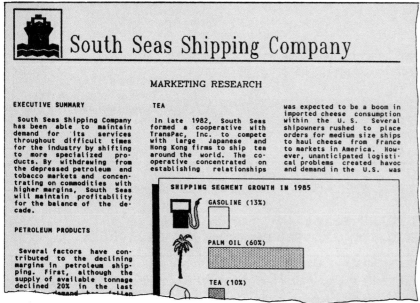

**FIGURE 10**
**Sample output from a laser
printer**

**Laser printers** convert data from the personal computer into a beam of laser light that is focused on a photoconductor, forming the images to be printed. The photoconductor attracts particles of toner that are fused onto paper to produce an image. An advantage of the laser printer is that numbers and alphabetic data can be printed in varying sizes and type styles. The output produced is very high quality (Figure 10), with the images resembling professional printing rather than typewritten characters. Laser printers for microcomputers can cost from $1,500 to over $8,000. They can print six to eight pages of text and graphics per minute.

## Computer Screens

The computer you use probably has a screen sometimes called a **monitor** or **CRT** (cathode ray tube). The **screen** displays the data entered on the keyboard and messages from the computer.

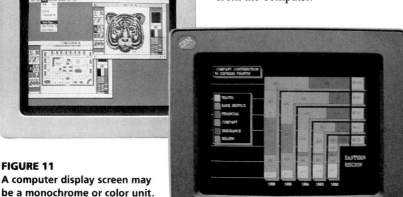

**FIGURE 11**
**A computer display screen may
be a monochrome or color unit.**

Two general types of screens are used on computers. A **monochrome** screen (Figure 11) uses a single color (green, amber, or white) to display text against a dark background. Some monochrome screens are designed to display only characters; others can display both characters and graphics. Although they cannot display multiple colors, some monochrome screens simulate full color output by using up to 64 shades of the screen's single color.

The second type of screen is a color display. These devices are generally able to display 256 colors at once from a range of more than 256,000 choices.

**Computer graphics**, charts, graphs, or pictures, can also be displayed on a screen so that the information can be easily and quickly understood. Graphics are often used to present information to others, for example, to help people make business decisions.

## Auxiliary Storage

Main memory is not large enough to store the instructions and data for all your applications at one time, so data not in use must be stored elsewhere. **Auxiliary storage** devices are used to store instructions and data when they are not being used in main memory.

**Diskettes**   One type of auxiliary storage you will use often with microcomputers is the **diskette**. A diskette is a circular piece of oxide-coated plastic that stores data as magnetic spots. Diskettes are available in various sizes. Microcomputers most commonly use diskettes that are 5¼ inches or 3½ inches in diameter (Figure 12).

To read data stored on a diskette or to store data on a diskette, you insert the diskette in a diskette drive (Figure 13). You can tell that the computer is reading data on the diskette or writing data on it because a light on the disk drive will come on while read/write operations are taking place. Do not try to insert or remove a diskette when the light is on. You could easily cause permanent damage to the data stored on it.

The storage capacities of diskette drives and the related diskettes can vary widely (Figure 14). The number of characters that can be stored on a diskette by a diskette drive depends on three factors: (1) the number of sides of the diskette used; (2) the recording density of the bits on a track; and (3) the number of tracks on the diskette.

Early diskettes and diskette drives were designed so that data could be recorded only on one side of the diskette. These drives are called **single-sided drives**. **Double-sided diskettes**, the typical type of diskette used now, provide increased storage capacity because data can be recorded on both sides of the diskette. Diskette drives found on many microcomputers are 5¼-inch, double-sided disk drives that can store approximately 360,000 bytes on the diskette. Another popular type is the 3½-inch diskette, which, although physically smaller, stores from 720,000 to 1.44 million bytes—over twice the capacity of the 5¼-inch diskette. An added benefit of the 3½-inch diskette is its rigid plastic housing, which protects the magnetic surface of the diskette.

The second factor affecting diskette storage capacity is the **recording density** provided by the diskette drive. (The recording density is stated in technical literature as the bpi—the number of bits that can be recorded on a diskette in a one-inch circumference of the innermost track on the diskette.) For the user, the diskettes and diskette drives are identified as being **single density**, **double density**, or **high density**. You need to be aware of the density of diskettes used by your system because data stored on high-density diskettes, for example, cannot be processed by a computer that has only double-density diskette drives.

The third factor that influences the number of characters that can be stored on a diskette is the number of tracks on the diskette. A **track** is a very narrow recording band forming a full circle around the diskette (Figure 15 on the following page). The width of this recording band depends on the number of tracks on the diskette. The recording bands are separated from each other by a very narrow blank gap. The tracks are established by the diskette drive using the diskette, and they are not visible.

**FIGURE 12**
Diskettes come in both 5 1/4-inch and 3 1/2-inch sizes. One advantage of the 3 1/2-inch type is its rigid plastic housing, which helps prevent damage to the diskette.

**FIGURE 13**
To read from a diskette or to store data on it, you must insert the diskette into the computer's diskette drive.

| DIAMETER SIZE (INCHES) | DESCRIPTION | CAPACITY (BYTES) |
|---|---|---|
| 5.25 | Single-sided, double-density | 160KB/180KB |
| 5.25 | Double-sided, double-density | 320KB/360KB |
| 5.25 | High-capacity, double-density | 1.25MB |
| 3.5 | Double-sided | 720KB |
| 3.5 | Double-sided, double-density | 1.44MB |

**FIGURE 14**
Types of diskettes and their capacities

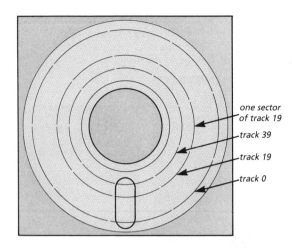

**FIGURE 15**
**How a diskette is formatted**

one sector
of track 19

track 39

track 19

track 0

Each track on a diskette is divided into sectors. **Sectors** are the basic units for diskette storage. When data is read from a diskette, a minimum of one full sector is read. When data is stored on a diskette, one full sector is written at one time. The number of sectors per track and the number of characters that can be stored in each sector are defined by a special formatting program that is used with the computer.

Data stored in sectors on a diskette must be retrieved and placed into main memory to be processed. The time required to access and retrieve data, called the **access time**, can be important in some applications. The access time for diskettes varies from about 175 milliseconds (one millisecond equals 1/1000 of a second) to approximately 300 milliseconds. On average, data stored in a single sector on a diskette can be retrieved in approximately 1/5 to 1/3 of a second.

Diskette care is important to preserve stored data. Properly handled, diskettes can store data indefinitely. However, the surface of the diskette can be damaged and the data stored can be lost if the diskette is handled improperly. A diskette will give you very good service if you follow a few simple procedures (Figure 16):

Don't touch the disk surface. It is easily contaminated, which causes errors.

Don't use near magnetic field including a telephone. Data can be lost if exposed.

Keep disk in protective envelope when not in use.

Don't bend or fold the disk.

Don't place heavy objects on the disk.

Insert disk carefully. Grasp upper edge and place it into the disk drive.

Don't use rubber bands or paper clips on the disk.

Don't expose the disk to excessive heat for sunlight.

Don't write on the index label with pencil or ballpoint. Use felt-tip pen only.

Don't use erasers on the disk label.

**FIGURE 16**
**How to care for and handle diskettes**

1. Store the diskette in its protective envelope when not in use. This procedure is especially necessary for the 5¼-inch diskette that has an oval opening, the **access window**, which permits the read/write heads to access the diskette but also allows the diskette to be easily damaged or soiled.

2. Keep diskettes in their original box or in a special diskette storage box to protect the diskette from dirt and dust and prevent it from being accidentally bent. Store the container away from heat and direct sunlight. Magnetic and electrical equipment, including telephones, radios, and televisions, can erase the data on a diskette so do not place diskettes near such devices. Do not place heavy objects on the diskette, because the weight can pinch the covering, causing damage when the disk drive attempts to rotate the diskette.

3. To affix one of the self-adhesive labels supplied with most diskettes, write or type the information on the label *before* placing the label on the diskette. If the label is already on the diskette, *do not* use an eraser to change the label. If you must write on the label after it is on the diskette, use only a felt-tip pen, *not* a pen or pencil, and press lightly.

4. To use the diskette, carefully remove it from the envelope by grasping the diskette on the side away from the side to be inserted into the disk drive. Slide the diskette carefully into the slot on the disk drive. If the disk drive has a latch or door, close it. If it is difficult to close the disk drive door, do not force it—the diskette may not be inserted fully, and forcing the door closed may damage the diskette. Reinsert the diskette if necessary, and try again to close the door.

The diskette **write-protect** feature (see Figure 17) prevents the accidental erasure of the data stored on a diskette by preventing the diskette drive from writing new data or erasing

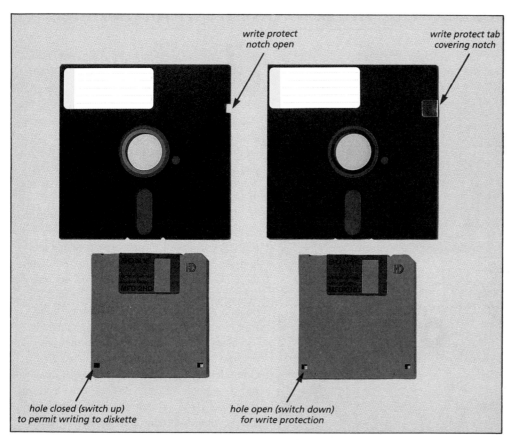

write protect
notch open

write protect tab
covering notch

hole closed (switch up)
to permit writing to diskette

hole open (switch down)
for write protection

**FIGURE 17**
The write-protect notch of the 5 1/4-inch disk on the left is open and therefore data could be written to the disk. The notch of the 5 1/4-inch disk on the right, however, is covered. Data could not be written to this disk. The reverse situation is true for the 3 1/2-inch disk. Data cannot be written on the 3 1/2-inch disk on the right because the small black piece of plastic is not covering the window in the lower left corner. Plastic covers the window of the 3 1/2-inch disk on the left, so data can be written on this disk.

existing data. On a 5¼-inch diskette, a **write-protect notch** is located on the side of the diskette. A special **write-protect label** is placed over this notch whenever you want to protect the data. On the 3½-inch diskette, a small switch can slide to cover and uncover the write protection notch. On a 3½-inch diskette, when the notch is uncovered the data is protected.

**Hard Disk**   Another form of auxiliary storage is a hard disk. A **hard disk** consists of one or more rigid metal platters coated with a metal oxide material that allows data to be magnetically recorded on the surface of the platters (Figure 18). Although hard disks are available in cartridge form, most hard disks cannot be removed from the computer and thus are called "fixed disks." As with diskettes, the data is recorded on hard disks on a series of tracks. The tracks are divided into sectors when the disk is formatted.

The hard disk platters spin at high rate of speed, typically 3,600 revolutions per minute. When reading data from the disk, the read head senses the magnetic spots that are recorded on the disk along the various tracks and transfers that data to main memory. When writing, the data is transferred from main memory and is stored as magnetic spots on the tracks on the recording surface of one or more of the disks. Unlike diskette drives, the read/write heads on a fixed disk drive do not actually touch the surface of the disk.

The number of platters permanently mounted on the spindle of a hard disk varies from one to four. On most drives each surface of the platter can be used to store data. Thus, if a hard disk drive uses one platter, two surfaces are available for data. If the drive uses two platters, four sets of read/write heads read and record data from the four surfaces. Storage capacities of fixed disks for microcomputers range from five million characters to over 100 million characters.

**FIGURE 18**
Cutaway of typical hard disk construction.

## SUMMARY OF THE COMPONENTS OF A COMPUTER

*T*he components of a complete computer are illustrated in Figure 19. (Compare this illustration to the computer you will be using.) Input to the computer occurs through the keyboard. As data is keyed on the keyboard, the data is transferred to main memory. In addition, the keyed data is displayed on the computer display screen. The output may be printed on a printer or may be displayed on the computer screen.

The processor unit, which contains main memory and the central processing unit (CPU), consists of circuit boards inside a housing called the **system unit**. In addition to the CPU and main memory, circuit boards inside the system unit contain electronic components that allow communication with the input, output, and auxiliary storage devices.

Data can be transferred from main memory and stored on a diskette or a hard disk. Computers may have a single diskette drive, two diskette drives, one diskette drive and one hard disk drive, or several other combinations. The keyboard, system unit, printer, screen, and auxiliary storage devices are called **computer hardware**.

**FIGURE 19**
A computer system

## WHAT IS COMPUTER SOFTWARE?

*A* computer's input, processing, output, and storage operations are controlled by instructions collectively called a **computer program** or **software**. A computer program specifies the sequence in which operations are to occur in the computer. For example, a person may give instructions that allow data to be entered from a keyboard and stored in main memory. Another time the program might issue an instruction to perform a calculation using data in main memory. When a task has been completed, a program could give instructions to direct the computer to print a report, display information on the screen, draw a color graph on a color display unit, or store data on a diskette. When directing the operations to be performed, a program must be stored in main memory. Computer programs are written by computer programmers.

Most computer users purchase the software they need for their computer systems. The two major categories of computer software are (1) application software and (2) system software.

## Application Software

**Application software** allows you to perform an application-related function on a computer. A wide variety of programs is available, but for microcomputers the three most widely used types of application software are word processing, spreadsheet, and database management.

**Word Processing Software**   **Word processing software** such as WordPerfect enables you to use a computer to create documents.

As you use a word processing program, words are keyed in, displayed on the screen, and stored in main memory. If necessary, you can easily correct errors by adding or deleting words, sentences, paragraphs, or pages. You can also establish margins, define page lengths, and perform many other functions involving the manipulation of the written word.

After you have created and corrected your text, you can print it and store it on auxiliary storage for reuse or future reference.

**Spreadsheet Software**   **Spreadsheet software** is used for reporting and decision making within organizations. At home, you can use a spreadsheet program for budgeting, income tax planning, or tracking your favorite team's scores. You might choose VP Planner or Lotus 1-2-3 to enter the values and formulas needed to perform the desired calculations.

One of the more powerful features of spreadsheet application software is its ability to handle "what-if" questions such as, "What would be the effect on profit if sales increased 12% this year?" The values on the worksheet could easily be recalculated to provide the answer.

**Database Software**   **Database software** is used to store, organize, update, and retrieve data. Packages such as **dBASE III Plus** store data in a series of files. A **file** is a collection of related data. The data can be organized in the manner you select for your particular application. Once stored in the database, data can be retrieved for use in a variety of ways. For example, data can be retrieved based on the name of an employee in an employee file and full reports can be generated.

## System Software

**System software** consists of programs that start up the computer—load, execute, store, and retrieve files—and perform a series of utility functions. A part of the system software available with most computers is the operating system. An **operating system** is a collection of programs that provides an interface between you or your application programs and the computer hardware itself to control and manage the operation of the computer.

System software, including operating systems, available on computers performs the following basic functions: (1) booting, or starting, the computer operation, (2) interfacing with users, and (3) coordinating the system's access to its various devices.

**"Booting" the Computer**   When a computer is turned on, the operating system is loaded into main memory by a set of instructions contained internally within the hardware of the computer. This process is called **booting** the computer. When the operating system is loaded into main memory, it is stored in a portion of main memory.

**Interface with Users**   To communicate with the operating system, the user must enter commands that the operating system can interpret and act upon. The commands can vary from copying a file from one diskette to another, to loading and executing application software.

**Coordinating System Devices**   Computer hardware is constructed with electrical connections from one device to another. The operating system translates a program's requirements to access a specific hardware device, such as a printer. The operating system can also sense whether the devices are ready for use, or if there is some problem in using a device, such as a printer not being turned on and, therefore, not ready to receive output.

## SUMMARY OF INTRODUCTION TO COMPUTERS

 s you learn to use the software taught in this book, you will also become familiar with the components and operation of your computer system. You can refer to this introduction when you need help understanding how the components of your system function.

## SUMMARY

1. A **computer** is an electronic device operating under the control of instructions stored in its memory unit.
2. All computers perform basically the same four operations: input, processing, output, and storage.
3. **Data** may be defined as the numbers, words, and phrases that are suitable for processing on a computer to produce information. The production of information from data is called **information processing**.
4. The four basic components of a computer are input unit, processor unit, output unit, and auxiliary storage units.
5. The **keyboard** is the most common input unit. It consists of typewriterlike keys, a numeric keypad, cursor control keys, and programmable function keys.
6. The computer's **processing unit** consists of the central processing unit (CPU) and main memory.
7. Output units consist primarily of displays and printers. **Displays** may be single color (monochrome) or full color. **Printers** may be impact or nonimpact printers.
8. A **dot matrix printer**, the type most commonly used for personal computing, forms characters by printing series of dots to form the character.
9. **Auxiliary storage** on a personal computer is generally disk storage. Disk storage may be on a 5¼-inch or 3½-inch **diskette**, or it may be on an internal **hard disk**.
10. New diskettes must be formatted before they can be used to store data.
11. Computer software can be classified as either **system software**, such as the **operating system**, or as **application software**, such as a word processing, spreadsheet, or database program.

## STUDENT ASSIGNMENTS

### True-False Questions

**Instructions:**   Circle T if the statement is true or F if the statement is false.

T   F   1. The basic operations performed by a computersystem are input operations, processing operations, output operations, and storage operations.
T   F   2. Data may be defined as numbers, words, or phrases suitable for processing to produce information.
T   F   3. A commonly used input unit on most personal computers is the keyboard.
T   F   4. A mouse is a hand-held scanner device for input.
T   F   5. The central processing unit contains the processor unit and main memory.
T   F   6. Typical personal computer memory is limited to a range of approximately 256,000 to 512,000 bytes of main memory.
T   F   7. Auxiliary storage is used to store instructions and data when they are not being used in main memory.
T   F   8. The diskette or floppy disk is considered to be a form of main memory.

T  F    9. A commonly used 5¼-inch double-sided double-density diskette can store approximately 360,000 characters.
T  F  10. Diskettes can normally store more data than hard disks.
T  F  11. A computer program is often referred to as computer software.
T  F  12. A computer program must be permanently stored in main memory.
T  F  13. Programs such as database management, spreadsheet, and word processing software are called system software.
T  F  14. The cursor is a mechanical device attached to the keyboard.
T  F  15. PgUp, PgDn, Home, and End are Function keys.
T  F  16. A laser printer is one form of impact printer.
T  F  17. A dot matrix printer forms characters or graphics by forming images as a closely spaced series of dots.
T  F  18. Application software is the type of program you will use to perform activities such as word processing on a computer.
T  F  19. The operating system is a collection of programs that provides an interface between you and the computer.

## Multiple Choice Questions

1. Which of the following activities will a personal computer *not* be able to perform?
   a. word processing
   b. taking orders in a restaurant
   c. making airline reservations
   d. replacing human decision making

2. The four operations performed by a computer include
   a. input, control, output, storage
   b. interface, processing, output, memory
   c. input, output, arithmetic/logical, storage
   d. input, logical/rational, arithmetic, output

3. Data may be defined as
   a. a typed report       c. a graph
   b. raw facts            d. both a and c

4. PgUp, PgDn, Home, and End keys are
   a. word processing control keys
   b. function keys
   c. optional data entry keys
   d. cursor control keys

5. A hand-held input device that controls the cursor location is
   a. the cursor control keyboard
   b. a mouse
   c. a scanner
   d. the CRT

6. A printer that forms images without striking the paper is
   a. an impact printer       c. an ink jet printer
   b. a nonimpact printer     d. both b and d

7. A screen that displays only a single color is
   a. a multichrome monitor
   b. an upper-lower character display
   c. a 7-by-9 matrix screen
   d. a monochrome screen

8. Auxiliary storage is the name given to
   a. the computer's main memory
   b. diskette drives
   c. instruction storage buffers
   d. none of the above

9. A diskette
   a. is a nonremovable form of storage
   b. is available in 5¼- and 3½-inch sizes
   c. is a form of magnetic data storage
   d. both b and c

10. The amount of storage provided by a diskette is a function of
   a. whether the diskette records on one or both sides
   b. the recording pattern or density of bits on the diskette
   c. the number of recording tracks used on the track
   d. all of the above

11. Some diskettes have an access window that is used to
   a. pick up and insert the diskette into a diskette drive
   b. provide access for cleaning
   c. provide access for the read/write head of the diskette drive
   d. verify data stored on the diskette

12. When not in use, diskettes
   a. should be placed in their protective envelopes
   b. should be stored away from heat, magnetic fields, and direct sunlight
   c. should be stored in a diskette box or cabinet
   d. all of the above

13. A hard disk is
   a. an alternate form of removable storage
   b. a rigid platter with magnetic coating
   c. a storage system that remains installed in the computer
   d. both a and b

14. Storage capacities of hard disks
    a. are about the same as for diskettes
    b. range from 80,000 to 256,000 bytes
    c. range from five million to over 100 million
    d. vary with the type of program used

15. Software is classified as
    a. utility and applied systems
    b. operating systems and application programs
    c. language translators and task managers
    d. word processing and spreadsheet programs

## Projects

1. Popular computer magazines contain many articles and advertisements that inform computer users of the latest in computing trends. Review a few recent articles and report on the apparent trends you have noted. Discuss which hardware features seem to be the most in demand. What are the differences between the alternative hardware choices? Discuss the implications these choices may have on the type of software chosen by a computer owner.

2. Software changes as computer users become more knowledgeable. According to your reading of computer magazines, what software innovations seem to have the greatest promise? Which specific features or styles of user interfaces seem to offer new computing capabilities? Discuss any particular program that seems to be a style setter in its field.

3. Visit local computer retail stores to compare the various types of computers and supporting equipment available. Ask about warranties, repair services, hardware setup, training, and related issues. Report on the knowledge of the sales staff assisting you and their willingness to answer your questions. Does the store have standard hardware "packages," or are they willing to configure a system to your specific needs? Would you feel confident about buying a computer from this store?

## INDEX

**Photo Credits:**    **Opening Page**, International Business Machines Corp.; **Figure 1**, International Business Machines Corp.; Compaq Computer Corp.; **Figure 2**, Intel Corp.; **Figure 4**, (a) Curtis Fukuda, (b) International Business Machines Corp.; **Figure 5**, Logitech, Inc.; **Figure 6**, International Business Machines Corp.; **Figure 9 and 10**, Hewlett-Packard Company; **Figure 11**, (left) Wyse Technology; (right) International Business Machines Corp.; **Figures 12, 13, and 17**, Curtis Fukuda; **Figure 18**, Seagate Technology; **Figure 19**, International Business Machines Corp.

# Introduction to DOS

# Introduction to DOS

## OBJECTIVES

You will have mastered the basics of using DOS when you can:

- "Boot" your microcomputer
- Enter the time and date, if required
- Establish the system default disk drive
- List a disk directory
- Cancel commands
- Format diskettes, using /S and /V
- Use file specifications to address files on various disks

- Copy files on the same disk and from one disk to another
- Rename and erase files
- Organize and manage file subdirectories on a hard disk
- Start application programs

## INTRODUCTION

An **operating system** is one or more programs that control and manage the operation of the computer. These programs provide an interface among the user, the computer equipment, and the application programs. For instance, to use a computer to print a memo, you'd first use the operating system to start the computer. Next, you would enter a keyboard command that the operating system processes to activate the word processing program. When the word processing program instructs the computer to print the memo, the operating system finds the proper file on the disk, retrieves the data from the disk, and routes the output to the printer. The operating system is not part of the application program itself, but it provides essential services that the application program uses to perform its functions.

### Operating Systems for IBM PCs

Microsoft Corporation joined forces with IBM to develop the program known as **DOS**, an acronym for **Disk Operating System**, used since 1981 in IBM PC and IBM-compatible computers. **PC-DOS** is the name for versions of DOS distributed by IBM for its Personal Computer and Personal System/2 lines. All IBM-compatible computers use versions of this operating system distributed by Microsoft as **MS-DOS**. This book uses the term DOS to refer to any of the various editions of PC- or MS-DOS and covers information applicable to all versions of DOS, unless otherwise noted.

## DOS Versions

The numbers following the abbreviation DOS indicate the specific version and release of the product (Figure 1). The **version** number is the whole number and signifies a major improvement of the product. The **release** number is the decimal number and identifies minor corrections or changes to a version of the product. For example, DOS 1.1 corrected some minor problems with DOS 1.0.

Software developers try to maintain **upward compatibility**, that is, that all the features of an earlier version remain supported by a later one. However, "downward" compatibility is not common. Programs or equipment that require the features of DOS 3.3, for example, will not function with DOS 3.2 or earlier versions.

| DOS VERSION RELEASE | MAJOR FEATURE SUPPORTED | YEAR |
|---|---|---|
| 3.3 | Introduction of PS/2 | 1987 |
| 3.2 | Token-Ring Networks, 3.5" Diskette | |
| 3.1 | Addition of Networking, 1.2 mb 5.25 Diskette | |
| 3.0 | Introduction of PC/AT | 1985 |
| 2.1 | Enhancements to 2.0 | |
| 2.0 | Introduction of PC/XT | 1983 |
| 1.1 | Enhancements to 1.0 | |
| 1.0 | Introduction of IBM/PC | 1981 |

**FIGURE 1**

# USING THE DISK OPERATING SYSTEM (DOS)

## Starting the Computer

**D**OS programs are normally stored on a diskette or on a hard disk. To begin using the operating system, it must be read into main memory, a process known as **booting**. If you are using a system with two diskette drives, insert the diskette containing DOS into drive A of the computer and turn on the computer (Figure 2). If you are using a system with a hard disk, DOS is already available on the hard disk. Turn on the computer (Figure 3) and be certain you do not insert a diskette before the system has completed its startup process. If the computer is already on and your DOS diskette is in drive A (or DOS is on the hard disk and drive A is empty), you can restart the system by pressing the CTRL, ALT, and DEL keys simultaneously (Figure 4).

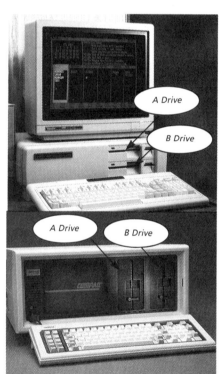

**FIGURE 2**

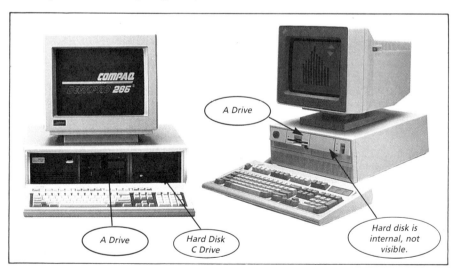

**FIGURE 3**

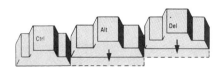

**FIGURE 4**

**The Cold Start.**   Starting the computer by turning on the power switch is known as a **cold start** or **cold boot**. The computer will first run some tests to diagnose its own circuitry (known on some computers as a **power-on self-test**, or **POST** process). After running this test, the computer will begin to read the DOS diskette.

**The Warm Start or Reset.**   Restarting the operating system by pressing the CTRL, ALT, and DEL keys simultaneously is called a **warm start**, or **warm boot**, because the computer has already been turned on. This procedure does not repeat the POST process, but it does erase all programs and data from main memory and reloads DOS. Do not worry about losing data from diskettes during this process, however, because data properly stored on diskettes will remain there.

**Loading DOS.**   While the system is being booted, the status light on the disk drive flashes on and off, and the disk drive whirls for a few seconds. During this time, the program from the operating system is being loaded into main memory. When DOS has been loaded into main memory, an image similar to Figure 5 appears on the screen. When DOS has been loaded into main memory, the system will perform various activities depending upon how the startup procedure has been tailored for the specific computer.

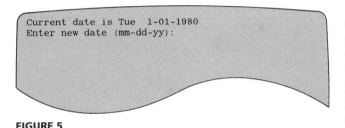

**FIGURE 5**

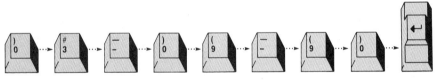

## Setting the Date and Time

Although not required, it is a good practice to enter the date and time so that files you create are accurately documented. Enter the current date when the computer screen displays the message shown in Figure 6. To enter the date, always enter the month, day, and year separated by hyphens (-), slashes (/), or, in DOS 3.30 and later versions, periods (.). For example, assume that today is March 9, 1990. Type 03-09-90. Then press the Enter key (Figure 7).

If the date displayed is already correct—which it may be if your computer has an internal clock—you do not need to enter the date. Instead, press the Enter key when the message "Enter new date:" appears on the screen.

You enter the time in the format hh:mm:ss.xx, where hh stands for hours, mm stands for minutes, ss stands for seconds, and xx stands for hundredths of a second. As with the date, you are not required to enter the time, although it is a good practice to do so. For practice, type the time as 11:50 and press the Enter key (Figure 8). (If you do not include seconds and hundredths of seconds, the operating system assumes a value of zero for them.)

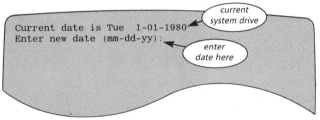

**FIGURE 6**

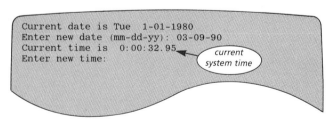

**FIGURE 7**

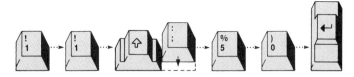

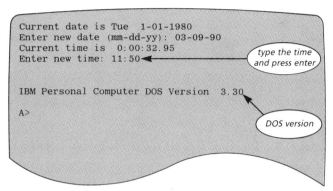

```
Current date is Tue  1-01-1980
Enter new date (mm-dd-yy): 03-09-90
Current time is  0:00:32.95
Enter new time: 11:50◄          type the time
                                and press enter

IBM Personal Computer DOS Version  3.30

A>                                    DOS version
```

**FIGURE 8**

## The Default Drive

The default drive assignment will vary depending upon the specific hardware you are using. A two-diskette system typically assigns drive A as the default drive (Figure 9). If your computer has a hard disk, the default drive will initially be drive C, and the prompt will appear as it is shown in Figure 10.

At times you will need to change the default drive assignment. Before you do so, be certain that the new drive is ready. A hard disk is always installed, but in a two-diskette system the disk drive must have a diskette inserted before it can be assigned as the default drive. If the drive does not have a diskette in it, the computer will give you an error message.

To change the drive assignment, type the letter of the new drive to be used, followed by a colon, and then press the Enter key. For example, to change the default to drive B, type the letter B, followed by a colon (:), and then press the Enter key (Figure 11, step 1). The prompt will display drive B as the default drive. Now, change the default drive back to drive A by typing A:← (Figure 11, step 2).

## The DOS Prompt

After the messages are displayed, the **system prompt** indicates that the operating system is ready to receive your commands (Figures 9 and 10). The letter displayed within the prompt > indicates which drive has been assigned as the default disk drive. The **default drive** is the disk drive in which the operating system assumes the disk or diskette containing the operating system and other programs is located. Another term used for the default drive is **current drive**, because it is the drive that is assumed to be in current use.

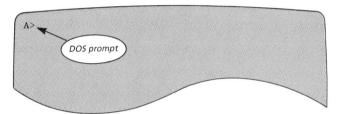

**FIGURE 9**

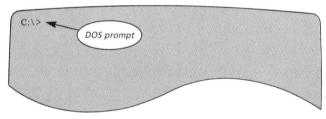

**FIGURE 10**

**FIGURE 11**

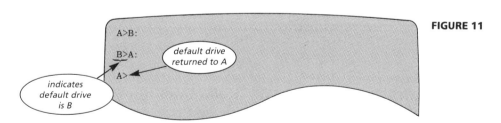

Step 1: Change the default drive from A to B.   Step 2: Change the default drive from B to A.

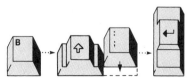
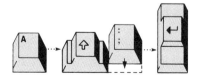

In most of the examples in this text, the default drive will be drive A. You will be told when the procedures for a hard disk are different than those for a diskette system. Figure 12 shows how to change the default drive for a hard disk system from drive C to drive A (step 1) and back to drive C (step 2).

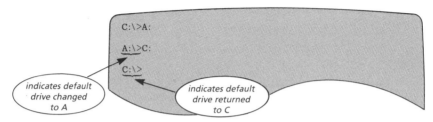

C:\>A:

A:\>C:

C:\>

*indicates default drive changed to A*

*indicates default drive returned to C*

**Step 1: Change the default drive from C to A.**     **Step 2: Change the default drive from A to C.**

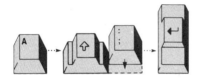          

**FIGURE 12**

# ENTERING DISK OPERATING SYSTEM (DOS) COMMANDS

Now that you have booted the DOS system, you are able to enter commands to instruct the computer. DOS includes a variety of commands to assist you in using the computer. Some of the commands might be called "status" or "informative" commands because they instruct DOS to give you information about the system's operation. The directory command, DIR, is one such informative command. It lists the names of files stored on a disk. Other commands support DOS functions, helping you use the computer. FORMAT, for instance, prepares a new disk for use in storing files.

The DOS commands you have entered so far have been typed in capital letters. You can type capital letters either by pressing the Caps Lock key or by holding down one of the two shift keys. However, you do not have to enter all DOS commands in capital letters. Commands, drive specifiers, and other entries to the operating system can be entered in any combination of uppercase and lowercase letters.

## Internal and External Commands

An **internal command** is part of the operating system program. Once you have loaded DOS into main memory, an internal command is always started there. You can enter an internal command at any time. It does not matter whether the DOS system diskette is in the default drive. DIR, COPY, CLS, ERASE, RENAME, and DEL are examples of internal commands.

**External commands**, on the other hand, are stored on the DOS system disk as program files. They must be read from the disk into main memory before they can be executed. This means that the DOS system disk must be in the default drive or the specified drive so that the program can be found on the disk and loaded into main memory for execution. FORMAT and CHKDSK are examples of external commands. Another easy way to identify external commands is to look for the extensions .BAT, .COM, or .EXE following the filename, such as FORMAT.EXE.

# DIRECTORY COMMAND (DIR)

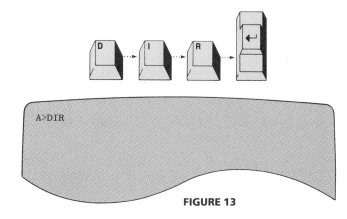

**FIGURE 13**

O ne of the functions of the operating system is to store files containing both programs and data on diskettes. To facilitate that storage, the operating system maintains a directory of all the files stored on a diskette. To display the directory of the diskette you have placed in drive A of your computer, use the **DIR command**. At the A > prompt, type DIR and press the Enter key (Figure 13).

The directory of the diskette in the default drive will then be displayed as in Figure 14. Because the default drive is drive A (as specified by the system's A > prompt), the directory of the diskette in drive A is displayed. If you are using a hard disk and your default disk is drive C, the DIR command will display the directory of your hard disk.

The directory itself consists of the names of the files on the diskette, the number of bytes required to store the file on the diskette, the date of the last change of the file, and for some files, the time of the last change of the file. The message at the end of the directory listing indicates the number of files on the diskette (in Figure 14 there are 15 files on the diskette) and the remaining space available on the diskette (181248 unused bytes remain on the diskette in Figure 14). At the end of the directory display, the system prompt reappears on the screen, indicating that the system is ready for your next command.

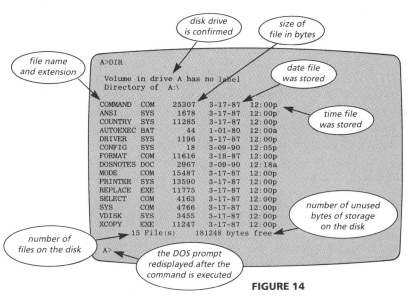

**FIGURE 14**

## Displaying Directories of Other Disks

The directories of files on diskettes in other disk drives of the computer can be displayed as well. For practice, remove your system diskette from drive A and move it to drive B. To display the directory, type the command DIR B: and press the Enter key, as in Figure 15. You have directed the operating system to display the directory of the diskette located in drive B. The entry B: specifies that drive B is to be used.

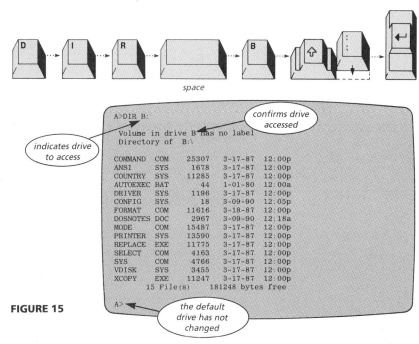

**FIGURE 15**

If your computer has a hard disk and you have been using drive C as the default drive, you can insert a diskette into drive A and then list the directory of that diskette drive by typing DIR A: and pressing the Enter key (Figure 16).

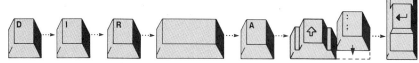

**FIGURE 16**

Note the use of the **colon**, **:**, with the disk drive letter. Whenever you refer to a specific disk drive, type the letter designating the drive followed by the colon, such as A:, B:, or C:.

## Pausing Directory Listings

The directory of your diskette will often contain more files than can be displayed on the screen at one time. DOS has two methods of handling this situation: the pause screen option and the DIR command options.

**Pause Screen (Control S).** To use a **pause screen** function, first make certain that your DOS diskette is in drive A. Type DIR and press the Enter key (Figure 17, step 1). When approximately one screenful of information is displayed, press Control-S. The directory display immediately halts (Figure 17, step 2). You can then examine the screen for any information you require. To continue the display, press any character key on the keyboard. The directory display will continue to scroll as if it had never halted. This pause screen operation can be used with many DOS commands.

**Step 1: Display a directory of the default drive.**

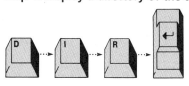

**Step 2: Halt the directory listing.**

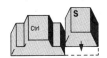

**Step 3: Continue the display by pressing any character key.**

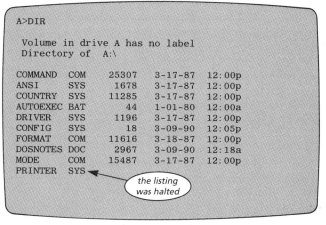

```
A>DIR

 Volume in drive A has no label
 Directory of  A:\

COMMAND   COM    25307    3-17-87   12:00p
ANSI      SYS     1678    3-17-87   12:00p
COUNTRY   SYS    11285    3-17-87   12:00p
AUTOEXEC  BAT       44    1-01-80   12:00a
DRIVER    SYS     1196    3-17-87   12:00p
CONFIG    SYS       18    3-09-90   12:05p
FORMAT    COM    11616    3-18-87   12:00p
DOSNOTES  DOC     2967    3-09-90   12:18a
MODE      COM    15487    3-17-87   12:00p
PRINTER   SYS
```

the listing was halted

**FIGURE 17**

**DIR Command Options.** It is not always easy to pause the directory listing where you want it. Therefore, you might want to use two other options with the DIR command. One option, /P, causes the screen to pause. The second option, /W, displays more data on the screen by increasing the **width** of the display area.

**/P—the Pause Option.** To demonstrate the pause option, type DIR followed by /P and press the Enter key (Figure 18). When the screen is full, the listing stops and the message "Strike a key when ready . . ." appears at the bottom of the screen. When you are ready to continue the listing, press any character key.

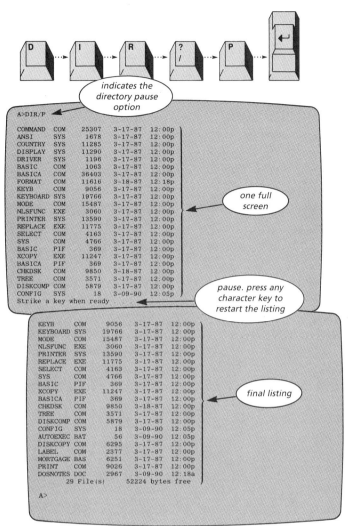

**FIGURE 18**

# FORMATTING A DISKETTE

Y ou cannot use a brand new diskette to store files. The diskette must first be formatted using the DOS FORMAT program. The **formatting** process establishes sectors on the diskette and performs other functions that allow the diskette to store files. Be careful when selecting disks to be used with the FORMAT command. Formatting a diskette destroys all files previously stored on the diskette. Therefore, you must be extremely careful to place the correct diskette in the drive and to make the correct drive letter designation. With a hard disk, extra precaution is necessary to avoid losing files by formatting the hard disk accidentally. DOS versions 3.0 and later provide some protection against accidental formatting of a hard disk, but your own precautions are still the best insurance.

**/W—the Wide Display Option.** The second option for displaying a long list of files is the **/W option**, which displays the information in a wide format. To use the /W option, type DIR /W, then press the Enter key (Figure 19). Note that only the file and directory names are listed, not the size, time, or date of the files.

## Canceling a Command (Break)

In some cases, you only need to see a portion of the directory and so you might want to cancel the DIR command after you have seen that portion. To cancel a command you use the Break key. Locate this key on your keyboard; on many keyboards it is on the side of a key, often on the Scroll Lock key or the Pause key. When you press Ctrl-Break the characters ^C appear on the screen and the system prompt reappears. You will often hear this keystroke combination referred to as **Control-Break** or the **Break key**. The characters ^C indicate that you canceled the command by using the Break key. In general, you can cancel any DOS command that has been initiated by pressing Control-Break. An alternate method of canceling DOS commands is pressing Control-C (Figure 20).

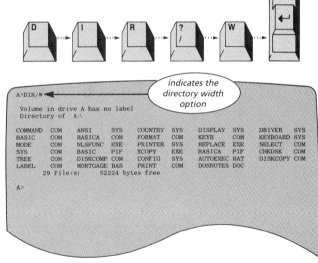

**FIGURE 19**

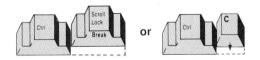

**FIGURE 20**

## The FORMAT Command

To initiate the FORMAT program, select a new diskette, or one that may be erased. (Use the DIR command to check the contents of your diskette if you are not certain it may be erased.) Because FORMAT is an external DOS command, the FORMAT.COM program file must be on the system disk in the computer when you use this command.

To format a diskette on a two-diskette system, place the DOS diskette in drive A. Type the command FORMAT B: and press the Enter key (Figure 21).

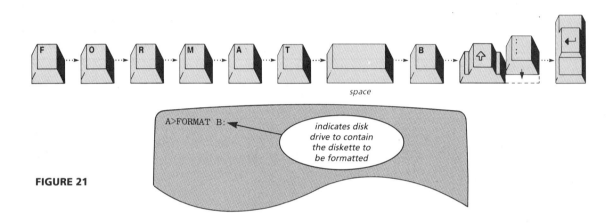

**FIGURE 21**

When you press the Enter key, the FORMAT program is loaded into main memory and is executed. A message appears on the screen instructing you to "Insert new diskette for drive B: and strike ENTER when ready" (Figure 22). If the disk you want to format is already in drive B, simply press the Enter key.

**Step 1: View the message and insert diskette.**

**Step 2: Press Enter.**

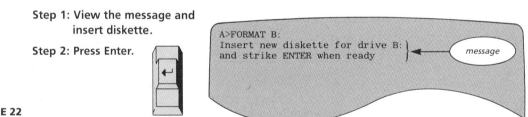

**FIGURE 22**

The FORMAT procedure on a hard-disk system is essentially the same as for a two-diskette system, except that the FORMAT program is stored on drive C, the hard disk. Be careful NOT to format drive C accidentally. To format a diskette in drive A at the C> prompt, type FORMAT A: and press the Enter key (Figure 23). The program will instruct you when to place the diskette to be formatted into drive A (Figure 24).

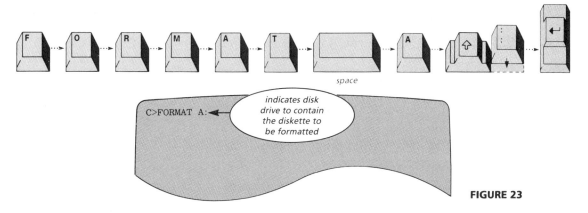

C>FORMAT A:

*indicates disk drive to contain the diskette to be formatted*

**FIGURE 23**

To complete the format process, place the diskette to be formatted into the appropriate drive (drive B for a two-diskette system; drive A for a computer with a hard-disk) and press the Enter key. While formatting occurs, a message appears indicating that the process is underway. Figure 25 shows the message from a two diskette system and Figure 26 illustrates the message on a computer with a hard-disk. Messages may differ slightly depending upon the version of DOS you are using. When the formatting process is complete, the messages shown in Figure 27 or 28 appear.

```
C:\>FORMAT A:
Insert new diskette for drive A:
and strike ENTER when ready
```

*message*

**FIGURE 24**

```
A>FORMAT B:
Insert new diskette for drive B:
and strike ENTER when ready

Head: 0 Cylinder: 16
```

*indicates area of diskette currently being formatted*

**FIGURE 25**

```
C:\FORMAT A:
Insert new diskette for drive B:
and strike ENTER when ready
Head: 0 Cylinder: 16
```

*indicates area of diskette being formatted*

**FIGURE 26**

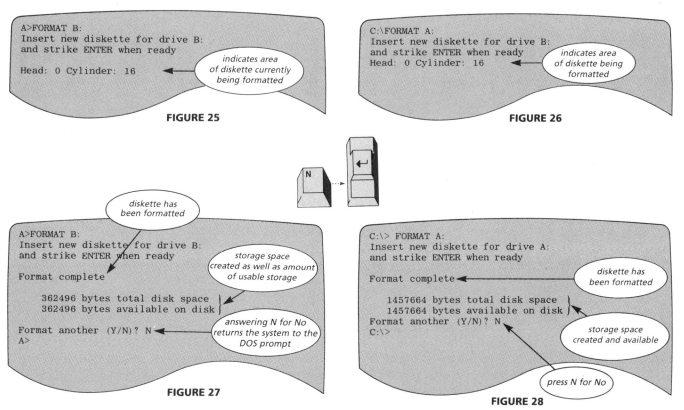

*diskette has been formatted*

```
A>FORMAT B:
Insert new diskette for drive B:
and strike ENTER when ready

Format complete

    362496 bytes total disk space
    362496 bytes available on disk

Format another (Y/N)? N
A>
```

*storage space created as well as amount of usable storage*

*answering N for No returns the system to the DOS prompt*

**FIGURE 27**

```
C:\> FORMAT A:
Insert new diskette for drive A:
and strike ENTER when ready

Format complete

    1457664 bytes total disk space
    1457664 bytes available on disk
Format another (Y/N)? N
C:\>
```

*diskette has been formatted*

*storage space created and available*

*press N for No*

**FIGURE 28**

The FORMAT program specifies that the diskette is formatted for a total number of bytes and that all of these bytes are available for storage. Finally, the FORMAT program asks if there are other diskettes to be formatted. If there are, press the letter Y and then the Enter key to continue the formatting process. If there are not more diskettes to be formatted, press the letter N and then the Enter key to end the FORMAT program.

## Formatting a System Disk (/S Option)

The FORMAT command shown in Figures 26 and 27 will format a diskette so that it can be used for both data files and program files. However, the diskette cannot be used to boot the system because it does not contain the special system programs that are required for booting. To format a diskette so that it contains these special programs, thus creating what is called a **system disk**, you must use the **/S option**.

Use the same diskette you used in the last exercise. If you are using a two-diskette system, use the following commands. If you are using a hard-disk system, use drive C as the default drive and place the diskette to be formatted in drive A. Be very certain NOT to format drive C accidentally.

To create a system disk on a two-diskette system, type FORMAT B:/S and press the Enter key (Figure 29). On a hard-disk system, type FORMAT A:/S. You will be prompted to insert a new diskette in drive B (or A); if the diskette you formatted earlier is still in the disk drive, simply press the Enter key. After the diskette is formatted, the "System transferred" message appears. In general, if you are formatting a diskette to be used only for storing data files, do not place system programs on the diskette so that more space is available for the data files.

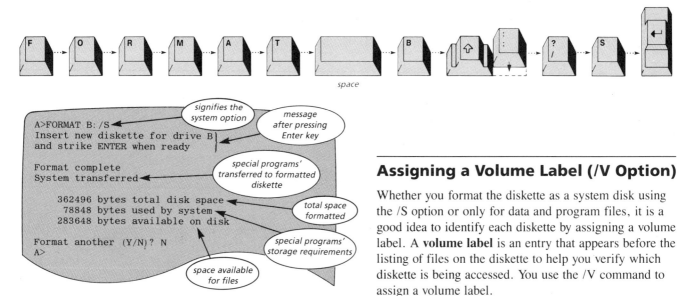

**FIGURE 29**

## Assigning a Volume Label (/V Option)

Whether you format the diskette as a system disk using the /S option or only for data and program files, it is a good idea to identify each diskette by assigning a volume label. A **volume label** is an entry that appears before the listing of files on the diskette to help you verify which diskette is being accessed. You use the /V command to assign a volume label.

To assign a volume label, you would type FORMAT B:/V and press the Enter key (Figure 30). You will again be instructed to insert a diskette into drive B. Insert a new diskette, or press the Enter key if the diskette from the previous exercise is still in drive B. When the format process is complete, you will receive the message "Volume label (11 characters, ENTER for none)?" as a prompt to enter your label. You may use 11 characters—letters, numbers, or spaces—but not punctuation or special characters. After you enter a label and press the Enter key, a message appears asking if you want to format another diskette. You would press N and the Enter key to return to the DOS prompt.

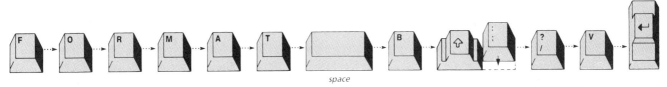

**FIGURE 30**

# CLS COMMAND

Quite often, as you issue several commands or perform lengthy processes, the display screen will become crowded and difficult to read and interpret (Figure 31). To clear the screen and place the system prompt on the first line of the screen, you can use the CLS (Clear Screen) command. Type the letters CLS, then press the Enter key to execute the Clear Screen command.

# MANAGING DATA AND PROGRAM FILES ON DISKS

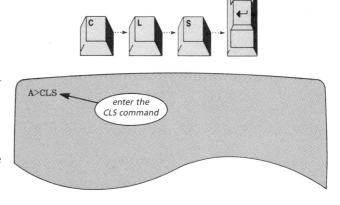

A **data file** is a collection of data created by application or system programs and used by the programs. The data can be the figures used for a spreadsheet showing sales revenues, names and addresses in a database file, or a word processing document announcing the arrival of a new employee. A **program file** contains machine-readable instructions that the computer follows to perform its tasks. The program might be an operating system program or one of the application programs such as word processing that uses data files. Both data files and program files require your attention to be stored on a disk correctly.

**FIGURE 31**

## Assigning File Specifications

DOS identifies the files on a disk by a combination of several specifications (Figure 32). A **file specification** lets DOS know exactly where to search for a file and gives its exact name. There are four parts to a DOS file specification: (1) the drive specifier, which you already know as drive A: or B: or C:, if there is a hard disk; (2) a directory specification (explained later); (3) the filename; (4) the filename extension.

**FIGURE 32**

| LEGEND | DEFINITION |
|--------|------------|
| d: | The disk drive letter specifies the drive containing the file you are requesting. For example, A: specifies disk drive A. If you omit the drive letter, DOS assumes the file is located on the default drive. A disk drive letter is always followed by a colon (:). |
| \path | A path is an optional reference to a subdirectory of files on the specified disk. It is preceded, and sometimes followed, by a backslash (\). |
| filename | The filename consists of from one to eight characters. |
| .ext | A filename may contain an optional extension of a period followed by from one to three characters. The extension is used to add further identity to files. |

**Filenames.** Regardless of the type of data in the file, you must assign a filename to every data file, as well as to every program file. A **filename** consists of one to eight characters and is used by DOS to identify a specific file. You may use any combination of characters except: period (.), quotation mark ("), slash (/), backslash (\), brackets ([ ]), colon (:), less than (<), greater than (>), plus (+), equals (=), semicolon (;), and comma (,).

In general, your filename should reflect the data stored in it. For example, if your file contains employee records, it is more meaningful to use the filename EMPLOYEE than to use the filename FILE1, even though DOS will accept either filename.

**Filename Extensions.** A filename can be made more specific by an optional extension. A **filename extension** consists of a period followed by one to three characters. The same characters that are permitted for a filename are permitted for a filename extension. The filename extension can identify a file more specifically or describe its purpose (Figure 33). For example, if you wish to create a copy of the EMPLOYEE file, you could use the filename extension .CPY to identify the file as a copied file. The entire file specification for the file would be EMPLOYEE.CPY.

**FIGURE 33**

| .COM Files | | .EXE Files | | .BAT Files | |
|---|---|---|---|---|---|
| COMMAND | COM | APPEND | EXE | AUTOEXEC | BAT |
| ASSIGN | COM | ATTRIB | EXE | WP | BAT |
| BACKUP | COM | FASTOPEN | EXE | INSTALL | BAT |
| BASIC | COM | FIND | EXE | | |
| BASICA | COM | JOIN | EXE | | |
| CHKDSK | COM | NLSFUNC | EXE | | |
| COMP | COM | REPLACE | EXE | | |
| DEBUG | COM | | | | |
| DISKCOMP | COM | | | | |
| DISKCOPY | COM | | | | |
| FORMAT | COM | | | | |
| LABEL | COM | | | | |

Certain programs associated with the Disk Operating System use special filename extensions. All files with the filename extensions .COM or .EXE are executable programs. Files with the extension .BAT are **DOS batch files** and contain a series of DOS commands to be executed in sequence. Any DOS command with one of these filename extensions is an external command. You can execute any external command simply by typing the filename (the extension is not required) and pressing the Enter key.

# COPY COMMAND

*O*nce you have formatted a diskette and are ready to use it to store data or program files, you will need a method of placing these files on the diskette. Use the **COPY command** to copy one file or a series of files to the same or a different diskette. As a DOS internal command, COPY may be used at any time, with or without the system disk.

## Using the COPY Command

The COPY command is often used to make working copies of program and data diskettes. Copying original files from one diskette creates a second diskette that can be used for everyday work to protect the original disk from damage. A similar use for COPY is to make a **backup copy** of a diskette to guard against accidental loss of data. One frequently used technique is to make a backup copy of a file whenever you work on revisions to an existing file. In fact, some application programs will make a backup file automatically, using the filename extension .BAK or .BAC to indicate that it is a backup file.

## Copying Files from One Diskette to Another

In the following examples of the COPY command, you will copy files from drive A to drive B. Check to see that you have the practice diskette provided with this book in drive A and your formatted diskette in drive B. If you are using a hard disk system, use drive C as the default drive, copying the files to drive A.

For practice, copy the file DOSNOTES.DOC from drive A to drive B. Your instructor will make the DOSNOTES.DOC file available to you or will give you the name of another file to copy. Type COPY DOSNOTES.DOC B: and press the Enter key. Note that after the word COPY you leave one or more spaces, then state the file specification of the file to be copied. In DOS terminology, this file is called the **source file**. In Figure 34, the filename DOSNO-TES.DOC is specified as the source file. Since no drive specification is included, the operating system assumes the file is located on the default drive, drive A.

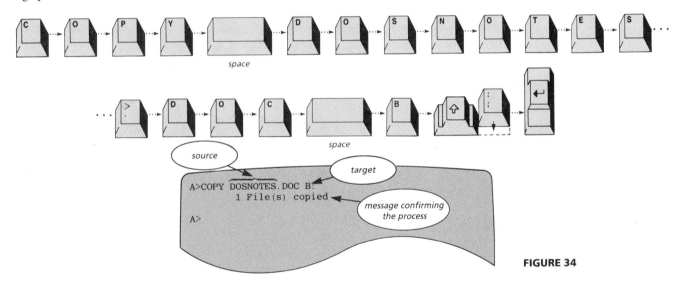

**FIGURE 34**

Following the source file is one or more blank spaces. Then, the **file specification**, which can include the drive specification, and the name of the **target file**, that is, the filename and filename extension of the source file after it is copied, is specified. In Figure 34, the drive specification B: states that the file is to be copied to a diskette in drive B. Because no filename is specified for the target file on drive B, DOS defaults to the same name as the source file, and so the name of the file on drive B will be DOSNOTES.DOC. The message "1 File(s) copied" signals that the command is completed.

When you copy a file from a diskette in one drive to a diskette in another drive, you can assign a new name to the target file. To copy the file DOSNOTES.DOC from the diskette in drive A to the diskette in drive B, giving the new file the name NOTECOPY on drive B, type COPY DOSNOTES.DOC B:NOTECOPY and press the Enter key (Figure 35). Again, the message "1 File(s) copied" appears when the task is completed, as in Figure 34.

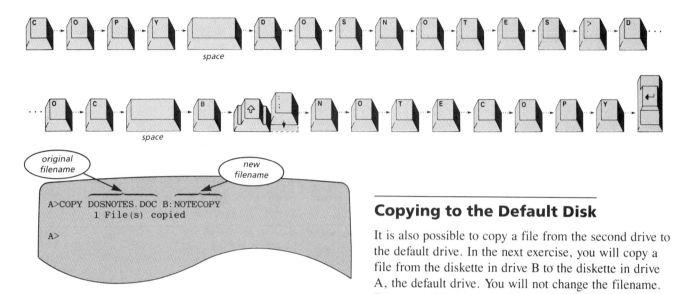

original filename

new filename

A>COPY DOSNOTES.DOC B:NOTECOPY
    1 File(s) copied

A>

**FIGURE 35**

## Copying to the Default Disk

It is also possible to copy a file from the second drive to the default drive. In the next exercise, you will copy a file from the diskette in drive B to the diskette in drive A, the default drive. You will not change the filename. To accomplish this procedure, type COPY B:NOTE-COPY A: and press the Enter key. This command copies the file named NOTECOPY from the diskette in drive B to the diskette in drive A. When the message "1 File(s) copied" appears, as in Figure 36, the copying process is completed. Because no target filename was given in the command, the file NOTECOPY will be on drive A under the same name as it is on drive B.

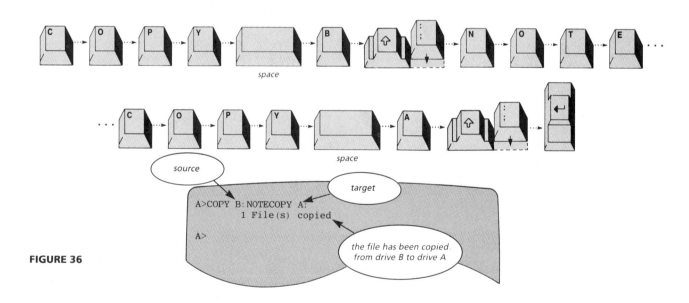

source

target

A>COPY B:NOTECOPY A:
       1 File(s) copied

A>

the file has been copied from drive B to drive A

**FIGURE 36**

## Copying a File to the Same Diskette

It is possible to copy a file to the same diskette, but you must use a different filename. For practice, copy the file named DOSNOTES.DOC stored on drive A onto the same diskette. Give the filename DOSNOTES.BAK to the target file. Type the command COPY DOSNO-TES.DOC DOSNOTES.BAK and press the Enter key.

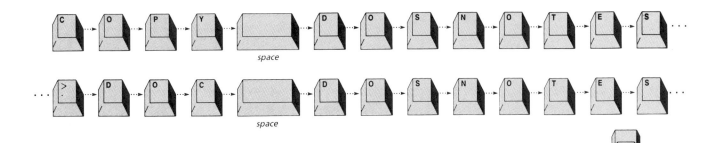

*space*

*space*

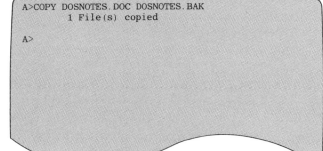

When your COPY command is executed, the file DOSNO-TES.DOC in drive A is copied to the same diskette on drive A as DOSNOTES.BAK (Figure 37). The file extension .BAK is used to distinguish the files. If you had used the same filename to designate both the target and source files on the same diskette, an error message would be displayed, stating that a file cannot be copied into itself. You would then have to reenter the COPY command using a different name for the target file.

```
A>COPY DOSNOTES.DOC DOSNOTES.BAK
       1 File(s) copied

A>
```

**FIGURE 37**

## Global Filename Characters ("Wildcards")

You can copy more than one file at a time using a single COPY command. To copy more than one file, you use **global characters**, or **wildcards**. These are special characters indicating that any character may occupy that specific location in the filename. The two global characters are the **\*** (asterisk) and the **?** (question mark).

To use wildcards, you need to know the files stored on the diskette. Figure 38 shows the directory of the diskette in drive A. Notice that the files DOSNOTES.BAK and NOTECOPY appear, a result of the COPY commands you used earlier. Notice also that several files have the same filename extensions. It is not uncommon, on any disk with many files, to find several files with similarities in filenames or extensions. These similarities can be exploited by using wildcard characters.

```
Volume in drive A has no label
Directory of  A:\

COMMAND   COM    25307   3-17-87   12:00p
ANSI      SYS     1678   3-17-87   12:00p
COUNTRY   SYS    11285   3-17-87   12:00p
AUTOEXEC  BAT       44   1-01-80   12:00a
DRIVER    SYS     1196   3-17-87   12:00p
CONFIG    SYS       18   3-09-90   12:05p
NOTECOPY          2967   3-09-90   12:18a
FORMAT    COM    11616   3-18-87   12:00p
COPYNOTE          2967   3-09-90   12:18a
DOSNOTES  DOC     2967   3-09-90   12:18a
MODE      COM    15487   3-17-87   12:00p
DOSNOTES  BAK     2967   3-09-90   12:18a
PRINTER   SYS    13590   3-17-87   12:00p
REPLACE   EXE    11775   3-17-87   12:00p
SELECT    COM     4163   3-17-87   12:00p
SYS       COM     4766   3-17-87   12:00p
VDISK     SYS     3455   3-17-87   12:00p
XCOPY     EXE    11247   3-17-87   12:00p
      18 File(s)    172032 bytes free

A>
```

**The \* Character.** You can use the global character **\*** (asterisk) to indicate a portion of the filename or extension. When the \* global character appears, any character can occupy that position and all the remaining positions in the filename or the filename extension.

For example, let us use the wildcard asterisk (\*) to copy files with the filename extension **FIGURE 38** .COM from the diskette in drive A to the diskette in drive B. Type COPY \*.COM B: and press the Enter key. In Figure 39, the source files are specified by the entry \*.COM. The asterisk (\*) in the filename portion of the specification means that any filename can be used. The file extension .COM states that the file specification must include the file extension .COM. In Figure 38, five filenames satisfy this criterion: COMMAND.COM, FORMAT-.COM, MODE.COM, SELECT.COM, and SYS.COM.

**FIGURE 39**

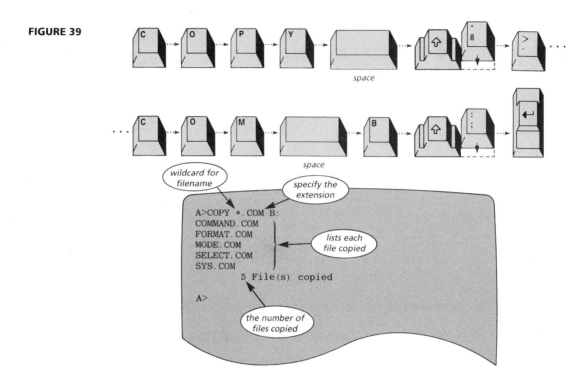

These files are copied to the diskette in disk drive B. The filenames for the copied files on the diskette in drive B remain the same as the source filenames on the diskette in drive A because you specified no new names in the copy command. When you copy files with a COPY command using the * global character, all files copied are listed by the COPY command. Figure 39 lists the five copied files.

You can also specify the global character * as the filename extension to copy a specific filename with any extension. For example, the diskette contains two files with the name DOSNOTES, DOSNOTES.BAK and DOSNOTES.DOC. Type the command COPY DOS-NOTES.* B: as in Figure 40 and press the Enter key to copy both the files with the filename DOSNOTES to drive B.

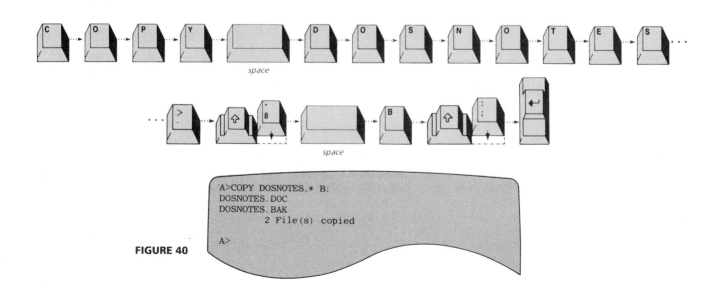

**FIGURE 40**

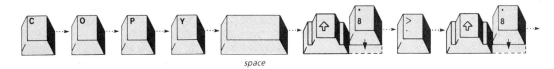

space

### Copying All Files from One Diskette to Another.

You can also use the COPY command to copy all of the files on one diskette to another diskette by using the * global character. This technique is useful in making backup or working copies of entire diskettes. You use the * wildcard in both the filename and extension positions to signify "all filenames.all extensions" in the command. Practice by typing COPY *.* B: and pressing the Enter key to copy all files on drive A to drive B (Figure 41).

**The ? Character.**   The ? (question mark) global character can also be used to represent any character occupying the position in which the wildcard character appears. However, the ? represents only a single character replacement, whereas the * can represent one or more characters. You can use a single ? or several in a command to identify files. Practice this option by typing COPY DOSNOTES.BA? B: and pressing the Enter key to copy DOSNOTES.BAK to drive B (Figure 42).

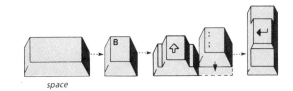

space

```
A>COPY *.* B:
COMMAND.COM
ANSI.SYS
COUNTRY.SYS
AUTOEXEC.BAT
DRIVER.SYS
CONFIG.SYS
NOTECOPY
FORMAT.COM
COPYNOTE
DOSNOTES.DOC
MODE.COM
DOSNOTES.BAK
PRINTER.SYS
REPLACE.EXE
SELECT.COM
SYS.COM
VDISK.SYS
XCOPY.EXE
        18 File(s) copied

A>
```

**FIGURE 41**

## Using Wildcards with DOS Commands

You have learned to use the wildcard characters with the COPY command. Many DOS commands support the use of global replacement characters. For example, you can use the wildcards with the DIR command to look for files of a common type. To look at all DOS batch files on a diskette, you would type the command DIR *.BAT and press the Enter key to display all files with the filename extension .BAT.

space

space

## RENAME COMMAND

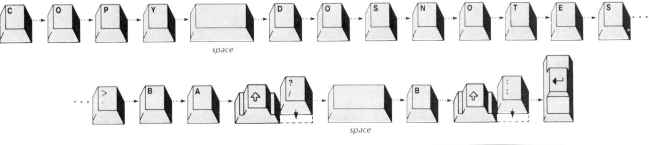

A>COPY DOSNOTES.BA? B:
DOSNOTES.BAK ◄——— *the ? is replaced by the letter K*
        1 File(s) copied

A>

**FIGURE 42**

*U*se the **RENAME command** when you want to rename a file on a diskette. If you assign a file-name already used by a file currently on the disk-ette, DOS creates the new file on the diskette and destroys the previously existing file with that name. You will not receive any warning that this has happened. Thus, you should periodically check the filenames on a diskette to avoid accidental replacement of files. If you discover a file-name you might reuse, you can use the RENAME command to change the name of the file.

In the example in Figure 43, the file with the filename NOTECOPY on drive A is to be renamed DOSFILE. Type the command RENAME NOTECOPY DOSFILE immediately after the system prompt and press the Enter key. When you press the Enter key, the filename on the diskette in drive A is changed from NOTECOPY to DOSFILE.

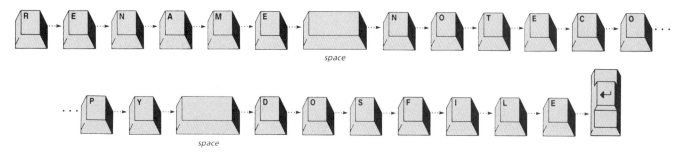

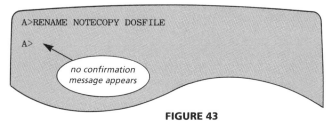

**FIGURE 43**

You can use the global characters * and ? with the RENAME command. In Figure 44, all files with the file extension .BAK are renamed with a file extension .BAC. Type the wildcard character * with the command RENAME *.BAK *.BAC and press the Enter key. All characters represented by the * will remain the same in the new filename. Thus, in Figure 44, all the filenames in the renamed files will remain the same, but the file extensions will change from .BAK to .BAC. RENAME does not confirm the operation on the screen, so you should use the DIR command before and after you use the RENAME command to assure the command was executed (Figure 45).

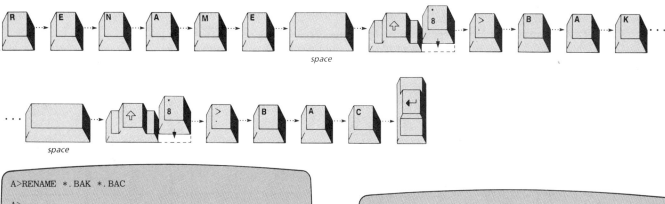

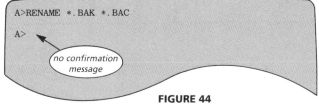

**FIGURE 44**

```
A>DIR

Volume in drive A has no label
Directory of  A:\

COMMAND  COM    25307   3-17-87   12:00p
ANSI     SYS     1678   3-17-87   12:00p
COUNTRY  SYS    11285   3-17-87   12:00p
AUTOEXEC BAT       44   1-01-80   12:00a
DRIVER   SYS     1196   3-17-87   12:00p
CONFIG   SYS       18   3-09-90   12:05p
DOSFILE          2967   3-09-90   12:18a
FORMAT   COM    11616   3-18-87   12:00p
COPYNOTE         2967   3-09-90   12:18a
DOSNOTES DOC     2967   3-09-90   12:18a
MODE     COM    15487   3-17-87   12:00p
DOSNOTES BAC     2967   3-09-90   12:18a
PRINTER  SYS    13590   3-17-87   12:00p
REPLACE  EXE    11775   3-17-87   12:00p
SELECT   COM     4163   3-17-87   12:00p
SYS      COM     4766   3-17-87   12:00p
VDISK    SYS     3455   3-17-87   12:00p
XCOPY    EXE    11247   3-17-87   12:00p
      18 File(s)    172032 bytes free

A>
```

one file renamed; other files not changed

**FIGURE 45**

# ERASE AND DEL COMMANDS

s a part of diskette file management, you should periodically remove unneeded files from your diskette. The **ERASE command** will erase, or remove, a file from a diskette. An alternative command that functions like the erase command is the **DEL** (delete) command. Take care when using the ERASE or DEL commands, because once a file has been erased from the directory, it cannot be easily recovered. Such inadvertent erasing of a file is another reason for keeping backup files.

## Removing Files

We will begin by removing a single file, DOSFILE, from drive A. Type ERASE DOSFILE and press the Enter key, as shown in Figure 46. (You could use the DEL command instead, typing DEL DOSFILE and pressing the Enter key.) Use the DIR command to assure that the file has been removed from the diskette.

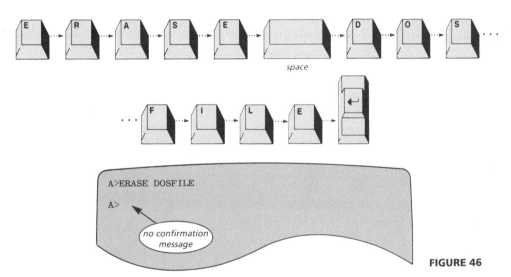

**FIGURE 46**

# USING DIRECTORIES AND SUBDIRECTORIES

## Directory Entries and Subdirectories

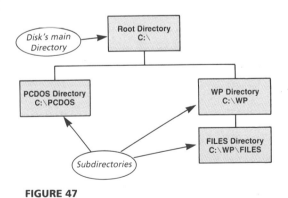

**FIGURE 47**

When you need to view the files on any disk, the computer does not actually read the entire disk looking for the file. Instead, a **file directory** or listing of each of the filenames on the disk is searched. This directory, created when the diskette is formatted, is called the **root directory**. Entries for subdirectories are made in the root directory. The root directory is the highest level directory of a disk (Figure 47).

You can make three types of entries into a disk directory: (1) the filename and extension, (2) the volume label, (3) a subdirectory entry. We have previously discussed (1) and (2).

You can create a **subdirectory** to group all files of a similar type together (Figure 47). For example, you can create a subdirectory containing all the files related to DOS.

There are at least two good reasons to use subdirectories. First, the operating system provides a limited number of entries in the file directory. A diskette has room for only 112 entries; a hard disk allows up to 512 entries. This capacity may be sufficient on a diskette, but a hard disk with many millions of bytes of storage may have more files than the directory permits.

It is also easier to find files that are organized by related groups than to search randomly through all the files on a disk.

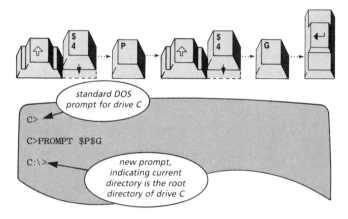

**FIGURE 48**

## The PROMPT Command

The standard DOS prompt, A >, B >, or C >, does not tell you what subdirectories you are using. DOS provides a way for you to monitor which directory is in use through the **PROMPT command**. To have DOS include the sub-directory information as a part of the DOS prompt, type PROMPT $P$G and press the Enter key (Figure 48). Whenever you change disk drive addresses, you will see the sub-directory information as a part of the prompt.

## Making Subdirectories

To create a subdirectory, use the **MKDIR command**, usually abbreviated as **MD**. If you have a hard disk, and *if your instructor approves*, create a subdirectory on drive C. Otherwise, practice the command on a diskette in drive A. To create a subdirectory called "PCDOS" on your diskette or disk drive, type MD A:\PCDOS and press the Enter key (Figure 49).

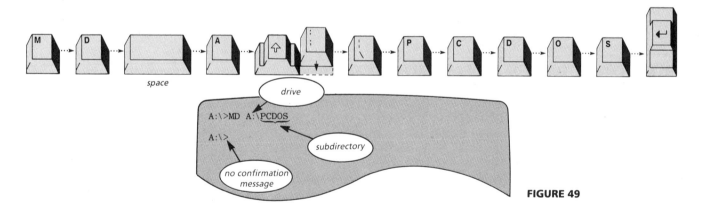

**FIGURE 49**

There are specific steps to the MD command. (1) Start a subdirectory entry with the drive designation. If the directory is to be on drive C, enter C: immediately after the MD command. Use the command MD A:\PCDOS to use drive A on a diskette. You can omit the drive specification if you are creating the directory on the default drive.

(2) Begin a subdirectory entry with the **backslash** character, \. The root directory for your hard disk is designated by a backslash alone. For example, C:\ designates the root

directory of drive C. The subdirectory made for the DOS files is C:\PCDOS. Notice that because you have issued the PROMPT command, the DOS prompt now includes the root or subdirectory name, C:\> or C:\PCDOS>.

(3) The subdirectory name, like any filename, can contain one to eight characters, followed optionally by a period and one to three characters in an extension. (Generally, subdirectory names do not include extensions.)

(4) You can assign a subdirectory entry to an existing subdirectory. For instance, you can create a subdirectory for a word processing program and a subordinate subdirectory for the data files created by the program. To create the word processing subdirectories shown in Figures 50 and 51, make the word processing subdirectory by typing MD A:\WP and press the Enter key. To make the subordinate subdirectory, type MD A:\WP\FILES and press the Enter key. The program subdirectory is A:\WP, and the word processing files can be stored in a second subdirectory, A:\WP\FILES. These two operations result in a series of related directories. Refer back to Figure 47 to see the relationships among the directories and subdirectories we have created.

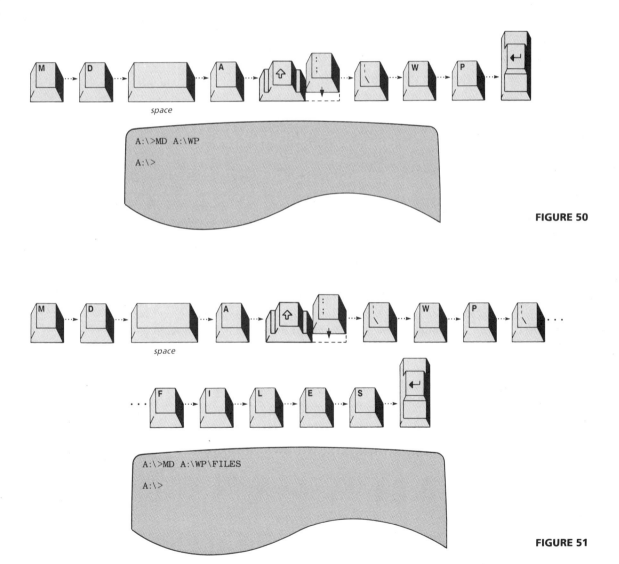

**FIGURE 50**

**FIGURE 51**

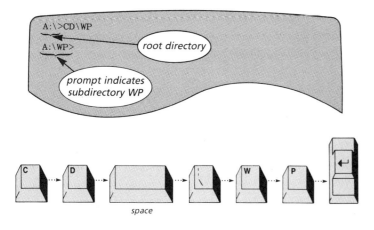

**FIGURE 52**

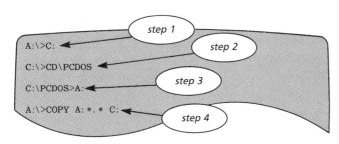

## Changing Directories

Use the **CHDIR command** to move from one directory to another. Enter the letters CD immediately following the DOS prompt. Then type the backslash character and the subdirectory name and press the Enter key. To change from the root directory to the WP directory, for instance, type the entry CD \WP and press the Enter key. The result shown in Figure 52 should appear on your screen. To move to a lower subdirectory, such as the FILES subdirectory, type CD \WP\FILES and press the Enter key.

If you are moving to a directory that is subordinate to the current subdirectory, you can simply type CD and the subdirectory name. For instance, if your current directory is WP, you can move to the FILES subdirectory by entering CD FILES. Note that the entry omits both the reference to WP (the current directory) and the backslash character.

To return to the root directory simply type CD\ and press the Enter key. The backslash character entered by itself signifies the root directory.

**The Current Directory.** Just as there is a default or current disk drive, there is a current directory. The **current directory** is the one in which you are currently working. When you first access a disk, the root directory is the current directory. You can, however, direct DOS to a subdirectory, which then becomes the current directory for that disk. If you temporarily set another drive as the default drive, the named directory remains the current directory for the first disk.

**FIGURE 53**

For practice, set your default drive to drive C by entering C: (Figure 53, step 1). Then set PCDOS as the current subdirectory for drive C by entering CD \PCDOS (step 2). Switch to drive A as the default drive (step 3) and copy files from drive A to drive C: type the copy command COPY A:*.* C: (step 4). Files are copied from the A drive to the PCDOS subdirectory on drive C even though the subdirectory is not specified in the copy command.

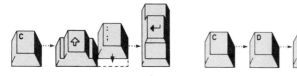

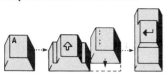

**Step 1: Change default to drive C.** **Step 2: Change from root directory of drive C to PCDOS directory.**

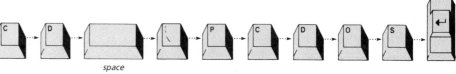

**Step 3: Return to A drive.** **Step 4: Copy files from drive A to the subdirectory PCDOS on drive C.**

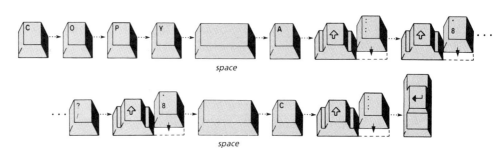

## Specifying a Path to Subdirectories and Files

You will find it very convenient to group files in subdirectories. To use the technique you must learn to specify the path to a file. The **path** includes three components: (1) the drive, (2) the name of the subdirectories, (3) the name of the file. The path specifies the route DOS is to take from the root directory through subdirectories leading to a file. Specify the path whenever you wish to access a file for DIR, COPY, or similar commands. Unless you specify a path, DOS may not find the file you desire because it would search only the current directory of the default drive.

**Specifying Paths in Commands.**   One way to specify the path is to include it in the command you are using. For example, to make a backup copy on a diskette of a file named DOSNOTES.DOC stored in the FILES subdirectory under the WP subdirectory, type the command COPY C:\WP-\FILES\DOSNOTES.DOC A:. The COPY command includes the source drive (C:), both directories specified together (\WP\FILES), and the filename preceded by a backslash (\DOSNOTES.DOC). On drive A, the file is stored simply as DOSNOTES.DOC under the root directory, because no subdirectory has been made or referenced on that disk.

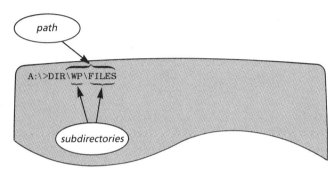

**FIGURE 54**

You can use this style with other DOS commands and when specifying files in many programs. For example, to display the file contents of the FILES subdirectory, enter DIR \WP\FILES and press the Enter key (Figure 54). Enter DIR \WP to list the program files for the word processing software stored under the WP subdirectory.

## Managing Files Within Subdirectories

To copy files or data to subdirectories, you can use the COPY command or any file storage techniques offered by your application program. Some programs may not recognize the subdirectory structure on your diskette, so you may need to set the current directory before you use the program. The RENAME, DIR, ERASE, and other DOS commands work in subdirectories in nearly the same way as they do in the main directory.

## Removing Subdirectories

When you no longer need a subdirectory, you can remove it. Use the **RMDIR command**, abbreviated to **RD**, to remove a specified directory from a disk.

**Erasing Subdirectory Files.**   To remove a subdirectory, you must first remove all files stored within it. You can do so by using the global character * with the ERASE command. You can issue this command from the subdirectory to be removed or from another directory if you give the full path specification. If you issue the command from another directory, make certain to use the correct subdirectory and path information or you might inadvertently erase files from another part of the disk.

For practice, delete the FILES subdirectory (Figure 55). First, enter the FILES subdirectory by typing the command CD\WP\FILES and pressing the Enter key. Next, empty the subdirectory of files by typing ERASE *.* and pressing the Enter key. You will receive the message "Are you sure (Y/N)?", to which you must press Y and then the Enter key.

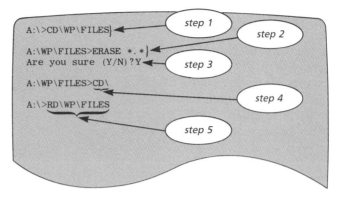

**Step 1: Change the directory to WP\FILES.**

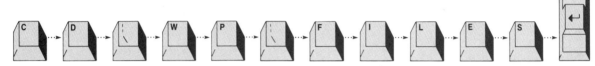

**Step 2: Erase all files.**

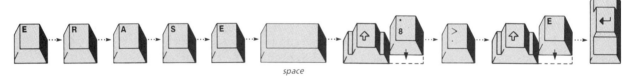

space

**Step 3: Respond "Yes" to the prompt.**    **Step 4: Change to the root directory.**

**Step 5: Remove the FILES subdirectory.**

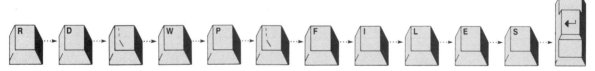

**FIGURE 55**            **Removing a Subdirectory.**    After you have emptied the subdirectory files, you can remove the subdirectory. Enter the root directory by typing the command CD\ and pressing the Enter key. To remove the FILES subdirectory, enter RD \WP\FILES and press the Enter key. Note that you must specify the full path, even though the WP directory is to remain. You must specify the full path so that DOS follows the path from the root directory, where the WP directory entry is stored, through the WP directory to find and remove the FILES entry.

## LOADING A PROGRAM

 **program** is a series of instructions that specifies the steps your computer must perform to accomplish a specific purpose. To execute a program, you must first load the program into main memory from diskette or disk storage. The program must be stored either on a diskette, which you have inserted into one of the disk drives, or on the internal hard disk. If you are using a two-diskette system, place the diskette containing the program to be executed in the default drive, usually drive A. Then type the program name (or name abbreviation) and press the Enter key. (Notice that loading and executing an application program is essentially the same as issuing an external DOS command.)

## SUMMARY

1. An **operating system** is one or more programs that control and manage the operation of a computer.
2. The operating system for an IBM Personal Computer is **PC-DOS**. Other compatible computers use a similar program called **MS-DOS**.
3. The **version** number of a program is the whole number and signifies a major improvement of the product. The **release** number is the decimal number and identifies minor corrections or changes to a version of the product.
4. "**Booting**" the computer refers to loading the operating system from a disk into main memory.
5. The computer can be "booted" by turning it on with the operating system located on a disk in the computer. This is called a "cold start."
6. To reload the operating system when the computer is already switched on, hold down the **Control** and **Alternate** keys and press the **Delete** key. This process is called a "warm start" or "reset."
7. The operating system will **prompt** you for its commands. DOS has two general types of commands: (1) **internal commands** that are executed from the program stored in the main memory; (2) **external commands** that are programs loaded from a disk as the command is executed.
8. After the operating system has been loaded into main memory, you may be prompted to enter the date or time. Some systems have an internal clock that provides this information for you.
9. The **DOS prompt** includes the letter address of the **default disk drive**, the disk that is currently in use for data or program access.
10. The default drive of a two-diskette computer is usually drive A. A computer with a hard disk drive will generally use drive C as its default drive.
11. You can change the default drive by entering a valid drive letter, followed by a colon, and pressing the Enter key.
12. To examine files on a disk, issue the **DIR** (directory) command. Use the /P option to pause a long directory listing when the screen is full. Use the /W option to list files across the width of the screen.
13. Give the **pause-screen** command by holding down the Control key and pressing the S key.
14. Many commands can be canceled by holding down the **Control** key and pressing the **Break** key or by pressing Control-C.
15. Use the **FORMAT** command to prepare diskettes for storing data or program files. Several options are available for various types of diskettes. Use /S to format the diskette as a **system disk**. The /V option prompts a **volume label**.
16. Filenames must be created by following specific rules. A **filename** may consist of up to eight letters, numbers, or certain symbols. The filename **extension** is an optional one- to three-character addition, separated from the filename by a period.
17. Files with the extensions **.BAT**, **.COM**, or **.EXE** are external, executable command files.
18. Use the COPY command to transfer a file to another diskette or to create a backup file on the same diskette.
19. **Wildcards**, the * and ? characters, can be used in conjunction with many DOS commands to replace specific characters.
20. A file to be copied is the **source** file. The resulting copy is called the **target** file.
21. You can change a file's name by specifying the target file used during the COPY command or by using the **RENAME** command.
22. To remove a file from a diskette, execute the **ERASE** or the **DELETE** command.
23. Disks can be better organized through the use of **subdirectories**. A disk's primary directory is the **root** directory, signified by a **backslash** following the drive letter, such as C:\.
24. Use the **MKDIR** or the **MD** command to create a subdirectory. The entry includes the drive, backslash, and directory name, such as C:\WP.
25. To switch from one directory to another, use the **CHDIR** or **CD** command, for example, CD\WP.
26. A directory can be removed by first erasing all the files in the directory, then using the REMOVE DIRECTORY command, **RD**.
27. To **load a program** for execution, type the name of the program file at the DOS prompt.

# STUDENT ASSIGNMENTS

## True/False Questions

**Instructions:**   Circle T if the statement is true or F if the statement is false.

T   F   1. PC-DOS and MS-DOS are essentially the same operation system.

T   F   2. When DOS is updated for a new version, programs operating in prior versions may not work under the newer edition.

T   F   3. The programs comprising an operating system such as PC-DOS can be stored on a diskette.

T   F   4. "Booting" the computer refers to the procedure of starting the operating system.

T   F   5. DOS commands are divided into two types: internal and external commands.

T   F   6. As a part of the system startup procedures, you are requested to enter the computer's serial number.

T   F   7. After the operating system has been loaded, you can type the command DIR and press the Enter key to display a directory of the diskette in the default drive.

T   F   8. The computer may have a built-in clock that the operating system automatically accesses to input the date and time.

T   F   9. The symbol A: >, which appears on the computer screen, is called the DOS Interlock.

T   F   10. A default disk drive is one that improperly stores data.

T   F   11. To change the disk drive assignment to drive C, type C:↵.

T   F   12. All DOS commands must be entered in uppercase characters.

T   F   13. You can list the directory of the default disk drive by typing DIR and pressing the Enter key.

T   F   14. The option /P used with the DIR command will cause the listing to pause when the screen is full.

T   F   15. Holding down the Control key and then pressing the Break key will cancel a command function.

T   F   16. To format a diskette, put the diskette to be formatted in disk drive A and enter the command FORMAT B:.

T   F   17. The command Copy A: can be used to copy all files from one disk drive to another.

T   F   18. The ERASE command can be used to remove a file from the file directory.

T   F   19. To include the operating system on a formatted disk, use the command FORMAT B:/S.

T   F   20. When you use the FORMAT option /V, the system will prompt you to enter a volume label.

T   F   21. To cancel a command, hold down the ALT key and press the END key.

T   F   22. A DOS filename may contain from 1 to 11 characters plus an optional extension of 1 to 3 characters.

T   F   23. The disk containing the file to be copied is known as the source disk.

T   F   24. Global replacement characters include *, ?, and \.

T   F   25. Hard disk drives are generally addressed as drive C.

T   F   26. Subdirectories on disks are used to group filename entries for convenient storage and retrieval.

T   F   27. A disk's main file directory is called the root directory.

T   F   28. The current directory is the one in which you are currently working.

T   F   29. To move from one current directory to another, use the MD command.

T   F   30. A file address contains the disk drive letter, the subdirectory path, and the filename.

T   F   31. A program cannot be loaded from a disk unless the program disk is in the current drive.

## Multiple-Choice Questions

1. "Booting" the computer refers to
   a. loading the operating system
   b. placing covers over the disk drives
   c. using application programs to access disk drives
   d. the system interface
2. "DOS" stands for
   a. Digital Organizing Software
   b. Data Output Stream
   c. Disk Operating System
   d. Dielectric Orthanographic Startup
3. PC-DOS is used on IBM Personal Computers and Personal System/2 systems. IBM-compatible computers generally use
   a. PC-OMD
   b. MS-DOS
   c. XD-DOS
   d. CP/DUZ
4. A term describing your ability to use newer editions of software while retaining features and data used in earlier ones is
   a. software generation
   b. compatibility curve
   c. upward compatibility
   d. version control
5. When you start up the computer, you load the operating system
   a. from a diskette in drive A
   b. from the computer's internal memory
   c. from the fixed disk if the computer is so equipped
   d. both a and c
6. The term for restarting the operating system in a computer already powered on is
   a. warm start
   b. cold start
   c. warm boot
   d. both a and c
7. The symbol A>
   a. is called a DOS prompt
   b. indicates the name of a program
   c. indicates the default disk drive
   d. both a and c
8. Listing the files on a disk is accomplished by
   a. typing DIR and pressing the Enter key
   b. typing LIST and pressing the Enter key
   c. typing CHKDSK and pressing the Enter key
   d. typing RUN FILES and pressing the Enter key

9. To pause a listing on the screen, press
   a. Control and Break
   b. Alternate, Control, and Delete
   c. Control and S
   d. either b or c

10. To cancel a command, press
    a. Control and Break
    b. Alternate, Control, and Delete
    c. Control and S
    d. either c or d

11. The _____ command establishes sectors on a diskette and performs other functions that allow the diskette to store files.
    a. CHKDSK
    b. DIR
    c. REUSE
    d. FORMAT

12. A valid DOS filename specification consists of
    a. 10 alphanumeric characters
    b. a 9-character filename
    c. an 11-character name, separated by a period at any position within the name
    d. an 8-character filename plus an optional extension of a period followed by 3 characters

13. A common use of the COPY command is to make working copies of program and data disks, producing
    a. file disks
    b. backup copies
    c. extension disks
    d. authorized disks

14. To copy the file PROGRAM.EXE from drive A to drive B, type the command
    a. COPY PROGRAM.EXE TO DRIVE B
    c. COPY A:PROGRAM.EXE TO B:PROGRAM.EXE
    d. COPY A:PROGRAM.EXE B:
    3. either b or c

15. To copy all files on drive A to drive C, type the command
    a. COPY DRIVE A TO DRIVE C
    b. COPY ALL FILES TO C
    c. COPY A:?.* C:?.*
    d. COPY A: C:

16. To change the name of a file from FILEX.DOC to FILEA.DOC, enter
    a. ALTER FILEX.DOC TO FILEA.DOC
    b. CHANGE FILEX.DOC TO FILEA.DOC
    c. ASSIGN FILEX.DOC AS FILEA.DOC
    d. RENAME FILEX.DOC FILEA.DOC

17. To remove a file from a disk, type
    a. REMOVE FILE
    b. DELETE FILEX.DOC
    c. ERASE FILEX.DOC
    d. either b or c

18. Filenames are grouped on disks into
    a. index lists
    b. directories and subdirectories
    c. subject and filename entries
    d. internally labeled entries

19. The MKDIR, or MD, command will
    a. manage directory files
    b. make a directory on a disk
    c. create a file copy
    d. either a or b
20. To shift from the root directory to a directory of files under a word processing directory, type the command
    a. CH /FILES
    b. GOTO WP FILES
    c. CD \WP\FILES
    d. C:\WP\FILES\*.*

## Projects

1. Start your computer without a DOS disk in drive A. What is the display on the screen? Why did this display appear? Insert a DOS disk in drive A and restart the computer by pressing the Ctrl Alt Del keys simultaneously.
2. Start your computer with the DOS disk in the default disk drive. If permitted in your computer lab, prepare a new diskette as a system disk using the proper FORMAT command options for the task at hand and for the specific diskette your computer uses.
3. Prepare a diskette to be a file disk using the FORMAT command. Give the diskette a volume label using your own name. Determine the proper type of diskette to use on the computer and, after formatting, determine the amount of free space remaining on the diskette.
4. If permitted in your computer lab, create a working copy of your application program diskettes.
    a. First, format a new diskette. Will there be enough room on the diskette to contain both the operating system and the program? How can you know?
    b. Using one command, copy all files from the master copy of the disk to your newly prepared diskette.
5. Create a subdirectory named SUB1 on your diskette.
6. Make subdirectory SUB1 the current directory. Copy all .DOC files into SUB1 and display the directory.
7. Remove the subdirectory created in Assignment 8.

# DOS Index

**Photo Credits:**   **Opening Page and Figure 2a**, Radio Shack, a division of Tandy Corp.; **Figures 2b and 3a**, Compaq Computer Corp.; **Figure 3b**, International Business Machines Corp.

# Word Processing Using WordPerfect

# PROJECT 1

## Typing, Saving, and Printing a Simple Letter

### Objectives

You will have mastered the material in this project when you can:

- Load WordPerfect into main memory
- Explain the function of the WordPerfect template
- Move the cursor in all directions
- View the reveal codes
- Type, save, and print a short letter
- Exit WordPerfect and return to the A > prompt

**W**ordPerfect, developed by **WordPerfect Corporation**, Orem, Utah is a best-selling word processing program. WordPerfect is available for use on most microcomputers on the market. In this unit, you will learn how to use WordPerfect on an IBM personal computer (PC, XT, AT, PS/2, and compatibles) operating under MS-DOS, or PC-DOS. Like all word processing programs, WordPerfect is used to produce printed documents and is especially useful when documents require precise formatting and presentation. These documents can be prepared for many different applications, from business memos to student term papers.

In the following projects all the features of WordPerfect will not be explained. For an explanation of those features not covered, refer to the WordPerfect Reference Manual supplied with the software package by WordPerfect Corporation.

For the following Projects using WordPerfect we assume you are using a keyboard with the function keys at the *left* of the keyboard.

### Using the Training Version of WordPerfect

Boyd & Fraser Publishing Company, the publisher of this textbook, has contracted with WordPerfect Corporation to obtain the **Training Version of WordPerfect**, Release 4.2. This training version contains most of the features of the WordPerfect package available in the retail market. It was developed to help students *learn* the features of WordPerfect, not to be a fully usable tool for professional documents. The limitations of the training version are as follows:

- You may work with as large a document as you like in memory; however, you may save to disk a document no larger than about 4K (4,000 characters).
- A data file created with the training version can be used with the commercial version of WordPerfect, and a file created in the commercial version of WordPerfect can be used with the training version.
- Data files of any size may be printed through parallel printer port 1 without defining a printer.
- The training version supports one font but not the extended ASCII characters.
- The letters *WPC will appear randomly throughout your printed document. This is your indication that the document was prepared using the training version of WordPerfect.
- Using training examples, you will be able to learn all the functions of WordPerfect 4.2's speller and thesaurus. However, you may not use the speller and thesaurus with any of your own documents.
- The Help file of the training version allows you to view the function-key template on the screen, but as with the speller and the thesaurus, space does not allow the complete Help files to be included on the training disk.

Boyd & Fraser Publishing Company and the authors are grateful to WordPerfect Corporation for allowing students to have access to this word processing program.

# THE KEYBOARD

*I*n Project 1 you will become familiar with the keyboard and the template used with WordPerfect. To learn the position and feel of the keys, you will practice pressing certain keys before turning the computer on. Then, after turning the computer on and loading WordPerfect, you will type, save, and print the short letter in Figure 1-1. You will then practice moving the cursor on a blank screen, after which you will exit the WordPerfect program.

```
December 1, 1990


Mr. Joseph Wright
236 Santo Domingo Cir,
Fountain Valley, Ca 92708

Dear Mr. Wright:

I received your letter today and wish to thank you for it.

Sincerely,


Mary Martinez
Director
```

**FIGURE 1-1**
Letter for Project 1.

The **keyboard** is used as an **input** device to input data into the computer. Look over the entire keyboard in Figure 1-2. In addition to the familiar typewriter keyboard keys, you will see some other keys. To the left of the typewriter section (or on top of the keyboard, depending on which keyboard you are using), you will notice keys F1 through F10. These are called **function keys** (some computers also have function keys 11 and 12). To the right of the keyboard is a **numeric keypad**, which looks similar to a 10-key adding machine. In addition to numbers, most keys on this numeric keypad have arrows pointing in different directions, or words such as Home and End.

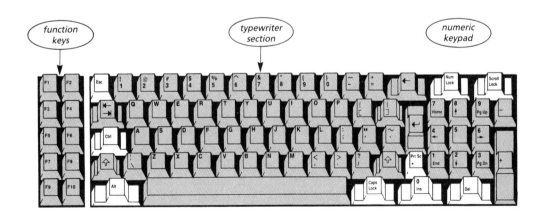

**FIGURE 1-2**
The computer keyboard
(console).

## The Typewriter Section

In the typewriter section of the keyboard, the **Shift** keys may look familiar, but the **Ctrl** (Control) and **Alt** (Alternate) keys may be new to you.

As you may know, the Shift key is used to make lowercase letters into CAPITAL LETTERS, or to type the symbols above the number (#, $, %, &, *, etc.) on the keyboard. The Ctrl and Alt keys, as well as the **Shift** keys (Figure 1-3), are used along with the function keys to achieve specific word processing goals.

To become familiar with these keys *before* you turn on the computer, press the Ctrl key down, then let it up. Now press the Alt key, then let it up. Press the Right Shift key down and while holding it press the R key, then let them both up. Now hold the Left Shift key down and press the 8 key. Had the machine been on and WordPerfect loaded, the R key would have typed a capital R and the 8 key would have typed the asterisk, *.

The **Tab** key (Figure 1-4) is used for indenting to the next tab setting to the right, just as on a typewriter. Press the Tab key, and notice that there is one arrow that faces forward → and one arrow that faces backward ←. That is because this key, when pressed with the Shift key, also allows you to release the left margin. Hold the Shift key down firmly and press the Tab key. Had the machine been on and WordPerfect loaded, the margin would have been released to the next tab setting to the *left* of the cursor.

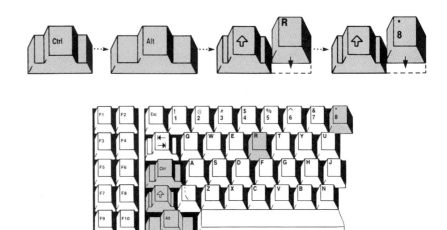

**FIGURE 1-3** The Ctrl, Alt, and Shift keys.

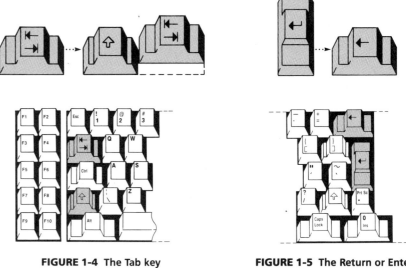

**FIGURE 1-4** The Tab key

**FIGURE 1-5** The Return or Enter and Backspace keys

The **Return** key (Figure 1-5), is used to do the same thing that the Return key is used for on a typewriter—to begin a new line. On most keyboards, however, the word **Enter** is on the key along with an arrow that looks like this ↵. That is because this key is also used to enter information into the computer.

Often while using a word processing package, such as WordPerfect, you will type a command and the letters or numbers you typed will stay on the screen; you may wonder what to do next. A good rule of thumb is that *if you have given a command and nothing happens, press Enter* ↵. In other words, the command you typed is only on the screen. It will not be entered into the memory of the computer until you press the Enter key. The few exceptions to this will be discussed individually. Now, for practice, press the Enter key.

Although Enter and Return are the same key, remember that sometimes the key will be referred to as Enter and sometimes as Return. When you were loading DOS into the computer, you had to type the date. After the date, you pressed the Enter key, because you wanted the date entered into the computer memory. When you press this key at the end of a paragraph or a short line, or when you want to add a blank line in your text, you refer to the key as the Return key, as you normally would if you were typing on a typewriter. Since the Enter (Return) key has an arrow like this ↵, many times throughout these projects you will see this arrow instead of the word Enter or Return. When you see the arrow, press the Enter key.

The **Backspace** key (Figure 1-5) is used to move the cursor backward on the screen, much like the Backspace key on a typewriter. However, in WordPerfect, as you backspace, the character or space directly to the left of the cursor (_) is deleted. Try pressing the Backspace key.

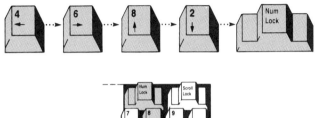

## The Numeric Keypad

Figure 1-6 shows the numeric keypad. The keys on the numeric keypad can be used to type numbers, but for most purposes it's better to use the number keys in the typewriter section of the keyboard to type numbers. It's more important to use the keys on the numeric keypad to move the cursor through the text on the screen. The arrow pointing to the left will move the cursor one character to the left. Press the **Left Arrow** key ← several times. The arrow pointing right will move the cursor one character to the right. Press the **Right Arrow** key → several times. The arrow pointing up will move the cursor up one line. Press the **Up Arrow** key ↑ several times. The arrow pointing down will move the cursor down one line. Press the **Down Arrow** key ↓ several times.

**FIGURE 1-6  The Numeric Keypad.**

If you wish to use the numeric keypad to type numbers instead of using it to move the cursor, you will have to "lock" the numbers to the "on" position by pressing the Num Lock key. For practice, press the Num Lock key several times.

## The Function Keys

Find the function keys on the far left side of the keyboard (or at the top). They are numbered 1 to 10, with an F in front of each number. These function keys are special keys programmed to execute commonly used commands. Functions can be margin changes, tab setting changes, boldfacing, correcting the spelling of a document, and so on.

To understand how the function keys work, first look at the keyboard. If you have any typing experience, you know that if you were to type the G key, you would see a lowercase g on the screen. If you hold down the Shift key and type the *same* G key, the Shift key changes the function of that key and makes it a capital G. You type the same key, but you get a different value, depending on whether you press the key alone or hold down the Shift key and press the G key.

The Function keys are very similar. If you press a function key alone, you will be able to perform a certain function, such as saving a document. But if you hold the Shift key down and press the same function key, you will be able to perform an entirely different function, such as centering.

Further, you can hold down the Alt key or the Ctrl key and press the same Function key to perform additional functions such as moving parts of your text. *Each* function key can have *four* different values, depending on whether you press it alone or with the Ctrl, Alt, or Shift keys.

## THE WORDPERFECT TEMPLATE

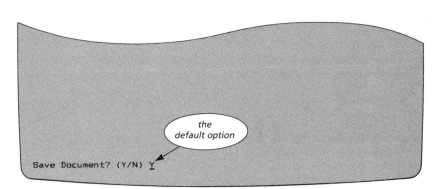

**FIGURE 1-7**
**Template around**
**Function keys.**

*F*igure 1-7 is a picture of the WordPerfect **Template**, showing how it fits over the function keys. Most word processors show command messages on the screen that take up valuable space. The template takes command messages off the screen and puts them next to the function keys to which they correspond. This not only makes it easier to learn the keystrokes, it also unclutters the screen, making it easier to read.

The template is color coded, starting at the bottom with black, then blue, green, and red on the top. The colors signify the following:

**Black** means you press the key alone.

**Blue** means you hold down the **Alt** key firmly while pressing the desired F key.

**Green** means you hold down the **Shift** key firmly while pressing the desired F key.

**Red** means you hold down the **Ctrl** key firmly while pressing the desired F key.

To understand how to use this template and its color coding, look to the right of the F6 key on the template. Notice that the bottom item, in black, says Bold. Therefore, if you desire to have your typing boldfaced you would press the F6 key alone. For practice, press the F6 key. If the computer had been turned on and WordPerfect was loaded, after you pressed the F6 key, any typing you did would have been boldfaced, until you "turned off" the boldface by pressing the F6 key again.

Let's try another example. Look at the template next to the F2 key. You will see the word Spell in red. Because red signifies the Ctrl key on the template, hold down the Ctrl key firmly and while holding it, lightly press the F2 key to perform the Spell function. For practice, hold down the Ctrl key and press the F2 key. If the machine had been turned on and WordPerfect was loaded, it would have been ready to check the spelling of your text.

In summary, whenever you see Ctrl, Alt, or Shift followed by a hyphen and a function key—such as Ctrl-F8 or Alt-F3— remember to hold down the first key and, while holding it down, lightly press the function key.

Common mistakes made by users of WordPerfect are that they try to press the Ctrl, Alt, or Shift key *simultaneously* with the function key, or they press the Ctrl, Alt, or Shift key, release that key, and then press the function key. If you make either of those mistakes, the computer will react as if you had pressed the function key *only*.

If you press the function keys in error and get a message on the lower left corner of the screen that you wish to remove, press the F1 (Cancel) key. That will usually undo that error and remove the message.

Practice on the keyboard for a few minutes to feel more comfortable with it. After you have practiced with the Ctrl, Alt, and Shift keys, you will have just the right touch.

## DEFAULTS

*O*ne word that you will see throughout this text is **default**. This word simply means that *unless instructed otherwise* this is the action to be taken. For example, you will often be asked to give a yes or no answer, as in the message in Figure 1-8. The Y (for yes) will automatically appear on the screen, which means that Y is the default. Notice that after the (Y/N),

Save Document? (Y/N) Y

the
default option

**FIGURE 1-8**

WordPerfect displays an option outside the parentheses, and the cursor will be under that option. You may type Y or N, whichever is your choice. However, the choice above the cursor is WordPerfect's default choice. If you want the default choice, you may either type the letter or press the Enter key, which automatically accepts the default.

## LOADING WORDPERFECT

**T**o place the WordPerfect training program into the memory of the computer, first load DOS into memory so that the A> prompt is displayed. Look at step 1 in Figure 1-9. Type b: and press the Enter key. This changes the default from drive A to drive B and enables your files to be saved to the disk in drive B. In step 2, at the B> prompt, type a:wp and press the Enter key. This instructs the computer to find the WordPerfect program in drive A.

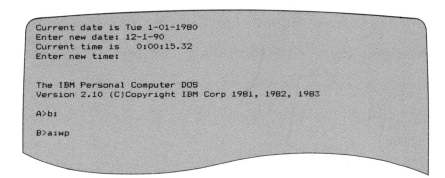

**FIGURE 1-9**

```
Current date is Tue 1-01-1980
Enter new date: 12-1-90
Current time is   0:00:15.32
Enter new time:


The IBM Personal Computer DOS
Version 2.10 (C)Copyright IBM Corp 1981, 1982, 1983

A>b:

B>a:wp
```

**Step 1: Change default to drive B**      **Step 2: Load WordPerfect into main memory**

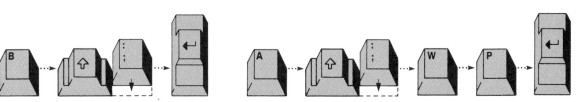

You hear the drives working, loading the WordPerfect program into the memory of the computer. Then you see the opening screen, informing you that you are using the training version of WordPerfect and explaining the licensing restrictions and the limitations of the training version (Figure 1-10). Press any key to continue. (If the last person to use the training version exited WordPerfect improperly, you may be stopped before this screen and asked, "Are other copies of WordPerfect currently running (Y/N)?" If you get this message, type N and WordPerfect will continue.)

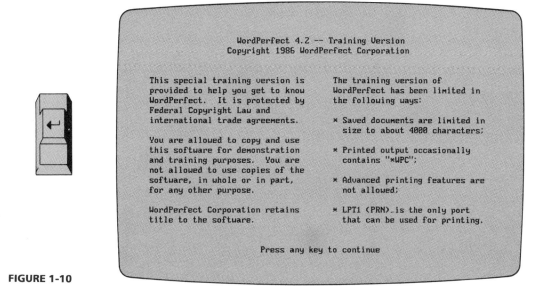

**FIGURE 1-10**

```
            WordPerfect 4.2 -- Training Version
            Copyright 1986 WordPerfect Corporation


This special training version is      The training version of
provided to help you get to know      WordPerfect has been limited in
WordPerfect.  It is protected by      the following ways:
Federal Copyright Law and
international trade agreements.        * Saved documents are limited in
                                        size to about 4000 characters;
You are allowed to copy and use
this software for demonstration       * Printed output occasionally
and training purposes.  You are         contains "*WPC";
not allowed to use copies of the
software, in whole or in part,        * Advanced printing features are
for any other purpose.                  not allowed;

WordPerfect Corporation retains       * LPT1 (PRN)_is the only port
title to the software.                   that can be used for printing.


            Press any key to continue
```

Some copies of the training version show a second screen welcoming you to WordPerfect, explaining how to use the function keys with the template and the Help function, and giving a few additional tips on how to use this software (Figure 1-11). If you see this screen, press any key to continue. If not, you are already into WordPerfect.

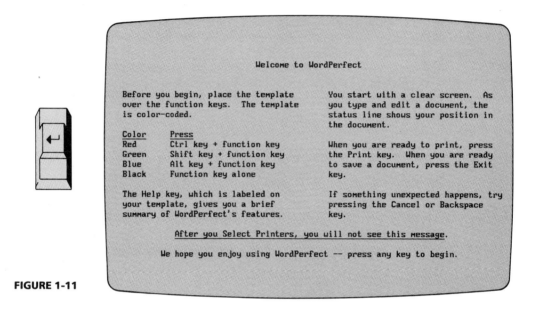

```
                    Welcome to WordPerfect

Before you begin, place the template        You start with a clear screen.  As
over the function keys.  The template       you type and edit a document, the
is color-coded.                             status line shows your position in
                                            the document.
Color     Press
Red       Ctrl key + function key           When you are ready to print, press
Green     Shift key + function key          the Print key.  When you are ready
Blue      Alt key + function key            to save a document, press the Exit
Black     Function key alone                key.

The Help key, which is labeled on           If something unexpected happens, try
your template, gives you a brief            pressing the Cancel or Backspace
summary of WordPerfect's features.          key.

           After you Select Printers, you will not see this message.

        We hope you enjoy using WordPerfect -- press any key to begin.
```

**FIGURE 1-11**

After you see the second opening screen, an almost blank screen appears, as shown in Figure 1-12. The only things on this screen are the status line and a blinking cursor. This blank screen is your work space, just as if you had put a blank piece of paper in your typewriter. The **cursor** is a visual reminder of where you are in the document. The **status line** informs you at all times about the exact document, page, line, and position of your cursor. For example, in Figure 1-12 the status line tells you that the cursor is in Document 1, on page 1, line 1, position 10.

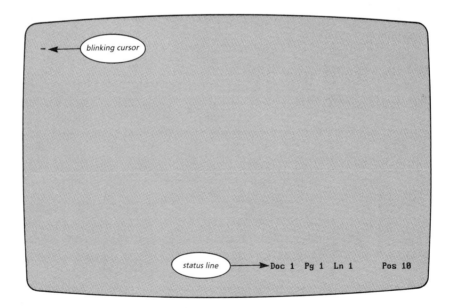

*blinking cursor*

*status line* ———▶ Doc 1  Pg 1  Ln 1          Pos 10

**FIGURE 1-12**

If you were typing on a typewriter, you would put one sheet of paper in at a time. Figure 1-13 illustrates how in WordPerfect all the pages seem to be attached together, with a so-called perforation between the pages. WordPerfect is programmed to advise you where the bottom of the page is and when you have started typing on the next page. When you have moved onto the next page, a line that looks much like a perforation will appear across the screen. After this line appears, the status line indicates that you are on the next page.

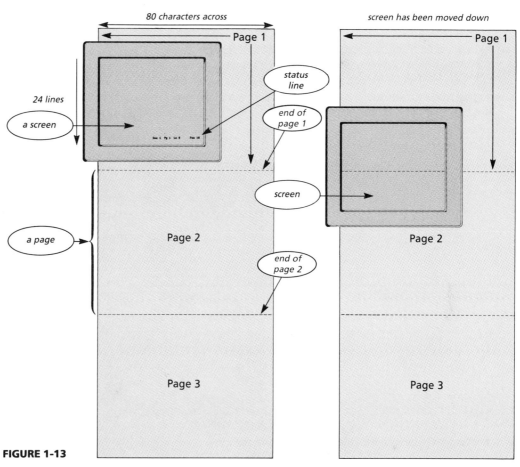

**FIGURE 1-13**

## THE SCREEN (OR WINDOW)

**A** **screen** or "window" is what appears on the computer monitor. Although you may have a four-page document, you can only view 24 lines down or 80 characters across at any one time on a screen. Imagine yourself looking out a window. You can only see a portion of the landscape outside. This does not mean that the rest of the world is not there, just that *your* view of the world is limited. If you went to another window, you would have a different view. This is the same as your "window" on your document. As Figure 1-13 shows, you can only see one screenful at a time. This does not mean that the rest of the document does not exist. Your view of your document depends on where your screen or "window" is situated.

## THE HELP FUNCTION

**I** f you need help, you could use the **Help Function**. This is a collection of screens that you can access any time you are working on a document. These screens contain quick reminders on how to use WordPerfect.

Because the amount of memory available for the training version of WordPerfect is limited, the full version of the help screens are not included on the training version WordPerfect diskette. To view the help screen that is included on the training version, look at the template next to the F3 key. In black you will see the word **Help**. Press the F3 key. This displays the help screen. To exit the help screen press the space bar.

## CREATING A DOCUMENT

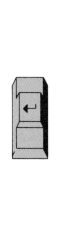

ow we are ready to create the letter to Mr. Wright (recall Figure 1-1). As you type, remember that if you type a mistake, all you need to do is press the Backspace key. As you do, your typing to the left of the Backspace key will be deleted. You can then retype correctly. If something unexpected happens, pressing the Backspace key may help. If you press a function key in error and you see a message at the bottom left corner of the screen, try pressing the **F1 (Cancel)** key.

Begin typing the first line of Figure 1-14, which is the date. As you type, notice that the position indicator (Pos) on the status line changes position with each letter or space you add.

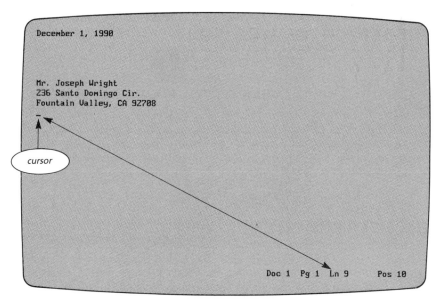

**FIGURE 1-14**

After typing the date, press the Return key. Pressing the Return key to start a new line is called a **hard return**. The cursor is now on line 2. Look at the status line for verification of the line where the cursor is. In order to insert four blank lines between the date and the addressee's name, press the Return key four more times. The status line now shows that the cursor is on line 6. Type the words Mr. Joseph Wright and then press the Return key, which takes the cursor to line 7. Type 236 Santo Domingo Cir. and press the Return key. The status line now indicates that the cursor is on line 8. Type the words Fountain Valley, CA 92708 and press the Return key. Figure 1-15 shows what your screen looks like with the date, name, and address.

**FIGURE 1-15**

Now that you have typed the name and address, you want a blank line between the last address line and the greeting to Mr. Wright. Simply press the Return key. That will insert a blank line. Your status line now indicates that the cursor is on line 10, position 10. Type the words Dear Mr. Wright: and press the Return key. Press the Return key again to insert another blank line. On line 12, type: I received your letter today and wish to thank you for it. Press the Return key. Press it again to insert a blank line. On line 14, type the word Sincerely, and press the Return key, which will move the cursor to line 15, position 10 (Figure 1-16).

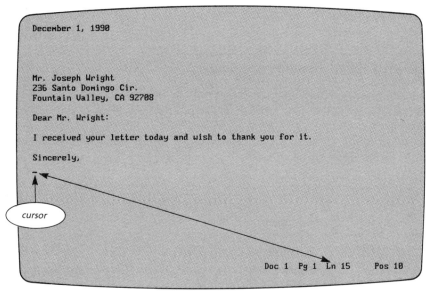

**FIGURE 1-16**

To add three more blank lines, press the Return key three more times. On line 18 type the words Mary Martinez followed by a Return. Type the word Director. The status line shows line 19, position 18. Press the Return key one more time, taking the cursor to line 20, position 10.

Figure 1-17 shows how the finished document should look on your screen.

If you neglected to insert a blank line somewhere, move the cursor to the beginning of that line and press Enter. If you omitted a word, move the cursor to the point where you wish to insert the word and type. All other text will move to accommodate the new text.

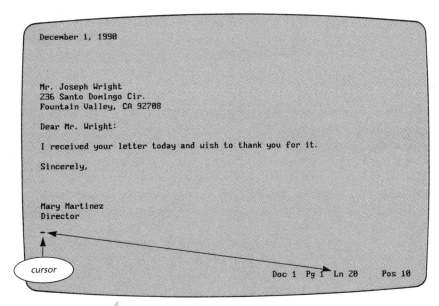

**FIGURE 1-17**

## REVEAL CODES

he WordPerfect software "remembers" each keystroke you make, whether a letter, number, or space. In addition, when you change margins or when you press the Return key, the Tab key, or other keys, the WordPerfect software embeds **codes** into the text, thereby recording each key you have pressed. To keep the screen clean and free of codes, WordPerfect stores these embedded codes in a hidden screen. You can view the codes at any time, however, by using the Alt and F3 keys. To learn about these codes first press the Up Arrow key until the cursor is at the top of the document.

### Learning How to Read the Reveal Codes

For each function you perform in WordPerfect, a unique code is embedded into the text. When you type a line and then perform a hard return, for example, that hard return is registered by the WordPerfect software and the code **[HRt]** is entered into the text at that point.

As you look at the screen you cannot see any of the codes, because they are on a hidden screen. Hold down the Alt key firmly and press the F3 key. Your screen will look like the one in Figure 1-18.

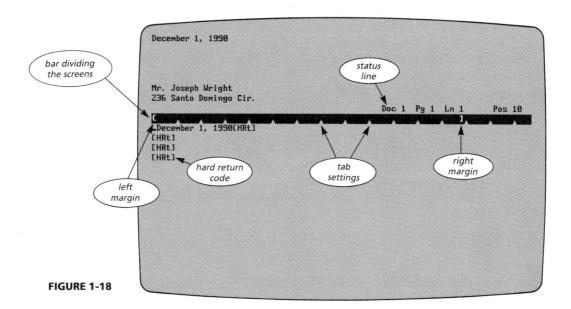

**FIGURE 1-18**

Look at your screen carefully. It appears that you have two different screens separated by a bar. First, look at the upper portion of the screen, at the numbers and letters above the bar. This is the screen you are used to viewing. You cannot see any codes, and your status line can still be viewed.

In the middle of the screen there appears to be a bar. On the left side you will notice a brace { . This indicates where your left margin is located. On the right side you will notice a bracket (]). This indicates where your right margin is located. The triangles ( ▲ ) you see between these symbols indicate where the tabs are currently set. Default is every five spaces.

On the bottom portion of the screen, notice that the text of the letter is the same as that on the top of the screen, with some differences. This lower screen is where your **reveal codes** are displayed. All the codes are in boldface. This is so that the codes will be easily recognized. The cursor in the reveal codes screen is also bolder than the cursor in the regular screen.

Figure 1-18 also shows, on the lower screen, that at the end of the first line you typed, you inserted a hard return. At the end of that line the code **[HRt]** is inserted, indicating that you pressed the Return key to start a new line.

Move your cursor one character to the right by pressing the Right Arrow → (step 1 in Figure 1-19). Notice that the cursor on the upper screen moves *underneath* each character, while the cursor on the lower screen moves *between* each character. Now move your cursor down one line by pressing the Down Arrow key ↓ (step 2 in Figure 1-19). Notice how both cursors move at the same time. They are, in fact, the same cursor, and move in relationship to each other.

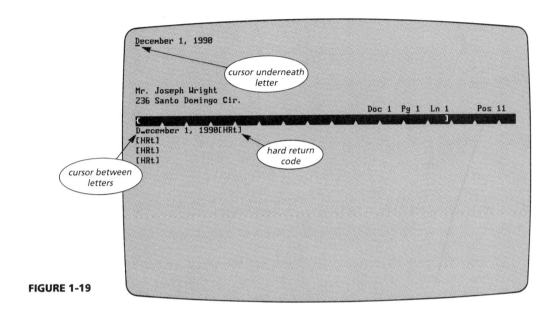

**FIGURE 1-19**

**Step 1: Move cursor one space to the right**

**Step 2: Move cursor down one line at a time**

**Step 3: Exit reveal codes**

*space*

Continue pressing the Down Arrow key ↓ until the status line indicates the cursor is on line 9. As you do this, notice how each time you pressed the Return key in the letter, the reveal codes indicate that a hard return code was embedded into the document. The reveal codes function is a valuable feature of WordPerfect. As you become more familiar with this feature, you will notice how much control you have over your word processing.

To exit from the reveal codes press the spacebar (step 3 in Figure 1-19). (The Enter or Cancel keys will also let you exit from the reveal codes).

Because you will be instructed many times in this text to display the reveal codes, practice this a few times. Hold down the Alt key, then press the F3 key. See how quickly the reveal codes are displayed. Press your spacebar to exit the reveal codes.

## SAVING A DOCUMENT

*T*he letter to Mr. Wright is now completed. Whenever a document is completed, it should be **saved** on a disk so that it can be retrieved for printing or modification at a later time. Look at the template next to the F10 key (Figure 1-20). Notice that the word Save is in black, indicating that the key is to be pressed alone. Now press the F10 key. At the lower left corner of your screen you will see the message "Document to be Saved:" (Figure 1-21).

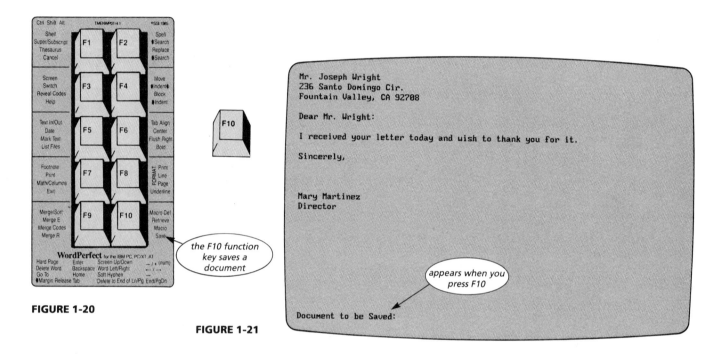

**FIGURE 1-20**

**FIGURE 1-21**

Type the name Wright (in upper-case, lowercase, or a combination). After you have typed Wright you will notice that nothing else happens. Remember: When nothing happens, press Enter (Figure 1-22).

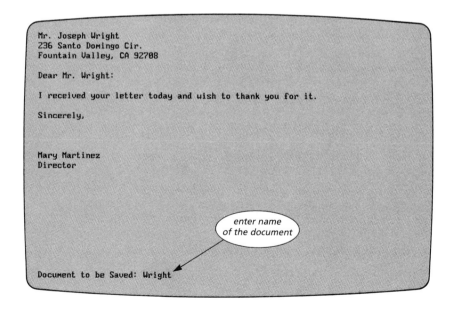

**FIGURE 1-22**

After you have pressed the Enter key you will notice that the light on drive B goes on, indicating that the document is being saved to drive B. That is because at the beginning of this project, before we loaded WordPerfect into the computer, we changed the default drive to B.

Your document is now named and saved. The name of your document appears in the lower left corner of your screen. As shown in Figure 1-13, the disk drive and directory that the document was saved to (B:\) are also displayed along with the document name.

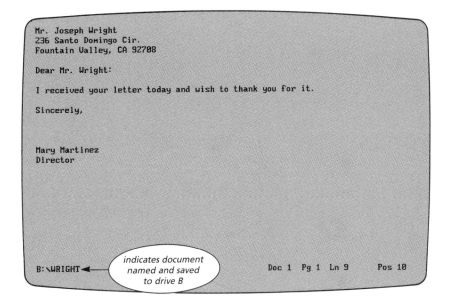

**FIGURE 1-23**

# PRINTING A DOCUMENT

fter the document is typed and stored on the disk, you usually want to **print** it on paper. Before continuing, be sure that your printer has continuous feed paper inserted and that the printer is turned on and ready to print.

To print your document look at the template next to the **F7** key. Notice the word Print in green (Figure 1-24).

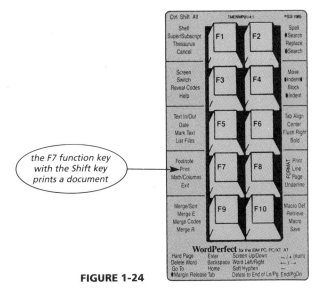

**FIGURE 1-24**

Hold down the Shift key and press the F7 key (step 1 in Figure 1-25). You will see the Print menu shown in Figure 1-25 at the bottom of your screen.

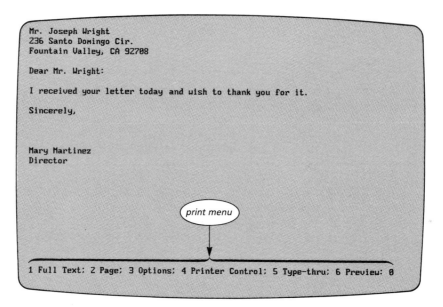

**FIGURE 1-25**

Step 1: Retrieve the Print menu

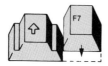

Step 2: Print the full text

Since we want to print the full text of this document, press the number 1 for full text (step 2 in Figure 1-25). At this point the printer will begin printing your document.

In Figure 1-26, notice that the document generated by the training version of WordPerfect contains the notation *WPC at random places throughout. This is your reminder that it is the training version and that it is copyrighted by WordPerfect Corporation.

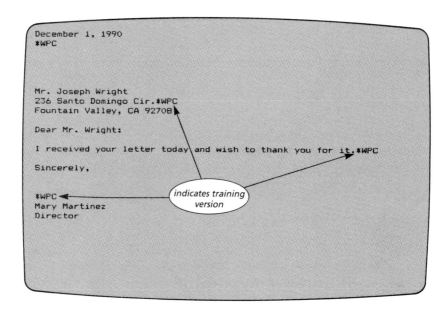

**FIGURE 1-26**

# MOVING THE CURSOR ON A BLANK SCREEN

Now that the letter to Mr. Wright has been typed, saved, and printed, we will use a blank screen to practice the Return, Tab, and spacebar functions. These are helpful keys for moving the cursor, shown in Figure 1-27. To be sure you are at the end of this document, press the **Home** key *two times*, then press the Down Arrow key ↓ one time (step 1 in Figure 1-28). This places the cursor at the end of your document. Press the Return key to insert a hard return (step 2 in Figure 1-28). This moves the cursor to a new line.

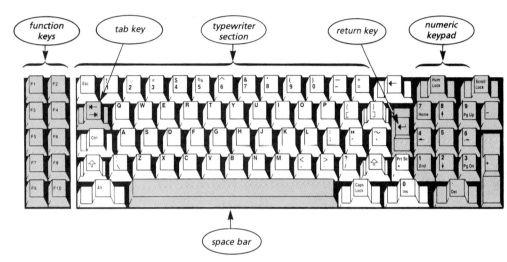

**FIGURE 1-27**

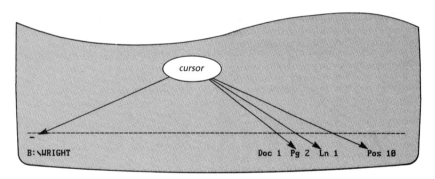

**FIGURE 1-28**

**Step 1: Move cursor to the end of the document**

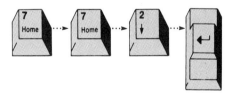

**Step 2: Move cursor to a new line**          **Step 3: Move to page 2, line 1**

Recall that when you press the Return key, the cursor moves down one line at a time. The status line also indicates when the cursor has moved down a line. Press the Return key until the status line indicates that the cursor is on page 1, line 54. If you then press the Return key one more time (step 3 in Figure 1-28), a dotted line appears on the screen. This dotted line marks the end of page 1. The status line indicates that the cursor is now on page 2, line 1 as shown in Figure 1-28.

Press the Tab key once and you will see the cursor move to the right five spaces at a time. The status line also indicates with the position number that the cursor has moved five spaces at a time.

Press the spacebar and you will see the cursor move to the right one space at a time. The status line will also indicate with the position number that the cursor has moved one space at a time.

Now that you understand the meanings of Pg (page), Ln (line), and Pos (position) on the status line, you may wonder about Doc (document) 1. WordPerfect allows you to work on two different documents at the same time. For example, suppose you were working on a 30-page document and you needed to stop and quickly type a letter and print it out. You could switch to Doc (document) 2. In fact, you could switch back and forth between the two documents, making changes, printing, saving, and so on. The changes or printing of document 1 would not affect document 2 at all. This is like having two computers.

Look at the template next to the F3 key and notice the word Switch in green (Figure 1-29). To see document 2, hold down the Shift key firmly and press the F3 key (step 1 in Figure 1-30). You could type, save, and print a letter in document 2 without disturbing your letter to Mr. Wright in document 1. When finished with the letter in document 2, you could switch back to document 1. Your cursor will revert to where it was in document 1, allowing you to continue.

To return to document 1, hold the Shift key down and press the F3 key (step 2 in Figure 1-30). You are now back in document 1.

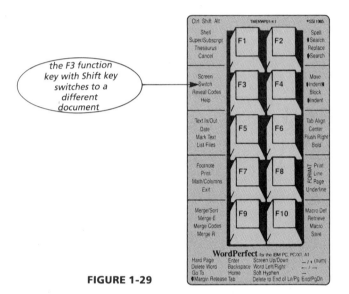

the F3 function key with Shift key switches to a different document

**FIGURE 1-29**

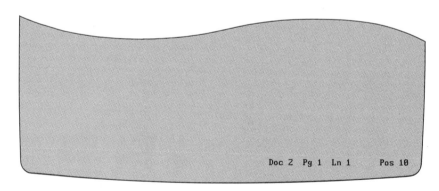

Doc 2   Pg 1   Ln 1      Pos 10

**FIGURE 1-30**

Step 1: Switch to Doc 2      Step 2: Return to Doc 1

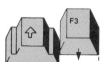

Since you have pressed the Return key, the spacebar, and the Tab key, you have changed your document. This altered document, with more spaces, tabs, and hard returns, has not been saved permanently to the disk, and we do not wish to do so. Remember that the *typed* portion of the document was saved. That saved portion was not changed on the disk. Since we want to exit from this document without saving again we will not use F10. To prepare to exit WordPerfect, move the cursor to the top of the document by pressing the Home key twice, then press the Up Arrow key ↑ (Figure 1-31). It is not necessary to move to the top of a document when exiting. We do so here to show that the letter to Mr. Wright is still in memory.

## EXITING WORDPERFECT

*T*o exit this document, as well as WordPerfect, first look at the template next to the F7 key. The word Exit is in black, indicating that you press only the F7 key (Figure 1-32).

Press the F7 key (step 1 in Figure 1-33). The message "Save Document? (Y/N) Y" is shown in the lower left corner of the screen.

**FIGURE 1-31**

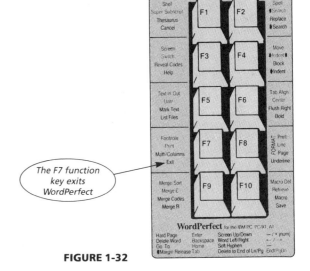

*The F7 function key exits WordPerfect*

**FIGURE 1-32**

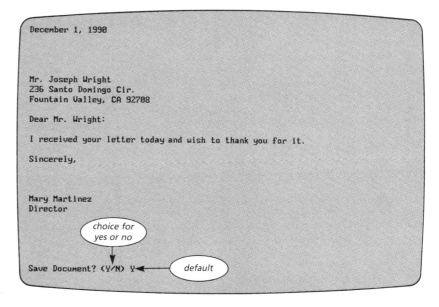

**FIGURE 1-33**

Step 1: Initiate exit

Step 2: Choose not to save document

The (Y/N) means that if you press the Y (for yes) you want to save the document. If you press the N (for no) you do not want to save the document. The Y outside the parentheses means that the WordPerfect software has defaulted the answer to yes, so if you press either the Enter key or the spacebar the computer will accept yes as the default. However, type N for no (step 2 in Figure 1-33). You will then see "Exit WP? (Y/N) N" on your screen (Figure 1-34). Since we do want to exit the program, type Y. (If you failed to complete the printing of the document you may see the message "Cancel all print jobs (Y/N)?N". If this appears, type Y for yes.)

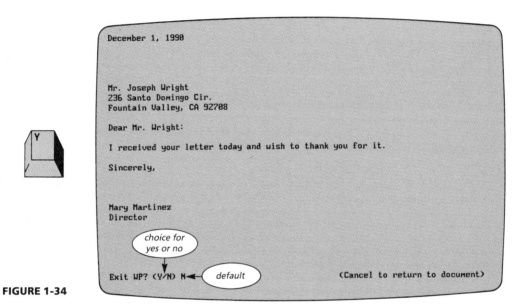

**FIGURE 1-34**

To exit properly we must return to the DOS prompt. After you have typed Y, the message "Insert COMMAND.COM disk in drive A and strike any key when ready" appears on the screen (Figure 1-35). On some copies of the training version or if you have a hard disk system the DOS prompt will appear immediately and you will not see the message.

If you see the message "Insert COMMAND.COM disk in drive A and strike any key when ready" take your WordPerfect training version out of drive A and insert your DOS disk. Press any key. You will then see the DOS prompt indicating that WordPerfect is no longer in the computer's memory (Figure 1-35).

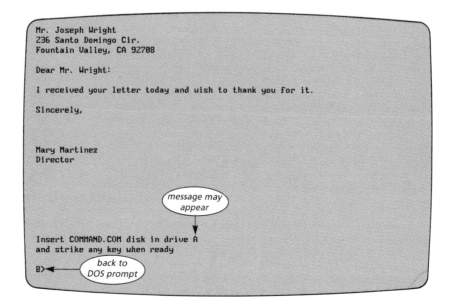

**FIGURE 1-35**

# PROJECT SUMMARY

*T*his project demonstrated how to use the function keys with the WordPerfect template. You learned how to enter the WordPerfect program and type a document using the hard return at the end of short sentences. You also learned the importance of reveal codes to a document, and that the hidden codes can be found by holding down the Alt key and pressing the F3 key. You learned how to save and print the document and how to move the cursor on a blank screen. Finally, you exited WordPerfect.

The following is a summary of the keystroke sequence we used in Project 1:

**SUMMARY OF KEYSTROKES—Project 1**

| STEPS | KEY(S) PRESSED | STEPS | KEY(S) PRESSED |
|---|---|---|---|
| 1 | b: [at the A> prompt] | 25 | ← |
| 2 | ← | 26 | Sincerely, |
| 3 | a:wp [at the B> prompt] | 27 | ← |
| 4 | ← | 28 | ← |
| 5 | ← [at first introductory screen] | 29 | ← |
| 6 | ← [only if you see a second intro-ductory screen] | 30 | ← |
| | | 31 | Mary Martinez |
| 7 | December 1, 1990 | 32 | ← |
| 8 | ← | 33 | Director |
| 9 | ← | 34 | ← |
| 10 | ← | 35 | [Alt-F3] |
| 11 | ← | 36 | [spacebar] |
| 12 | ← | 37 | [F10] |
| 13 | Mr. Joseph Wright | 38 | Wright |
| 14 | ← | 39 | ← |
| 15 | 236 Santo Domingo Cir. | 40 | [Shift-F7] |
| 16 | ← | 41 | 1 |
| 17 | Fountain Valley, CA 92708 | 42 | [F7] |
| 18 | ← | 43 | N |
| 19 | ← | 44 | Y |
| 20 | Dear Mr. Wright: | 45 | [remove disk from drive A if you see prompt "Insert COMMAND.COM disk in drive A and strike any key when ready"] |
| 21 | ← | | |
| 22 | ← | | |
| 23 | I received your letter today and wish to thank you for it. | 46 | [put DOS disk into drive A] |
| | | 47 | [press any key] |
| 24 | ← | 48 | [remove disks from both drives] |

## Project Summary (continued)

The following list summarizes the material covered in Project 1.

1. The **keyboard** is used as an input device to input data into the computer.
2. **Function keys** numbered F1 through F10 are located to the left or at the top of the keyboard. Each function key has been assigned four specific functions to execute commonly used commands.
3. The keys on the **numeric keypad**, to the right of the keyboard, are used to move the cursor. When the Num Lock key is pressed, these keys can also be used to type numbers.
4. The **Shift key** is used to make lowercase letters into capital letters and to type the symbols above the numbers. It is also used with the function keys to accomplish specific word processing goals.
5. The **Ctrl** key, used in tandem with function keys, performs special functions.
6. The **Alt** key, used in tandem with function keys, also performs special functions.
7. The **Tab** key moves the cursor to the next tab setting, and when used with the Shift key releases the left margin.
8. The **Enter** or **Return** key is used to enter data in the computer, or as a **hard return** at the end of a line or paragraph.
9. The **Backspace** key moves the cursor backward on the screen, deleting the character to the left of the cursor.
10. The **Left Arrow** key moves the cursor one character to the left.
11. The **Right Arrow** key moves the cursor one character to the right.
12. The **Up Arrow** key moves the cursor up one line.
13. The **Down Arrow** key moves the cursor down one line.
14. A color-coded **template** is placed over the function keys to identify the keys to be used for specific functions.
15. The **Help function** is a collection of screens that gives reminders on how to use WordPerfect.
16. A **default** option is a preassigned choice. Unless instructed otherwise, the default option will be chosen.
17. The **cursor** is the blinking underscore on the screen that designates the current position in a document.
18. The **status line**, at the bottom right of the screen, identifies the exact location of the cursor.
19. The **screen** (window) is the monitor of the computer. It shows what has been entered into the computer.
20. Press the **Cancel (F1)** key when an undesired message appears at the bottom left of the screen.
21. **Reveal codes** are the commands embedded in the document by the WordPerfect software. They control how the input document appears on the screen, as well as how it is printed on a printer.
22. The **hard return [HRt]** code indicates the end of a short line or paragraph, or where a blank line is to be inserted into the document.
23. Press the Alt and F3 keys to view the screen that reveals the embedded reveal codes that control the format of the document.
24. After a document has been entered into the computer, it must be **saved** to a disk for later retrieval or reference.
25. **Printing** a document that has been typed and stored produces a copy of the document on paper.

# STUDENT ASSIGNMENTS

## STUDENT ASSIGNMENT 1: True/False

**Instructions:** Circle T if the statement is true and F if the statement is false.

T  F    1. It is not necessary to use the Ctrl, Alt, or Shift keys with any other key.
T  F    2. A good rule of thumb is, if nothing happens on the screen, press Enter.
T  F    3. The WordPerfect template fits above or around the function keys.
T  F    4. When saving a document the file name must be typed in all capital letters.
T  F    5. To exit WordPerfect, use the F7 key.
T  F    6. To save a file, use the F10 key.
T  F    7. The numeric keypad is usually on the left side of the keyboard.
T  F    8. To print a document, use the Ctrl-F8 keys.
T  F    9. On most monitors, you can only view 24 lines of typing at a time.
T  F   10. To add a blank line, press the spacebar.

## STUDENT ASSIGNMENT 2: Multiple Choice

**Instructions:**    Circle the correct response.

1. The WordPerfect template is used in conjunction with the
   a. numeric keypad
   b. alphabet keys
   c. function keys
   d. 1 through 10 keys
2. On the template, functions typed in red are used with the
   a. Ctrl key
   b. Shift key
   c. Alt and Ctrl key
   d. none of the above
3. The numeric keypad can be used to
   a. type numbers
   b. move the cursor
   c. neither a nor b
   d. both a and b
4. When some function keys are pressed a message may appear at the
   a. upper left corner of the screen
   b. lower left corner of the screen
   c. upper right corner of the screen
   d. lower right corner of the screen
5. After you press some function keys and a message appears on the screen, you can cancel the message by pressing the
   a. F2 key
   b. F7 key
   c. Shift-F10 keys
   d. F1 key
6. The Right Arrow key moves the cursor
   a. one character or space to the right
   b. one word to the right
   c. to the right end of the line
   d. one line down
7. To exit from reveal codes you can
   a. press the Right Arrow key
   b. press the spacebar
   c. press the Down Arrow key
   d. press the Home key twice, then the Up Arrow key
8. The Return key is used to
   a. end a paragraph
   b. put a [HRt] code in the document
   c. insert a blank line
   d. all of the above

## STUDENT ASSIGNMENT 3: Matching

**Instructions:** Put the appropriate number next to the words in the second column.

1. Red
2. Blue
3. Black
4. Cancel
5. Save
6. Print
7. Bottom of document
8. Green
9. Exit
10. Reveal codes
11. Top of document

_____ Alt plus a function key
_____ Alt-F3
_____ Shift-F7
_____ Ctrl plus a function key
_____ Shift
_____ F7
_____ F1
_____ Function key alone
_____ Home, Home, Up Arrow
_____ Home, Home, Down Arrow
_____ F10

## STUDENT ASSIGNMENT 4: Fill in the Blanks

1. To enter the WordPerfect program at the B> prompt, type _____ and then press _____ .
2. When WordPerfect has been brought into the memory of the computer, a screen appears that is blank except for a _____ line at the lower right corner of the screen.
3. The status line contains the default settings of Doc _____ Pg _____ Ln _____ Pos _____ .
4. The screen or window can show _____ lines of the document at any one time.
5. If something unexpected happens on the screen—for example, an extra space or a hard return—pressing the _____ key may help.
6. When you press the Return key at the end of a line, the code that is embedded into the document is _____ .
7. When the screen is split to reveal codes, the codes can be viewed in the _____ screen.
8. The Down Arrow moves the cursor down _____ lines.
9. "Document to be Saved:" appears on the screen when you press the _____ key.
10. If an unwanted message appears on the screen, you can usually press the _____ key to cancel the message.

## STUDENT ASSIGNMENT 5: Fill in the Blanks

1. When pressing Ctrl, Alt, or Shift with a function key, it is incorrect to press the keys simultaneously. The correct way is _____ .
2. The ↵ key can be called either the _____ or the _____ key.
3. After pressing Shift-F7 to print, if you wish to print the full text, you must press the number _____ .
4. If you accept the tab default settings, the cursor will move _____ spaces when you press the Tab key.
5. After you press the Shift-F3 keys, the cursor will move to document _____ .
6. When you wish to exit, press the _____ key.
7. After you have pressed the Exit key, instead of exiting immediately, WordPerfect prompts: _____ Document? (Y/N) Y.
8. If you press N in answer to the message in question 7, the next prompt is: _____ WP? (Y/N) N.
9. If you press Y in answer to the message in question 8 you will then _____ from the WordPerfect program.

## STUDENT ASSIGNMENT 6

**Instructions:** On the keyboard shown here, label the keys with the names given below.

Ctrl
Shift (both keys)
Alt
Backspace
Tab
Enter (Return)
Spacebar

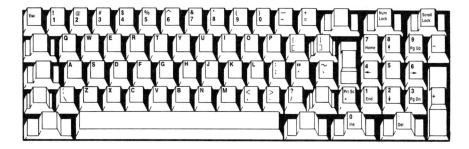

On the numeric keypad, fill in the correct direction of the cursor arrows.

Label function keys 1 through 10 (write F1, F2, etc.).

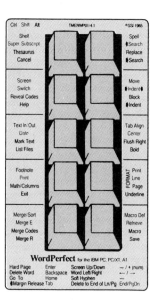

## STUDENT ASSIGNMENT 7: Correcting Errors

**Instructions:** The document illustrates the first part of a memo that is being prepared using WordPerfect. An error was made when typing the memo. The last word was typed todya. The word should be today. Explain in detail the steps necessary to correct the error.

Method of correction: _____

_____

_____

_____

_____

_____

_____

_____

```
December 1, 1990



Mr. Joseph Wright
236 Santo Domingo Cir.
Fountain Valley, CA 92708

Dear Mr. Wright:

I received your letter todya_
```

## STUDENT ASSIGNMENT 8: Correcting Errors

**Instructions:** The screen illustrates a letter that has been prepared using WordPerfect. There are no hard returns between the body of letter and the word Sincerely, and there is no space between the words thankyou. Explain in detail the steps required to add a blank line above the word Sincerely, and to put a space between the words thankyou.

```
December 1, 1990



Mr. Joseph Wright
236 Santo Domingo Cir.
Fountain Valley, CA 92708

Dear Mr. Wright:

I received your letter today and wish to thankyou for it.
Sincerely,


Mary Martinez
Director
```

Method of correction: _____

_____

_____

_____

## STUDENT ASSIGNMENT 9: Viewing Reveal Codes

Problem 1: Prepare the memo illustrated. Follow the step-by-step instructions you learned in this project.

```
TO:   All Employees
FROM:      Personnel Department
SUBJECT:   Vacation Schedules

The following are the rules for vacations:

1.   Each employee will have two weeks vacation.
2.   Vacations must be taken in June, July or August.
3.   You must notify personnel 4 weeks in advance.
4.   You must obtain approval from your supervisor.

Janet Fisher
Personnel Administrator
```

Problem 2: After you have typed the letter, press the Alt-F3 keys to reveal the codes. To send what is on your screen to the printer press the PrtSc (Print Screen) key (on some computers there is a Print Screen key, and on others you must press Shift-PrtSc). After you have a hard copy of what is on the screen, circle all [HRt] codes on the page.

Problem 3: Save on disk as schedule.1.

## STUDENT ASSIGNMENT 10: Creating and Printing a Document

**Instructions:**    Perform the following tasks.

1. Load the disk operating system into main memory.
2. Load the WordPerfect program into main memory by inserting the WordPerfect diskette into drive A and putting a data disk into drive B. Type b: and press Enter. At the B> prompt, type a:wp and press the Enter key.

Problem 1:  Prepare the letter illustrated below.

```
March 15, 1990


Ms. Roberta Weitzman
President, SpaceTek Inc.
44538 Scroll Avenue
Monnett, NJ 08773

Dear Ms. Weitzman:

This letter confirms our purchase of 13 Pin Brackets.

James R. McMillan, AirFrame Inc.
```

Problem 2: Save the document on disk. Use the file name Weitzman.1.

Problem 3: After the document has been saved on disk, produce a printed copy of the letter.

## STUDENT ASSIGNMENT 11: Creating and Printing a Document

**Instructions:**    Perform the following tasks.

1. Load the disk operating system into main memory.
2. Load the WordPerfect program into main memory by inserting the WordPerfect diskette into drive A and putting a data disk into drive B. Type b: and press enter. At the B> prompt, type a:wp and press the Enter key.

Problem 1:  Prepare the letter illustrated below.

```
March 15, 1990


Dear Employees:

You must notify the Personnel department of your vacation plans.

Janet Fisher
Personnel Administrator
```

Problem 2: Save the document on disk. Use the file name Vacation.

Problem 3: After the document has been saved on disk, produce a printed copy of the letter.

## PROJECT 2

## Creating a Document with Word Wrap

### Objectives

You will have mastered the material in this project when you can:

- Type documents using word wrap
- Move the cursor using more efficient keystrokes
- Delete and restore text

```
December 1, 1990


TO:  All Sales Managers
RE:  New Bonus Plan

The new bonus plan approved by the Board of Directors will become
effective January 1.  If you have questions, contact Hanna Butler
prior to January 1, 1991.  All sales people are affected by the
new plan.

Rita Moeller

cc:  Board of Directors
```

**FIGURE 2-1**

### Loading the WordPerfect Program

At the A> prompt, type b: and press Enter; at the B> prompt type a:wp and press Enter. WordPerfect loads into main memory. First you see the screen informing you that you are using the educational version of WordPerfect. Press any key to continue. Next, you may see the screen explaining the WordPerfect template colors; if you see this second screen, press any key to continue. The next screen is your clean work space. As you saw in Project 1, the only thing you see is the status line in the lower right corner, indicating that the cursor is in document 1 on page 1, line 1, position 10.

## LEARNING ABOUT WORD WRAP

When you type on a typewriter, the first thing you do after putting the paper in is set the margins. In WordPerfect, the default margins are position 10 at the left and position 74 at the right. *Default* means that the margins have been preset at these positions. Unless you instruct the software otherwise, these are the margins it will follow.

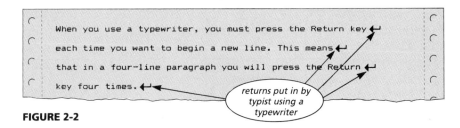

```
When you use a typewriter, you must press the Return key ←
each time you want to begin a new line. This means ←
that in a four-line paragraph you will press the Return ←
key four times. ←
```
*returns put in by typist using a typewriter*

**FIGURE 2-2**

When you type on a typewriter with the margins set, every time you approach the end of a line, you hear a "ding" from the typewriter. This indicates that the margin is approaching and you should finish typing the current word and press the Return ← key to return the carriage to the next line, as illustrated in Figure 2-2.

Most word processing software, unlike a typewriter, allows you to type continuously. The software automatically "wraps" the typing to the next line when it reaches the right margin, as illustrated in Figure 2-3. The term for this is **word wrap**. The only time you need to press the Return ↵ key is when you reach the end of a paragraph, when you want to insert a blank line, or when you want to terminate the line before word wrap can take effect. Such is the case in the first three lines of the memo you will be typing (see Figure 2-1). Word wrap allows you to enter data much faster than if you had to press Return after each line. The word wrap feature is a major advantage of most word processing programs, including WordPerfect.

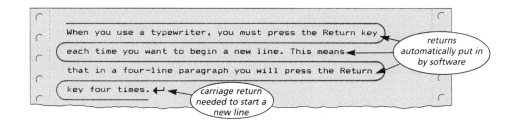

**FIGURE 2-3**

## Typing a Letter

Begin typing the memo in Figure 2-1. As you learned in Project 1, each time you press a key on the keyboard to enter a character, the cursor moves one position to the right, and the position number on the status line changes to indicate the cursor's position. The date line is not long enough to wrap. Therefore, after typing the date, press the Return ↵ key. The status line shows the cursor on line 2, position 10. Press the Return ↵ key four more times to move the cursor to line 6, position 10. Type TO: and press the Tab key, moving the cursor to position 15; then type the words All Sales Managers and press the Return ↵ key, putting the cursor on line 7, position 10.

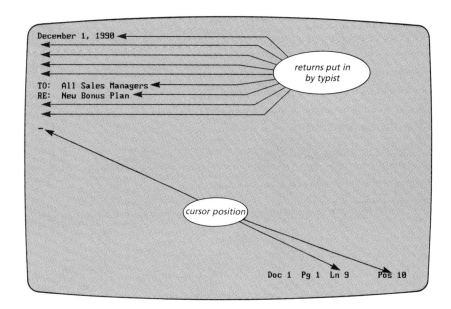

**FIGURE 2-4**

Type RE: and press the Tab key; then type the words New Bonus Plan. Press the Return key two times (↵ ↵), taking the cursor to line 9, position 10 (Figure 2-4).

Now type the paragraph of the memo. As you type remember to press the spacebar twice after each period at the end of each sentence. Also, remember *not* to press the Return key at the end of each line. As you approach the end of the first line, watch the screen. When you begin to type the word "effective", notice that the word is too long to fit on the line. But before the word is completely typed it wraps down to the next line.

Type the entire paragraph. After you have typed the last word, plan, followed by a period, the cursor is on line 12, position 19. Press the Return ↵ key because this last line of the paragraph is too short to wrap. Press the Return key again, moving the cursor to line 14, position 10. Type the name Rita Moeller and press the Return ↵ key two times. The cursor is now on line 16, position 10. Type the abbreviation cc:, then press the Tab key. Type the words Board of Directors.

The cursor should be on line 16, position 33. Press Return ↵, thereby putting the cursor on line 17, position 10 (Figure 2-5).

In Figure 2-5, all the text in the body of the memo has been typed. It consists of three full lines of text and a partial fourth line. Word wrap occurred for the three full lines of text. When you typed the fourth line of the paragraph, you reached the end of the text before word wrap took effect, so you pressed the Return to cause a hard return. When word wrap causes text to be moved to the next line, a **soft return** is said to have occurred.

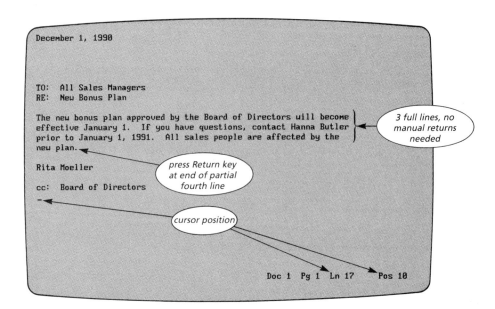

**FIGURE 2-5**

## Checking the Reveal Codes

It is always necessary to be conscious of the codes being embedded into your document. The entire format of your document is determined by the codes, and the printer is governed by codes. If something does not print the way you anticipated, it is wise to check the codes. As you learned in Project 1, the codes are embedded into the document automatically by the software and saved when the document is saved. Before you look at the codes, return to the top of the document. Press the Home, Home, Up Arrow ↑ keys (Figure 2-6). This takes the cursor immediately to the top of the document, line 1, position 10.

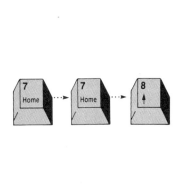

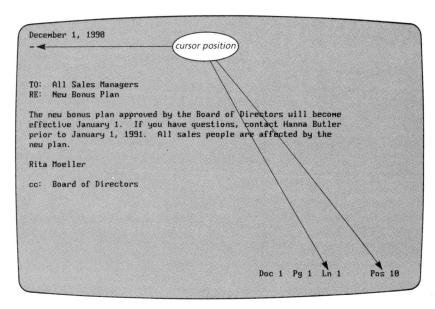

**FIGURE 2-6**

Look at the template next to the F3 key. Notice the words Reveal Codes in blue. Hold down the Alt key firmly and press the F3 key. When you do, the screen shown in Figure 2-7 appears.

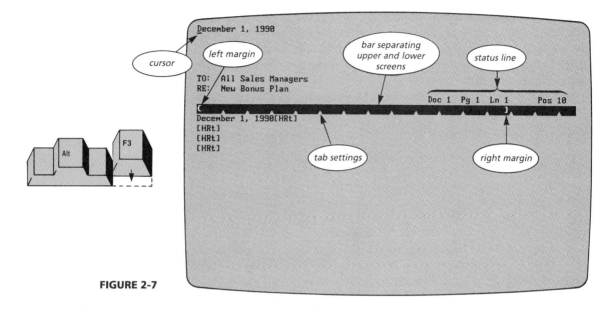

**FIGURE 2-7**

Look at your screen carefully. The bar indicating the left and right margins and tab settings separates the upper and lower screens. Above the bar is the screen you are familiar with. You cannot see any codes, and your status line can still be viewed.

Below the bar is the reveal codes screen. Notice that the typing is the same as on the upper screen, except the codes also appear. All the codes are in boldface so that they are easily recognizable (if you have a color monitor, boldface may appear as a particular color; in that case the codes will be that boldface color). The cursor in the lower screen is also bolder than the cursor in the regular screen.

In Figure 2-8, notice the [HRt] code at the end of line 1 where you typed the date. Move the cursor down to line 6 with the Down Arrow ↓ key. Notice that both cursors move at the same time. They are, in fact, the same cursor and move in relationship to each other.

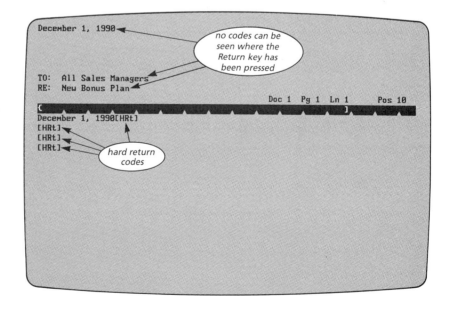

**FIGURE 2-8**

As you move the cursor, notice that wherever you inserted a hard return there is the [HRt] code. In Figure 2-9, on line 6 after TO: and on line 7 after RE: where you pressed the Tab key, notice the code **[TAB]**. Each of those lines is followed by a hard return.

Looking only at the lower screen, continue moving the cursor down with the Down Arrow ↓ key. When you get to the paragraph you typed, notice that instead of [HRt] codes at each line end, there are **[SRt]** codes (Figure 2-10). These are the lines where you allowed word wrap to occur, so there is a soft return [SRt] code at the end of each line.

With the Down Arrow ↓ key continue moving the cursor down to the end of the document, shown in Figure 2-11. The last code in the document is [HRt].

To exit from the reveal codes screen, press the spacebar or another key such as Enter.

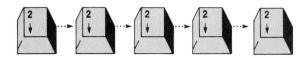

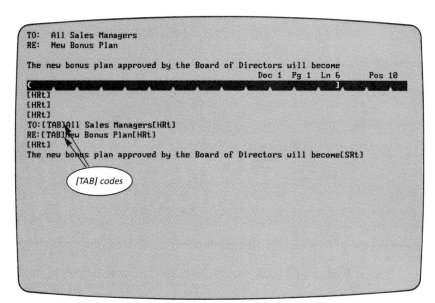

**FIGURE 2-9**

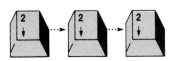

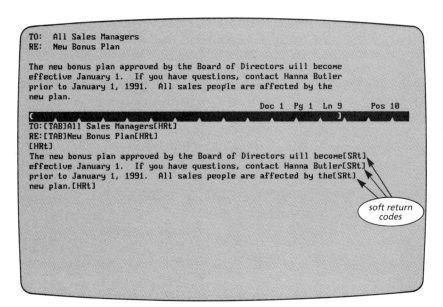

**FIGURE 2-10**

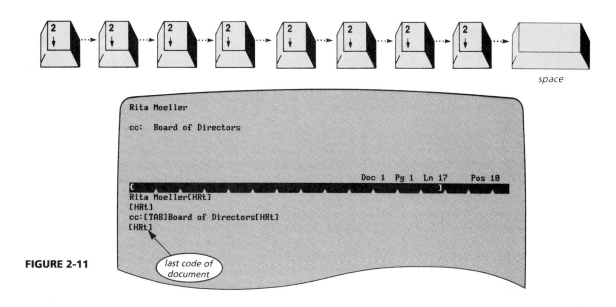

*space*

**FIGURE 2-11**

*last code of document*

## Saving a Document

The memo to the sales managers shown in Figure 2-1 is completed. Whenever a document is completed, it should be saved onto the disk so that it can be retrieved for printing or modification at a later time. Look at the template next to the F10 key. Notice the word Save in black. Press the F10 key (step 1 in Figure 2-12). At the lower left corner of your screen you see the message "Document to Be Saved:". To name the document type the word MEMO as shown in step 2 of Figure 2-12 (you can type it in uppercase, lowercase, or a combination). After you have typed MEMO, notice that nothing else happens. Press the Enter key ←.

After you press the Enter key, notice that the light on drive B goes on, indicating that the document is being saved to the diskette in drive B, the default disk drive.

Your document is now named and saved. The name of the document appears in the lower left corner of your screen. Although you did not enter B:\ before you typed the name, because WordPerfect defaults to drive B, B:\ appears to remind you that the document is saved to the diskette in drive B.

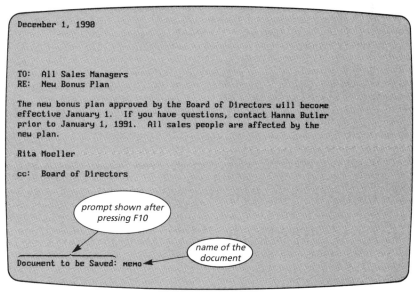

*prompt shown after pressing F10*

*name of the document*

**Step 1: Save the document**      **Step 2: Name the document**

**FIGURE 2-12**

Figure 2-13 shows that that designation is now part of the name of this document.

## Printing a Document

After the file is entered and stored on the disk, the next task is normally to print the document. Be sure your printer has paper inserted correctly and that the printer is turned on and is ready to print.

From Project 1, remember that to print your document you must invoke the Print function. While holding down the Shift key, press the F7 key. Figure 2-14 shows that when you press those keys the print menu appears at the bottom of the screen.

Since you wish to print the full text of this document, press the number 1 for full text. At this point the printer begins printing your document. The printed document is illustrated in Figure 2-15.

The document generated by the training version of WordPerfect contains random *WPC notations throughout. The notations are your reminder that you are using the WordPerfect training version copyrighted by WordPerfect Corporation.

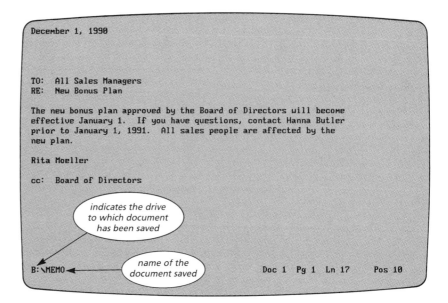

December 1, 1990

TO: All Sales Managers
RE: New Bonus Plan

The new bonus plan approved by the Board of Directors will become effective January 1. If you have questions, contact Hanna Butler prior to January 1, 1991. All sales people are affected by the new plan.

Rita Moeller

cc: Board of Directors

*indicates the drive to which document has been saved*

B:\MEMO ← *name of the document saved*   Doc 1   Pg 1   Ln 17   Pos 10

**FIGURE 2-13**

December 1, 1990

TO: All Sales Managers
RE: New Bonus Plan

The new bonus plan approved by the Board of Directors will become effective January 1. If you have questions, contact Hanna Butler prior to January 1, 1991. All sales people are affected by the new plan.

Rita Moeller

cc: Board of Directors

*option to print the complete text*        *the print menu*

1 Full Text; 2 Page; 3 Options; 4 Printer Control; 5 Type-thru; 6 Preview: 0

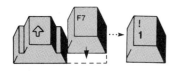

**FIGURE 2-14**

December 1, 1990
*WPC

TO: All Sales Managers
RE: New Bonus Plan*WPC

The new bonus plan approved by the Board of Directors will become effective January 1. If you have questions, contact Hanna Butler prior to January 1, 1991. All sales people are affected by the new plan.*WPC

Rita Moeller

cc: Board of Directors
*WPC

*indicates training version of WordPerfect*

**FIGURE 2-15**

# MOVING THE CURSOR

## Arrow Keys

s you have learned, the arrow keys are used to move the cursor on the screen. However, to save time by moving more efficiently through your document, WordPerfect allows many combinations of cursor movements. Table 2-1 presents a complete list of cursor movements. Refer to the table during the following discussion about cursor movements.

**TABLE 2-1** Summary of Cursor Keystrokes

| KEYSTROKES | RESULTS |
|---|---|
| ← | Moves cursor one character or space to the left. |
| → | Moves cursor one character or space to the right. |
| ↑ | Moves cursor up one line. |
| ↓ | Moves cursor down one line. |
| Ctrl → | Moves cursor to the first letter of the next word. |
| Ctrl ← | Moves cursor to the first letter of the previous word. |
| Home → | Moves cursor to the right edge of the current screen. If you continue to press Home, Right Arrow the cursor moves to the right edge of the next screen to the right. |
| Home ← | Moves cursor to the left edge of the current screen. If there are more screens to the left and you continue to press Home, Left Arrow, the cursor moves to the left edge of the next screen. |
| Home ↑ | Moves cursor to the top of the current screen, then to the top of the previous screen. |
| Home ↓ | Moves cursor to the bottom of the current screen, then to the bottom of the next screen. |
| − (on numeric keypad) | Moves cursor to the top of the current screen, then to the top of the previous screen (same as Home, Up Arrow). |
| + (on numeric keypad) | Moves cursor to the bottom of the current screen, then to the bottom of the next screen (same as Home, Down Arrow). |
| Home Home ↑ | Moves cursor to the top of the entire document. |
| Home Home ↓ | Moves cursor to the bottom of the entire document. |
| Home Home → | Moves cursor to the right end of the current line. |
| Home Home ← | Moves cursor to the beginning of the current line. |
| Home Home Home ← | Moves cursor in front of all codes and characters at the beginning of the current line. |
| End | Moves cursor to the right end of the current line. |
| PgDn | Moves cursor to line 1 of the next page. |
| PgUp | Moves cursor to line 1 of the previous page. |
| Ctrl-Home, page number, ← | "Go to" command. When "Go to" appears on the screen, type the page number desired and press Enter. Moves cursor to line 1 of page indicated. |
| Ctrl-Home ↑ | Moves cursor to line 1 of current page. |
| Ctrl-Home ↓ | Moves cursor to last line of current page. |
| Ctrl-Home Alt-F4 | Moves cursor to the beginning of a block. |
| Esc | Repeats the keystroke command the number of times indicated. The default number is 8. To change the number, type in the desired number when n = 8 appears on the screen. Refer to WordPerfect manual to change the default number permanently. |
| Esc ↓ | Moves cursor down the number of lines indicated, i.e., if n = 8, the cursor would move down 8 lines. |
| Esc ↑ | Moves cursor up the number of lines indicated. |
| Esc → | Moves cursor right the number of characters indicated. |
| Esc ← | Moves cursor left the number of characters indicated. |
| Esc PgDn | Moves cursor down the number of pages indicated. Cursor will be placed on line 1 of the new page. |
| Esc PgUp | Moves cursor up the number of pages indicated. Cursor will be placed on line 1 of the new page. |
| Tab | Moves the cursor right to the next tab setting, on the current line only when the Insert key has been pressed and the word Typeover appears on the screen. (Caution: if Typeover is not on, a [TAB] code will be inserted.) |

## Home Key Used with Arrow Keys

Move to the top of the document by pressing Home, Home, and then the Up Arrow key (Figure 2-16). To move to the end of the document, press Home, Home, and the Down Arrow key (step 1 in Figure 2-17). The cursor will go to the bottom of the document.

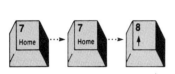

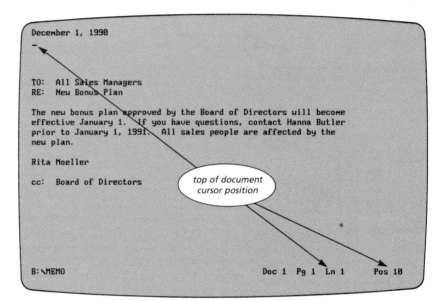

**FIGURE 2-16**

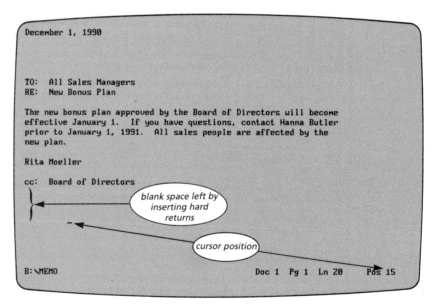

**FIGURE 2-17**

**Step 1: Move cursor to the end of the document**

**Step 2: Insert 3 lines**

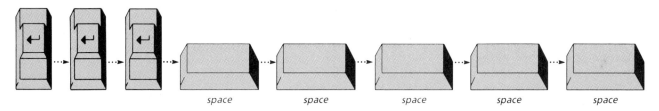

**Step 3: Move cursor to the top and bottom of the document**

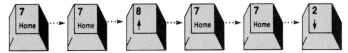

**FIGURE 2-17** (Steps 2 and 3)

The cursor cannot move past the bottom of the document, that is, it cannot move where there is no typing or codes. Press the Return key three times to put the cursor on line 20. Note the status line. Press the spacebar five times (step 2 in Figure 2-17), placing the cursor on line 20, position 15. Press Home, Home, and the Up Arrow key. The cursor returns to line 1, position 10. Then press Home, Home, and the Down Arrow key (step 3 in Figure 2-17). The cursor returns to line 20, position 15.

Many cursor movements can only be demonstrated over several pages of text. Since you have not yet typed several pages, do the following exercise first so you can practice additional cursor movements.

First, press a hard return ↵, which moves the cursor to line 21, position 10. Type the letter o followed by a hard return ↵. Continue to type the letter o followed by a hard return ↵ until the cursor is on line 54 of page 1 (this may seem awkward right now, but you will see its usefulness when we begin to move the cursor). Next type one more o followed by a hard return ↵ and as you do, watch for a dotted line to appear across the screen. This dotted line indicates that there has been a *page break*, which means that the document has moved from page 1 to page 2. Figure 2-18 shows that the status line also indicates that the cursor is now on page 2, line 1.

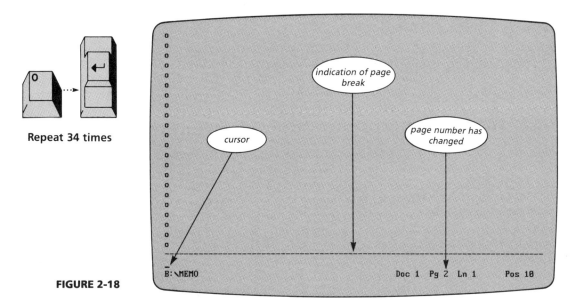

Repeat 34 times

**FIGURE 2-18**

On page 2, line 1 type the letter a, then press the Enter key ↵. Continue to do this until another page break appears and the status line indicates that the cursor is on page 3, line 1, as shown in step 1 of Figure 2-19. To complete this exercise, type the letter u and press the Enter key ↵. Continue to do so until the cursor is on line 14, position 10 of page 3 (step 2 of Figure 2-19). If you could now see your entire document, it would look like Figure 2-20.

The cursor is at the bottom of your document. That is, the *last* position of the cursor is the end of the document. Now press Home, Home, Up Arrow to move to the beginning of your document, page 1, line 1, position 10 (step 1 of Figure 2-21). Press the Down Arrow until you are on line 9 of page 1, the paragraph portion of your letter (step 2 of Figure 2-21).

To move the cursor to the right, press the Right Arrow → (step 3 of Figure 2-21). This moves the cursor to the right one character at a time. To move the cursor to the left, press the Left Arrow ← (step 4 of Figure 2-21). This moves the cursor to the left one character at a time.

## Control Key Used with Arrow Keys

Move the cursor to position 41 of line 9 so that it is under the letter t in the word the (step 1 in Figure 2-22). To move one word at a time, hold the Ctrl key down firmly and while holding, press the Right Arrow key → (step 2 in Figure 2-22). If you continue to press the Right Arrow key, the cursor moves one word at a time. Hold down the Right Arrow key firmly while holding the Ctrl key; notice how fast the cursor moves through the document.

Hold down the Ctrl key and press the Left Arrow key ←. The cursor moves to the left one word at a time (step 3 in Figure 2-22).

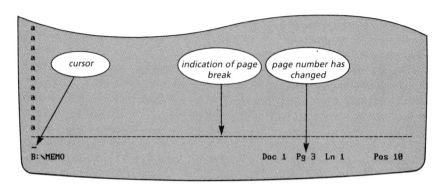

B:\MEMO                                    Doc 1  Pg 3  Ln 1        Pos 10

**Step 1: Repeat 54 times**     **Step 2: Repeat 13 times**

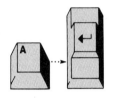     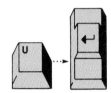

**FIGURE 2-19**

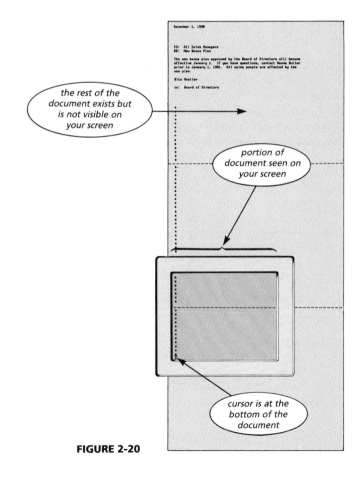

**FIGURE 2-20**

**Step 1: Move the cursor to top of the document**

**Step 2: Move the cursor to line 9**

**Step 3: Practice using the Right Arrow key**

**Step 4: Practice using the Left Arrow key**

**FIGURE 2-21**

**Step 1: Move the cursor to line 9, position 41**

**Step 2: Move the cursor to the beginning of the next word**

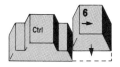

**Step 3: Move the cursor to the beginning of previous words**

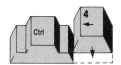

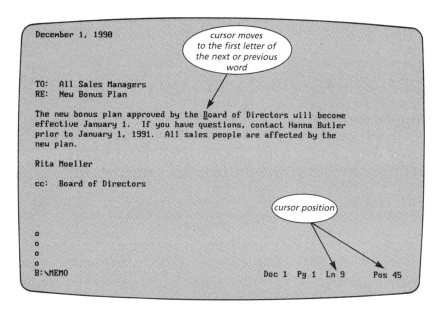

**FIGURE 2-22**

## End Key

Move the cursor again to line 9, position 10. Note that you are at the left edge of the line. Press the End key. Figure 2-23 shows how the End key moves the cursor to the end of the line.

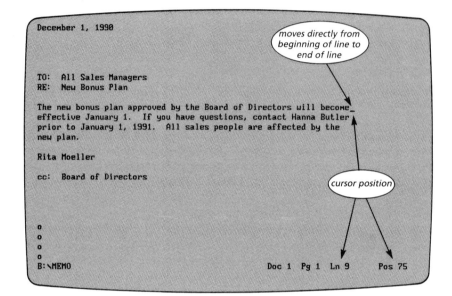

**FIGURE 2-23**

## More Home Key, Arrow Key Sequences

Move to the top of the document again by pressing Home, Home, Up Arrow. The cursor is now on page 1, line 1, position 10.

As you learned in Project 1, you may have a large document, but the monitor can only show you one screenful at a time. If you wish to move the cursor to the top, the bottom, the left, or the right edges of your present screen, press the Home key *once*, then the Up, Down, Left, or Right arrow keys. Try pressing the Home key, then the Down Arrow key ↓. That moves the cursor to line 24 (step 1 in Figure 2-24). Press the Home key, then the Up Arrow key ↑. That moves the cursor to line 1 (step 2 in Figure 2-24). Press Down Arrow ↓ to move the cursor down to line 9. Now press Home, then Right Arrow →. The cursor moves to the right end of the line (step 3 in Figure 2-24). Press Home, then Left Arrow ←. The cursor moves to the left edge of the screen, in this case the left end of the line (step 4 in Figure 2-24). Thus, pressing the Home key once in combination with an arrow key moves the cursor to the edges of the screen.

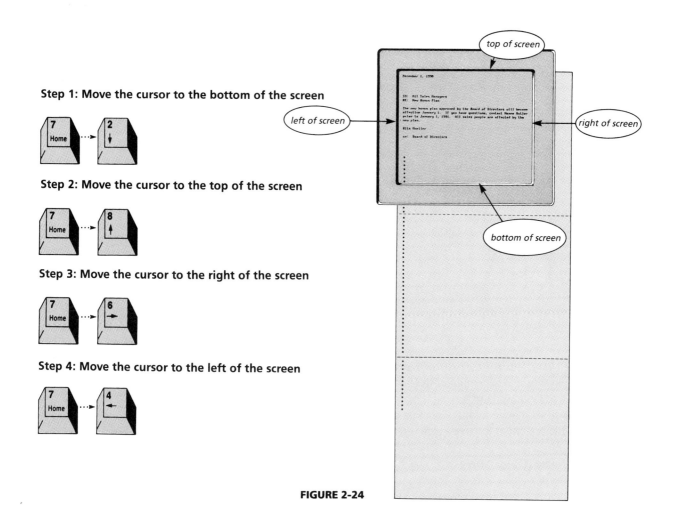

**Step 1: Move the cursor to the bottom of the screen**

**Step 2: Move the cursor to the top of the screen**

**Step 3: Move the cursor to the right of the screen**

**Step 4: Move the cursor to the left of the screen**

**FIGURE 2-24**

The margins of your document can be very wide, extending beyond the left or right edges of your screen, and you may wish to be able to move quickly to the left or right ends of a line in your document. With the cursor still on page 1, line 9, press Home, Home, Right Arrow (step 1 of Figure 2-25 on the following page). Notice that the cursor moves to the right end of the line, to position 75. Press Home, Home, Left Arrow, and the cursor moves back to position 10 at the left end of the line (step 2 in Figure 2-25). The cursor movements caused by Home, Right or Left Arrow, and Home, Home, Right or Left Arrow appear to be the same. But if you had lines longer than could be shown on one screen, you would notice that Home, Left or Right Arrow moves the cursor only to the edges of the screen you are viewing. Figure 2-25 illustrates that Home, Home, Right or Left Arrow causes the cursor to move immediately to the right or left ends of the line, even if the ends of the line cannot be seen on the current screen.

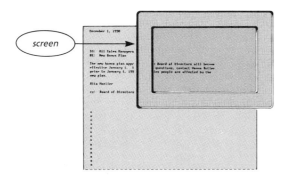 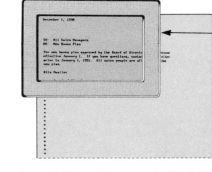

**Step 1: Move the cursor to the right end of the line**

**Step 2: Move the cursor to the left end of the line**

**FIGURE 2-25**

In addition to the Home, Home, Left Arrow function, you can use Home, Home, Home, Left Arrow. This keystroke sequence moves the cursor to the beginning of the line, even if codes are embedded at the beginning of the line. When text is moved, the codes have to be moved too.

Move your cursor to the bottom of the screen by pressing Home, Down Arrow ↓. The cursor is now on page 1, line 24, position 10. To go to the bottom of the *next* screen, press Home, Down Arrow ↓. The cursor is now on page 1, line 48, position 10.

When you press Home, Down Arrow or Home, Up Arrow, you will not miss viewing any lines of typing. The cursor moves down one screen at a time or up one screen at a time, without skipping any portions of the document. Figure 2-26 shows how the screen moves. Because WordPerfect automatically breaks a page at line 54, the next screen down shows the remainder of the lines on page 1, then the dotted line showing the break between the pages. The cursor is on line 17 of page 2. Press Home, Down Arrow again and again until the cursor is at the bottom of the document (page 3, line 14). Since that is as far as the cursor has been before, it cannot be moved any farther. To move the cursor up one screen at a time, press Home, Up Arrow ↑. The cursor moves to the top of the screen. Continue pressing Home, Up Arrow and watch how the cursor moves a screen at a time (watch the status line as well as the screen). Continue pressing Home, Up Arrow until the cursor is on page 1, line 1.

## Plus and Minus Keys on the Numeric Keypad

The **Plus** and **Minus** keys on the numeric keypad, when the Num Lock key is "off", perform the same functions as the Home, Up Arrow and Home, Down Arrow keys (Figure 2-27).

Look on the numeric keypad at the Plus ( + ) and the Minus (–) keys. Press the Plus key. Notice that the cursor moves to line 24, as shown in Figure 2-28.

**Step 1**

**Step 2**

**Step 3**

**Step 4**

**Step 5**

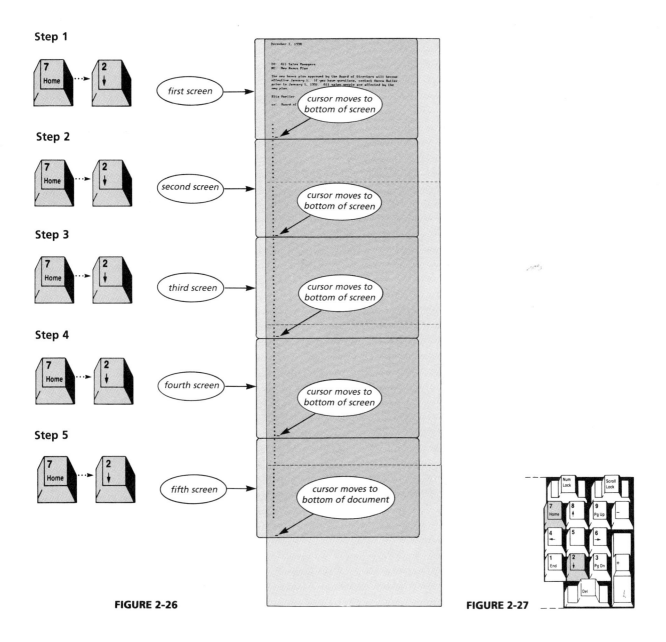

first screen

cursor moves to bottom of screen

second screen

cursor moves to bottom of screen

third screen

cursor moves to bottom of screen

fourth screen

cursor moves to bottom of screen

fifth screen

cursor moves to bottom of document

**FIGURE 2-26**

**FIGURE 2-27**

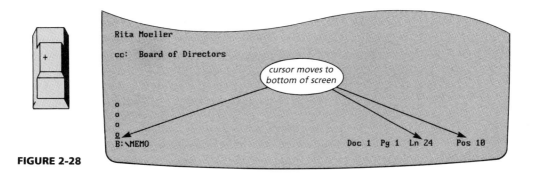

cursor moves to bottom of screen

**FIGURE 2-28**

Press the Plus key again and the cursor moves to line 48 (Figure 2-29). This is the same result you would get from pressing the Home, Down Arrow keys. Press the Minus key and the cursor moves to the top of the screen, line 25 (Figure 2-30), just as if you had pressed the Home, Up Arrow keys. Press the Minus key again and the cursor moves to line 1 of page 1.

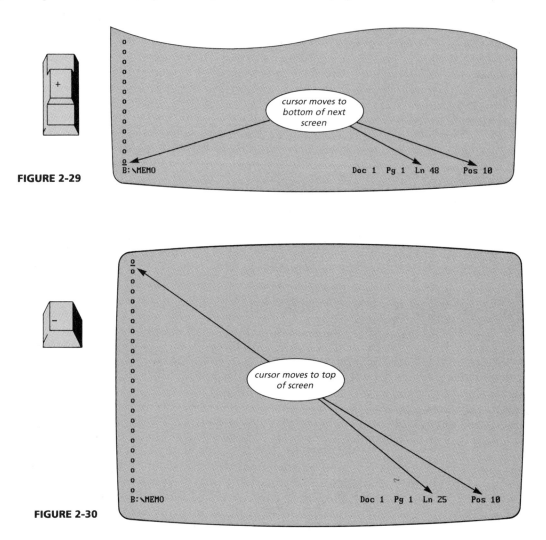

**FIGURE 2-29**

cursor moves to bottom of next screen

B:\MEMO                    Doc 1  Pg 1  Ln 48    Pos 10

**FIGURE 2-30**

cursor moves to top of screen

B:\MEMO                    Doc 1  Pg 1  Ln 25    Pos 10

## Page Down and Page Up Keys

The **PgDn** (Page Down) key moves the cursor to line 1 of the *next* page. The **PgUp** (Page Up) key moves the cursor to line 1 of the *previous* page.

With the cursor on page 1, line 1, press the PgDn key (step 1 of Figure 2-31). Notice that the cursor moves to line 1 of page 2. Press the PgDn key again and the cursor moves to line 1 of page 3 (step 2 of Figure 2-31).

Now move the cursor up only one line by pressing the Up Arrow ↑ key (step 1 of Figure 2-32). The cursor moves to line 54 of page 2. Press the PgDn key (step 2 of Figure 2-32). Note that the cursor moves only one line, but the status line indicates the cursor is on page 3 because PgDn moved the cursor to line 1 of page 3.

Press the Up Arrow ↑ one time, moving the cursor to line 54 of page 2. Because the status line states page 2, you know that the previous page is page 1. Therefore the PgUp key will take the cursor almost two full pages to line 1, page 1. Press the PgUp key.

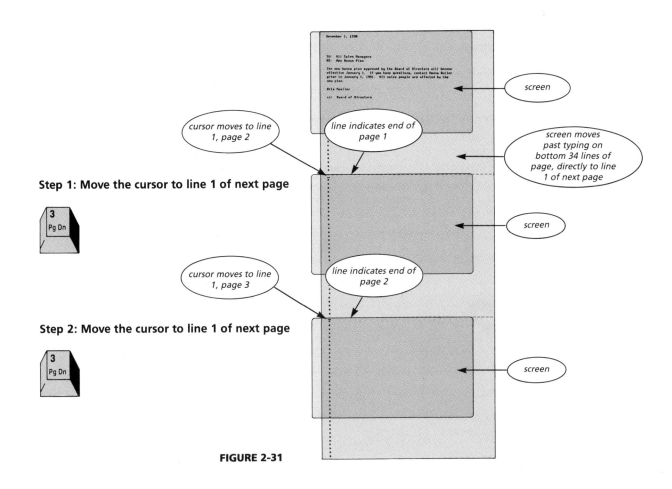

**Step 1: Move the cursor to line 1 of next page**

**Step 2: Move the cursor to line 1 of next page**

**FIGURE 2-31**

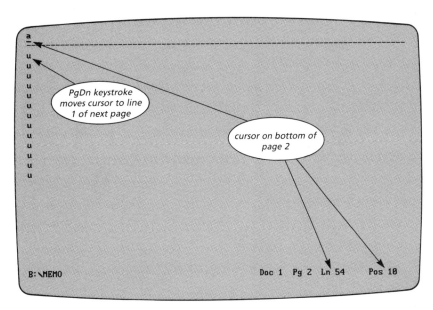

**FIGURE 2-32**

**Step 1: Move cursor up one line to line 54 of page 2**

**Step 2: Move cursor to line 1 of page 3**

## "Go to" Cursor Function

There may be times when you want to go directly to a specific page, but repeatedly pressing the PgDn key would take too long. For example, if you had a 30-page document and you wished to go to page 15, pressing PgDn 15 times would be too time consuming.

To move directly to a particular page, hold down the Ctrl key and while holding it, press the Home key (step 1 of Figure 2-33). You see the message "Go to" in the lower left corner of the screen. Type the number 3 and then press Enter ↵(step 2 of Figure 2-33). Notice that the cursor moves to page 3, line 1. To "Go to" a particular page, you can also go backward. While on page 3, line 1, hold the Ctrl key down and press the Home key (step 1 of Figure 2-34). The "Go to" message appears again. Type the number 2 and then press the Enter ↵ key (step 2 of Figure 2-34). The cursor is now on page 2, line 1. The cursor will always go to line 1 of the page number that you type.

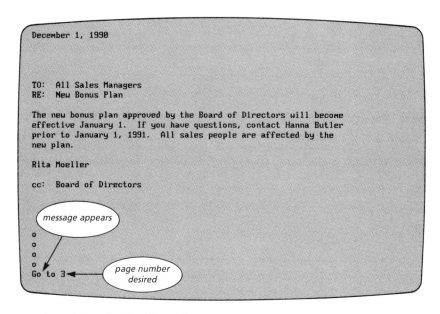

**FIGURE 2-33**

**Step 1: Invoke the "Go to" message**     **Step 2: Go to page 3**

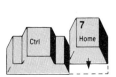

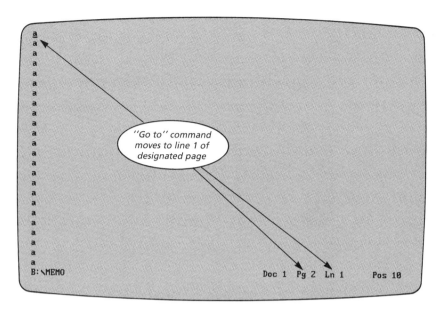

**FIGURE 2-34**

Step 1: Invoke the "Go to" message    Step 2: Go to page 2

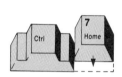

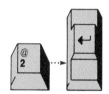

Another "Go to" command will take you either to the last line or the first line of the page you are currently on. The cursor should be on page 2, line 1. Hold down the Ctrl key and press the Home key. The "Go to" message appears. Press the Down Arrow key ↓ (see Figure 2-35). Look at the status line and notice that the cursor stayed on page 2, but went to the last line of that page, line 54.

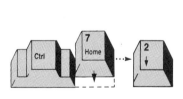

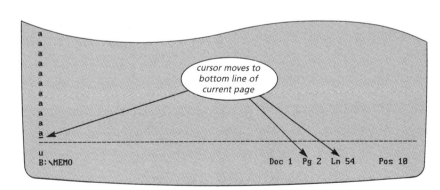

**FIGURE 2-35**

To move the cursor to the first line of page 2, hold the Ctrl key down and press the Home key. The "Go to" message appears. Press the Up Arrow ↑ key (see Figure 2-36). The cursor moves to page 2, line 1.

To move the cursor to the top of your document, press Home, Home, Up Arrow. The cursor is on page 1, line 1.

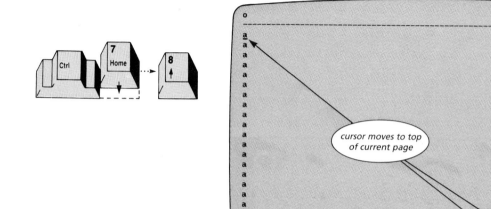

**FIGURE 2-36**

## Esc Key

Another key used to move the cursor is the **Esc** key. This is called a repeating key because it will repeat almost any stroke, whether a character or a cursor movement. For our purposes now, we will use it only to move the cursor.

Press the Esc key. Figure 2-37 shows the message "n = 8" at the bottom left corner of the screen. The message means that the default number is 8. Whatever keystroke you choose will be repeated eight times. After pressing Esc, press the Down Arrow ↓ key (step 1 of Figure 2-38). Instead of moving down one line, the cursor moves down eight lines, from line 1 to line 9. Press the Esc key again. The message "n = 8" appears again. Now press the Right Arrow key → (step 2 of Figure 2-38). The cursor moves to position 18 on line 9, moving eight characters to the right instead of just one.

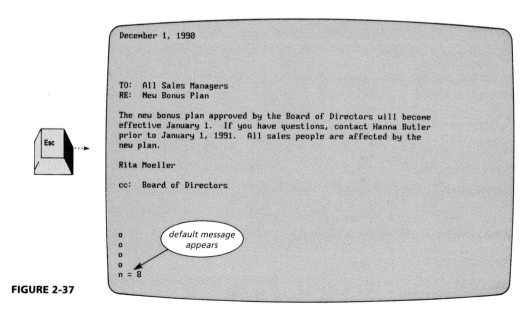

**FIGURE 2-37**

Moving the Cursor **WP 49**

You can also change the number of lines or characters that the cursor will move. Press the Esc key. The message "n = 8" appears on the screen. Instead of accepting the default, type the number 15. The 8 is replaced by the number 15 in the message. Next, press the Down Arrow key. The cursor moves down 15 lines to line 24, as shown in Figure 2-39.

You can see how important it is to memorize the keystroke sequences that move the cursor. You will save a lot of time by learning to use WordPerfect efficiently.

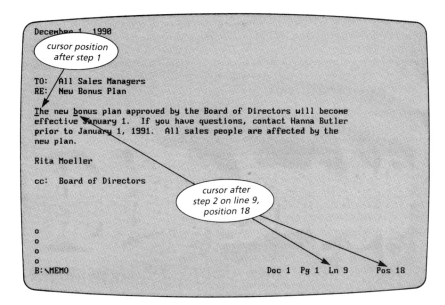

**FIGURE 2-38**

**Step 1: Move cursor down 8 lines**    **Step 2: Move cursor 8 characters to the right**

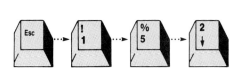

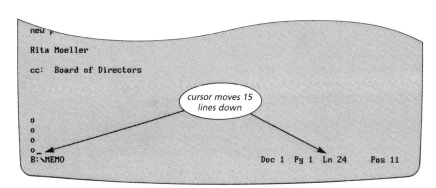

**FIGURE 2-39**

## DELETING TEXT

L earning how to use the deletion keys is as important as learning the cursor movements. Table 2-2 presents a comprehensive list of deletion keystrokes. Refer to the table during the following discussion about using the deletion keys.

Before we start, move the cursor to the bottom of the document by pressing Home, Home, Down Arrow. The cursor should be on page 3, line 14.

**TABLE 2-2**   Summary of Deletion Keystrokes

| KEYSTROKES | RESULTS |
|---|---|
| F1 1 | Restores deleted text. F1 highlights deleted text, then 1 restores that text. |
| Backspace | Deletes the character or code to the left of the cursor. |
| Delete | Deletes the character or code above the cursor moving to the right (as text is deleted, the typing to the right of the cursor moves left to the cursor). |
| Home Backspace | Deletes the word to the left of the cursor. |
| Ctrl-Backspace | Deletes the word above the cursor (as words are deleted, the typing to the right of the cursor moves left to the cursor). |
| Ctrl-End | Deletes from the cursor to the end of the current line. |
| Ctrl-PgDn | The prompt "Delete Remainder of Page? (Y/N) N" appears. Type the letter Y to delete from the cursor to the end of the current page. |
| Alt-F4 Delete | To delete a block place the cursor at the beginning of a block. Hold down the Alt key and press F4. Move the cursor to identify and highlight a block of text. Press the Delete key. At the prompt "Delete Block? (Y/N) N" type the letter Y. |

### Using the Backspace Key and Restoring Deleted Text

Type these words: This is how to use the Backspace key (see Figure 2-40). The cursor is now at position 46 in a blank space just to the right of the y in the word key. Think of the **Backspace** key as deleting *backward*. Press the Backspace key and notice that the character to the *left* of the cursor is deleted. Continue to press the Backspace key until you've deleted the words Backspace and key (Figure 2-40).

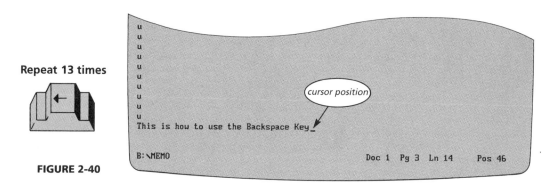

**Repeat 13 times**

FIGURE 2-40

If you deleted text in error, and you have not moved the cursor to another position in the document, you can restore your text. Look at the template next to the F1 key. Notice the word Cancel in black. Press the F1 key. The text that was deleted reappears and is highlighted on the screen. The menu on the bottom of the screen shows that pressing the numeric key 1 will "undelete" or restore the highlighted text. Press 1 to see the text restored, putting the cursor back to position 46 to the right of the y (Figure 2-41).

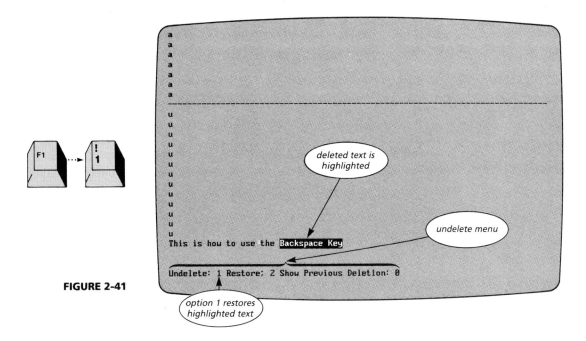

**FIGURE 2-41**

## Using the Delete Key and Restoring Deleted Text

The other key used to delete text is the Delete key. The **Delete** key deletes the space or character directly *above* the cursor. Think of the Delete key as deleting text going *forward*.

Press the Return key to move the cursor to page 3, line 15. Type these words: This is how to use the Delete key (see Figure 2-42). Press Home, Left Arrow to move the cursor to the beginning of the line, putting the cursor under the T in This. Press the Delete key and notice that the T that was directly above the cursor is deleted. Delete these words: This is how.

As before, to restore this deleted text press the F1 key. The "undelete" menu appears at the bottom of the screen. Press 1 to restore the highlighted text. The text is restored with the cursor on position 21.

**Repeat 11 times**

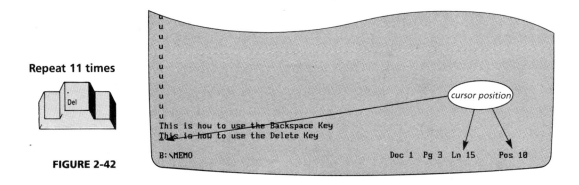

**FIGURE 2-42**

## Deleting One Line at a Time

To delete a line from where the cursor is to the end of the line, hold the Ctrl key down and press the End key. Figure 2-43 shows that the text from position 21 to the end of the line is deleted. To restore the deleted text, press the F1 key, then number 1.

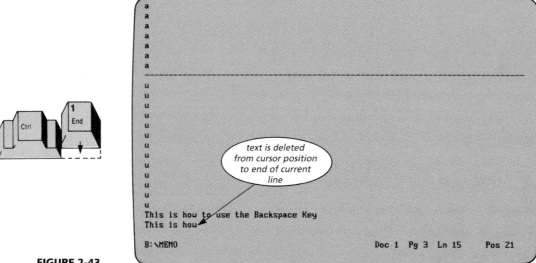

**FIGURE 2-43**

## Deleting One Page at a Time

The Ctrl-PgDn keys are used if you wish to delete from where the cursor is to the bottom of the page. Press Home, Home, Up Arrow to move the cursor to page 1, line 1. Since the cursor is on line 1, Ctrl-PgDn will delete from there to line 54, which is the bottom of this page. If your cursor were on line 9, Ctrl-PgDn would delete from there down to line 54. Hold down the Ctrl key and press the PgDn key (Figure 2-44). Since an entire page can contain a lot of work, WordPerfect has a built-in precaution. The message "Delete Remainder of Page? (Y/N) N" appears at the bottom left corner of the screen. The N at the end of the message means that the default is no. Therefore, if you press any key (besides Y), the answer no is accepted and nothing is deleted. Type the letter Y. Figure 2-45 shows that typing the letter Y deletes the entire text of page 1, bringing the text that was below page 1 up to line 1 of page 1.

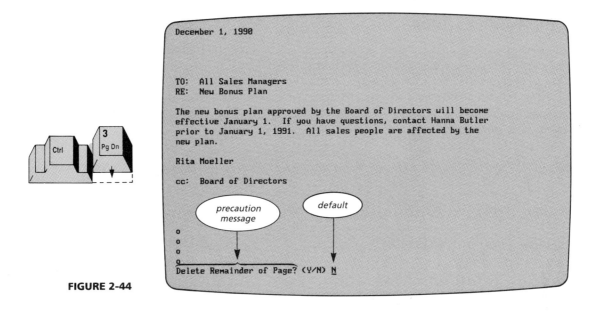

**FIGURE 2-44**

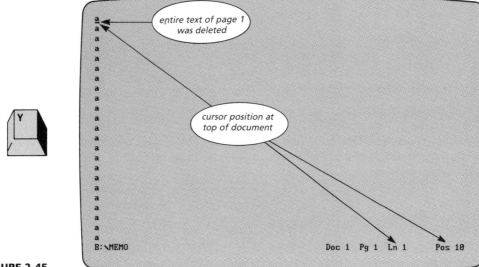

**FIGURE 2-45**

To restore the entire deleted text, press F1 to undelete and highlight the deleted text, then press the number 1 to restore the entire deleted text, bringing the cursor to line 54 on page 1. Press Home, Home, Up Arrow, moving the cursor to page 1, line 1. The entire text is restored.

## Deleting One Word at a Time

There will be times when you want to delete three or four words on a line. Move the cursor under the T in The, hold down the Ctrl key, and press the backspace key. Figure 2-46 shows that instead of just one character, the entire word The plus the space after it is deleted, bringing the first character of the next word to the cursor. Ctrl-Backspace deletes one word at a time going *forward* through the text. Continuing to hold down the Ctrl key and pressing the Backspace key, delete these words: new bonus plan. Then, to restore the deleted text, press the F1 key. Notice the highlight on the words The new bonus plan. Press the number 1 to restore those words to the text.

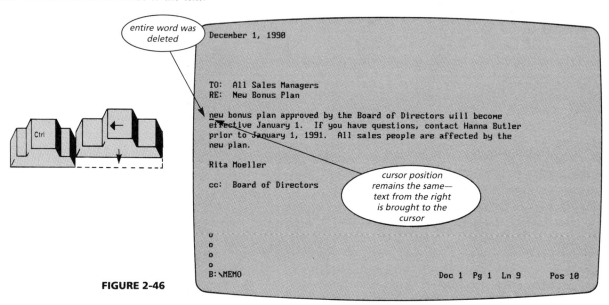

**FIGURE 2-46**

The cursor is at position 29 under the letter a in the word approved. To delete one word at a time going *backward* in your text, press the Home key once, then press the Backspace key. Notice that the word "plan" to the left of the cursor is deleted. Again press Home, then Backspace. The word "bonus" is deleted. Press Home, Backspace two more times, deleting first the word "new" and then the word "The" (see Figure 2-47). To restore these four words, press the F1 key and then the number 1. The text is restored to its original form.

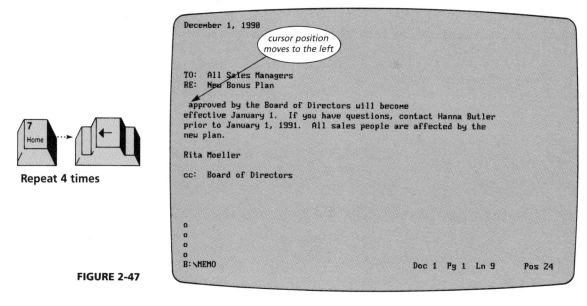

**Repeat 4 times**

**FIGURE 2-47**

## Deleting One Block at a Time

Sometimes you may wish to delete an entire block of text. The **Block** feature highlights an area or "block" of text, thereby isolating that text from the rest of the document. Once the desired text is highlighted you can invoke the desired function.

Press Home, Home, Up Arrow to move the cursor to the top of your document (page 1, line 1). Press the Esc key, then the Down Arrow ↓ key, moving the cursor to page 1, line 9.

Look at the template next to the F4 key. You see the word Block in blue. Hold down the Alt key and press the F4 key (step 1 in Figure 2-48). The "Block on" message blinks in the lower left corner of your screen. To highlight text you must move the cursor in any of the ways you have learned in this project (step 2 in Figure 2-48). For example, press the Right Arrow → key and as you continue to press it, you see the word "The" highlighted. To highlight one *word* at a time, hold down the Ctrl key and while holding it, press the Right Arrow → key two or three times. Notice that words are highlighted one at a time. Press Down Arrow ↓ and notice that you can highlight one line at a time. Move the cursor to line 12, position 19, thereby highlighting the entire paragraph. Figure 2-49 shows how the entire paragraph should be highlighted.

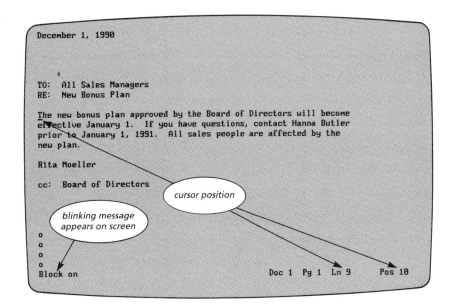

**Step 1: Invoke Block on**  **Step 2: Use cursor movements to highlight paragraph**

 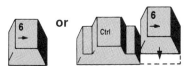 

**FIGURE 2-48**

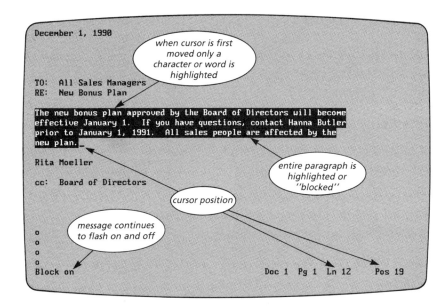

**FIGURE 2-49**

Now that the desired text is highlighted, press the Del key. Figure 2-50 shows that when you do, the message "Delete Block (Y/N)? N" appears at the bottom left corner of the screen. Delete the block of text you have highlighted by typing the letter Y. Restore the deleted text by pressing the F1 key. The deleted text is highlighted again. Press the number 1 and the text is restored.

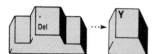

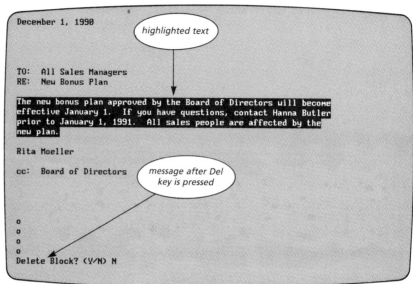

**FIGURE 2-50**

## EXITING PROJECT 2

Move the cursor to the top of the document by pressing Home, Home, Up Arrow. Look at the template next to the F7 key. Notice the word Exit in black. Press the F7 key (step 1 in Figure 2-51). The message "Save Document? (Y/N) Y" is shown in the lower left corner of the screen.

The (Y/N) indicates that if you press Y for yes, you would like to save the document. If you press N for no, you do not wish to save the document. The Y outside the brackets indicates that the default response to this question is yes, which means that if you press either the Enter key or the spacebar the software will process yes as your answer. In this project you altered the document since you last saved it to the disk. To save this latest version you should replace the old document with the newly revised version. To save the new version and replace the old version, press Y for yes (step 2 in Figure 2-51).

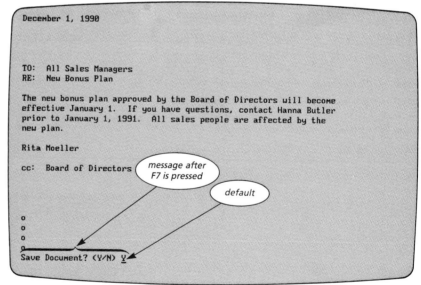

**Step 1: Invoke Exit**

**Step 2: Save the document**

**FIGURE 2-51**

Figure 2-52 shows that the message "Document to be Saved: B:\MEMO" appears at the bottom of the screen. It is not necessary to type MEMO again. Just press the Enter ← key. WordPerfect then presents the message "Replace B:\MEMO? (Y/N) N" (Figure 2-53). Type the letter Y. The light on drive B turns on, indicating that the document is being saved in its new form to the disk. Next, a message "Exit WP? (Y/N) N" appears (Figure 2-54). Type the letter Y. (If you failed to complete the printing of the document you may see the message "Cancel all print jobs (Y/N)? N" If this appears, type the letter Y for yes.)

As you learned in Project 1, to exit properly we must return to the DOS prompt. After you have typed the letter Y, the message "Insert COMMAND.COM disk in drive A and strike any key when ready" appears on the screen. On some copies of the training version or if you have a hard disk system, the DOS prompt will appear immediately and you will not see the message. If you see the message, take your WordPerfect training version out of drive A and insert your DOS disk. Press any key. You then see the DOS prompt indicating that WordPerfect is no longer in main memory.

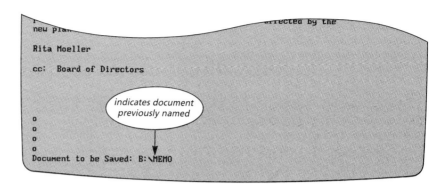

**FIGURE 2-52**

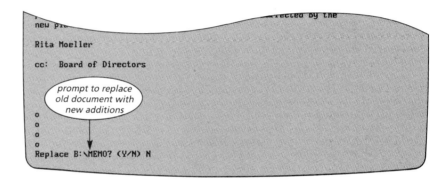

**FIGURE 2-53**

**FIGURE 2-54**

## PROJECT SUMMARY

In Project 2, you learned how to type a document using the word wrap feature. After the document was typed, you learned more about the reveal codes, including how to read the [TAB] code, the hard return [HRt] code, and the soft return [SRt] code.

After saving the document, you printed it. To understand how the cursor moves through several pages of text, you added typing to page 3. Then you practiced several keystrokes that help to move the cursor quickly through a document. You learned that the screen can only show certain portions of the document at a time. You also learned how to edit the text by using several deletion keystrokes or functions.

The following is a list of the keystroke sequence we used in Project 2:

**SUMMARY OF KEYSTROKES—Project 2**

| STEPS | KEY(S) PRESSED | STEPS | KEY(S) PRESSED |
|---|---|---|---|
| 1 | b: [at the A> prompt] | 27 | ↵ |
| 2 | ↵ | 28 | ↵ |
| 3 | a:wp [at the B> prompt] | 29 | Rita Moeller |
| 4 | ↵ | 30 | ↵ |
| 5 | ↵ [at first introductory screen] | 31 | ↵ |
| 6 | ↵ [only if you see a second introductory screen] | 32 | cc: |
| 7 | December 1, 1990 | 33 | [TAB] |
| 8 | ↵ | 34 | Board of Directors |
| 9 | ↵ | 35 | ↵ |
| 10 | ↵ | 36 | [F10] |
| 11 | ↵ | 37 | memo |
| 12 | ↵ | 38 | ↵ |
| 13 | [Caps Lock] | 39 | [Shift-F7] |
| 14 | TO: | 40 | 1 |
| 15 | [Caps Lock] | 41 | [practice in text cursor movements and deleting text] |
| 16 | [TAB] | 42 | [F7] |
| 17 | All Sales Managers | 43 | Y |
| 18 | ↵ | 44 | ↵ |
| 19 | [Caps Lock] | 45 | Y |
| 20 | RE: | 46 | Y |
| 21 | [Caps Lock] | 47 | [remove disk from drive A if you see prompt "Insert COMMAND.COM disk in drive A and strike any key when ready"] |
| 22 | [TAB] | | |
| 23 | New Bonus Plan | 48 | [put DOS disk into drive A] |
| 24 | ↵ | 49 | [press any key] |
| 25 | ↵ | 50 | [remove disks from both drives] |
| 26 | The new bonus plan approved by the Board of Directors will become effective January 1. If you have questions, contact Hanna Butler prior to January 1, 1991. All sales people are affected by the new plan. | | |

The following list summarizes the material covered in Project 2:

1. The **word wrap** function eliminates the need to press the Return (Enter) key until you come to the end of a paragraph, short line, or command, or if you want to insert a blank line.
2. A **soft return** has occurred when word wrap automatically moves text to the next line.
3. The **[SRt]** code is embedded in the document when a soft return occurs.
4. Pressing the Tab key embeds the **[TAB]** code into the document.
5. Cursor movement keys are the single keys or combinations of keys that move the cursor efficiently throughout the document (see Table 2-1).
6. The **Plus** and **Minus** keys on the numeric keypad perform the same functions as the Home, Up Arrow and Home, Down Arrow keys.
7. To move the cursor to line 1 of the next page, press the **PgDn** key. To move the cursor to line 1 of the previous page, press the **PgUp** key.
8. To move directly to a particular page, press Ctrl-Home, then enter the desired page number in response to the "**Go to**" message on the screen, and press Enter.
9. The **Esc** key lets you repeat a character or a cursor movement.
10. Deletion keys are the single keys or combinations of keys that delete a character, a word, a page, or blocks of text (see Table 2-2).
11. The **Backspace** key deletes the character or code to the left of the cursor.
12. The **Delete** key deletes the space or character directly above the cursor, moving to the right.
13. The **Block** function highlights a block of text in the document so that a specific function can be performed, such as deleting the text.

# STUDENT ASSIGNMENTS

## STUDENT ASSIGNMENT 1: True/False

**Instructions:**   Circle T if the statement is true and F if the statement is false.

T  F   1. When typing a paragraph at the computer, if you continue typing, the words will automatically wrap to the next line.
T  F   2. When word wrap occurs, the code inserted in the document is [HRt].
T  F   3. To view the reveal codes screen, press the Alt key, release it, and press F3.
T  F   4. When a word is in black on the template, it signifies that the function key is to be pressed alone.
T  F   5. To move the cursor to the bottom of the screen, press Home, Down Arrow.
T  F   6. To move the cursor to the top of the current screen you press Home, Up Arrow.
T  F   7. To move the cursor to the bottom of the document press the PgDn key.
T  F   8. The Backspace key deletes the character or space above the cursor.
T  F   9. To restore deleted text, press the F1 key, then 1.

## STUDENT ASSIGNMENT 2: Multiple Choice

**Instructions:**   Circle the correct response.

1. To load WordPerfect into main memory, with the WordPerfect disk in drive A, type
   a. the characters WPC at the DOS A> prompt
   b. the word WORDPERFECT at the DOS A> prompt
   c. the characters a:wp at the DOS B> prompt
   d. the word WORDPERFECT at the DOS B> prompt
2. Which of the following is a valid file name?
   a. MEMO
   b. memo
   c. Memo
   d. all of the above
3. When typing a paragraph
   a. press the Enter key at the end of each sentence
   b. press the Enter key at the end of each line
   c. press the Enter key at the end of each paragraph
   d. press the Enter key at the end of the document
4. The command to move the cursor to line 1 of the next page is
   a. Home, Home, Down Arrow
   b. Home, Down Arrow
   c. End
   d. PgDn
5. The command to delete from the cursor to the end of the line is
   a. End
   b. Ctrl-End
   c. Delete
   d. Ctrl-Backspace
6. If the cursor is on line 54 of page 1, how many lines will the cursor move if you press the PgDn key?
   a. 1
   b. 54
   c. 53
   d. 2
7. To repeat a certain keystroke, you can press the Esc key before the keystroke. The default number of keystrokes is (Esc = ?)
   a. 10
   b. 9
   c. 8
   d. 6
8. The Cancel key can be used to restore a deletion. The Cancel key is
   a. Esc
   b. F1
   c. Shift-F1
   d. Alt-F1
9. The command Ctrl-PgDn can be used to delete
   a. the current page from the cursor down
   b. the entire current page, no matter where the cursor is
   c. 54 lines of type
   d. half a page

10. To invoke the Block function, press
    a. Ctrl-F4
    b. F4
    c. Shift-F4
    d. Alt-F4

## STUDENT ASSIGNMENT 3: Matching

**Instructions:**   Put the appropriate number next to the words in the second column.

|  |  |
|---|---|
| 1. PgDn | _____ one word to the left |
| 2. Home, Home, Down Arrow | _____ line 1 of previous page |
| 3. Right Arrow | _____ line 1, page 3 |
| 4. Ctrl-Left Arrow | _____ top of document |
| 5. Esc, Down Arrow | _____ bottom of document |
| 6. PgUp | _____ right end of line |
| 7. End | _____ bottom line of current page |
| 8. Ctrl-Home, Down Arrow | _____ line 1 of next page |
| 9. Ctrl-Home, 3, Enter | _____ next right character |
| 10. Home, Home, Up Arrow | _____ 8 lines down |

## STUDENT ASSIGNMENT 4: Fill in the Blanks

**Instructions:**   Next to each keystroke or keystroke sequence, describe its effect.

**Keystroke(s)**          **Effect**

1. PgDn _____
2. PgUp _____
3. Right Arrow _____
4. Left Arrow _____
5. Down Arrow _____
6. Up Arrow _____
7. Home, Home, Up Arrow _____
8. Home, Home, Down Arrow _____
9. Ctrl-Left Arrow _____
10. Ctrl-Right Arrow _____
11. Home, Down Arrow _____
12. Home, Up Arrow _____
13. Home, Left Arrow _____
14. Home, Right Arrow _____

## STUDENT ASSIGNMENT 5: Fill in the Blanks

**Instructions:**  Next to each delete function below, describe the effect of that deletion.

| Delete Function | Effect |
| --- | --- |
| 1. Backspace | _____ |
| 2. Delete | _____ |
| 3. Ctrl-Backspace | _____ |
| 4. Ctrl-End | _____ |
| 5. Ctrl-PgDn, Y | _____ |
| 6. Alt-F4, Home, Home, Down arrow, Delete, Y | _____ |
| 7. F1, 1 | _____ |
| 8. Home, Backspace | _____ |

## STUDENT ASSIGNMENT 6: Deleting Text

**Instructions:**  The screen illustrates a memo that was prepared using WordPerfect. The words "approved by the Board of Directors" are to be deleted from the memo. Assume that the cursor is under the B in the word Board. Explain in detail the steps necessary to delete the words.

```
TO:   All Sales Managers
RE:   New Bonus Plan

The new bonus plan approved by the Board of Directors will become
effective January 1.  If you have questions, contact Hanna Butler
prior to January 1, 1991.  All sales people are affected by the
new plan.

Rita Moeller

cc:  Board of Directors




B:\DIRECTOR                              Doc 1  Pg 1  Ln 11     Pos 33
```

Method of correction: _____

_____

_____

_____

## STUDENT ASSIGNMENT 7: Reformatting the Text

**Instructions:**   The screen illustrates a memo that was prepared using the word wrap feature in WordPerfect. Words were then deleted in the first line of the paragraph. Explain in detail the steps necessary to reformat the text so that all lines wrap at the margins.

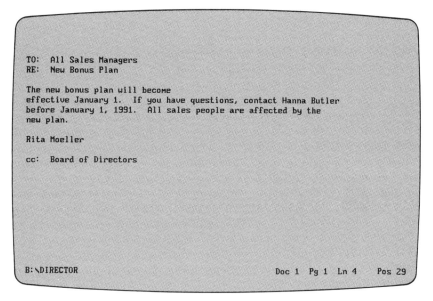

```
TO:   All Sales Managers
RE:   New Bonus Plan

The new bonus plan will become
effective January 1.  If you have questions, contact Hanna Butler
before January 1, 1991.  All sales people are affected by the
new plan.

Rita Moeller

cc:  Board of Directors




B:\DIRECTOR                                    Doc 1  Pg 1  Ln 4    Pos 29
```

Method of correction: _____

_____

_____

_____

## STUDENT ASSIGNMENT 8: Modifying a WordPerfect Document

**Instructions:**   Perform the following tasks.

1. Load DOS into main memory.
2. Load WordPerfect into main memory by inserting the WordPerfect diskette into drive A and putting a data disk into drive B. Type b:. At the B> prompt, type a:wp and press the Enter key.

Problem 1:  Type the letter illustrated at right without corrections.

Problem 2:  Make the corrections indicated and save the document. Name the document Director.

Problem 3:  Print the document.

```
TO:   All Sales Managers
RE:   New Bonus Plan
              new
The  bonus plan  approved by the Board of Directors  will become
effective January 1.  If you have questions, contact Hanna Butler
before  prior to  January 1, 1991.  All sales people are affected by the
new plan.

Rita Moeller

cc:  Board of Directors
```

## STUDENT ASSIGNMENT 9: Modifying a WordPerfect Document

**Instructions:**    Perform the following tasks.

1. Load DOS into main memory.
2. Load WordPerfect into main memory by inserting the WordPerfect diskette into drive A, and putting a data disk into drive B. Type b:. At the B> prompt, type a:wp and press the Enter key.

Problem 1: Type the document illustrated below. Then make the following changes to the document. *NOTE:* In pencil, note the changes to the memo on this page before modifying the document using WordPerfect.

```
TO:   All Employees
FROM:  Personnel Department
SUBJECT:  Vacation Schedules

All employees that have been employed for more than one year are
eligible for two weeks vacation each year.  The vacations must be
taken during the months of June, July, or August.  You must
notify the Personnel Department at least 4 weeks in advance.  You
must also obtain approval from your immediate supervisor.

Janet Fisher
Personnel Administrator
```

1. Begin the memo on line 12 of the page.
2. Add the current date on the line above the word TO.
3. Delete the words "each year" from the second line of the body of the memo.
4. Insert the word May, a comma, and a space before the word June in the third line of the body of the memo.
5. Delete the sentence "You must notify the Personnel Department at least 4 weeks in advance."
6. Delete the word "also" from the last sentence.
7. Delete the period after the word "supervisor" in the last sentence and add these words to the last sentence: at least 4 weeks in advance.

Problem 2: Save the modified document. Name the document Schedule.2.

Problem 3: Print the modified document.

## STUDENT ASSIGNMENT 10: Modifying a WordPerfect Document

**Instructions:**    Perform the following tasks.

1. Load DOS into main memory.
2. Load WordPerfect into main memory by inserting the WordPerfect diskette into drive A and putting a data disk into drive B. Type b:. At the B> prompt, type a:wp and press the Enter key.

```
DATE:      January 1, 1991
TO:   All Employees
FROM:  Personnel Department
SUBJECT:  Vacation Schedules

All employees that have been employed for more than one year are
eligible for two weeks vacation.  The vacations must be taken
during the months of May, June, July, or August.  You must obtain
approval from your immediate supervisor at least 4 weeks in
advance.

Janet Fisher
Personnel Administrator
```

Problem 1: Type the document illustrated below. Then make the following changes to the document. *NOTE:* In pencil, note the changes on the letter on this page before modifying the document using WordPerfect.

```
January 10, 1990



Ms. Roberta A. Morris
Editor, Computer Magazine
222 Edwin Drive
Arlington, VA 22289

Dear Ms. Morris:

Please enter my subscription to your magazine effective
immediately.  It is my understanding that you provide free
subscriptions to those employed in the computer industry.

Thank you for providing this valuable service to the computer
industry.

Sincerely,


Rodney C. Caine
Programmer/Analyst
Rockview International
111 Riverview Drive
Redlands, CA 92393
```

1. Begin the letter on line 8 of the page.
2. Change the name to Ms. Roberta A. Morrison.
3. Change the address to 222 Edwards Drive.
4. Delete the words "effective immediately" beginning on the first line of the text.
5. Add this sentence at the end of the first paragraph: I am currently employed as a programmer/analyst with Rockview International, Redlands, California.
6. Change the last sentence to: Thank you for providing this valuable service to those employed in the computer industry.

Problem 2: Save the modified document. Name it Morrison.

Problem 3: Print the modified document.

```
January 10, 1990



Ms. Roberta A. Morrison
Editor, Computer Magazine
222 Edwards Drive
Arlington, VA 22289

Dear Ms. Morris:

Please enter my subscription to your magazine.  It is my
understanding that you provide free subscriptions to those
employed in the computer industry.  I am currently employed as a
programmer/analyst with Rockview International, Redlands,
California.

Thank you for providing this valuable service to those employed
in the computer industry.

Sincerely,


Rodney C. Caine
Programmer/Analyst
Rockview International
111 Riverview Drive
Redlands, CA 92393
```

# PROJECT 3

## Learning Special Features

### Objectives

You will have mastered the material in this project when you can:

- Arrange text flush right and centered
- Underline and boldface text
- Insert text and typeover existing text
- Indent text using the indent key and the left/right indent function
- Save and replace a document

*I*n Project 3 you will create the document shown in Figure 3-1. Load WordPerfect as you have previously done for Projects 1 and 2. Note that correct typing practice requires you to press the spacebar *two times* after typing the period at the end of a sentence. Also note that Project 3 gives some instructions that do not coincide with the document shown in Figure 3-1. This is done purposely. Later in the project you will learn how to move the cursor back to these positions to change and correct the typing, so that eventually your document will be exactly like the one in Figure 3-1. Finally, we will hereafter abbreviate instructions whenever you are asked to hold down one key and, while holding it down, press another key. For example, Alt-F3, means hold down the Alt key and while holding it down press the F3 key.

```
                                        December 15, 1990

              LICENSING AGREEMENT

You should carefully read the following terms and conditions.
Your use of this program package indicates your acceptance of
them.  If you do not agree with them, you should not use this
software package.  Instead, you should return the package and
your money will be returned to you.

PerSoft Inc. provides this program and licenses you to use it.
You assume responsibility for the selection of this program to
achieve your intended results.  PerSoft Inc. assumes no
responsibility for the results you obtain from the use of this
software package.

LICENSE

You may perform the following functions:

     a.   Use the program on a single machine only.  Use on more
          than one machine is considered "pirating" this
          software.

     b.   Copy the program into any machine readable or printed
          form for backup or modification purposes in support of
          your use of the program on a single machine.  Certain
          programs from PerSoft Inc., however, may contain
          mechanisms to limit or inhibit copying.  These programs
          are marked "copy protected."

     c.   Modify or merge the program into another PerSoft Inc.
          program for use on the single machine.  Any portion of
          the program merged into another program will continue
          to be subject to the terms and conditions of this
          License.

You MAY NOT use, copy, modify, or transfer the program, in whole
or in part, except as expressly permitted in this Licensing
Agreement.  PerSoft Inc. also reserves the right to do the
following:

          Withdraw your license if this software package is used
          for any illegal or immoral purpose which, in the sole
          judgment of PerSoft Inc., may damage the reputation of
          PerSoft Inc.

If you transfer possession of any copy, modification, or merged
portion of the program to another person, YOUR LICENSE IS
AUTOMATICALLY TERMINATED.
```

**FIGURE 3-1**

# MOVING TEXT FLUSH RIGHT

**I**n Figure 3-1, notice that the date is against the right margin. The term to describe this placement of text is **flush right**. Look at the template next to the F6 key, as shown in Figure 3-2. You see the words Flush Right in blue. Press Alt-F3, (step 1 of Figure 3-3). The right margin defaults at position 74. Notice on the status line that the cursor is on position 75, just to the right of position 74. As you type, the text will move to the left of position 75. Type the date December 15, 1990. Figure 3-3 shows how the cursor is anchored at position 75 and how the letters move to the left as you type them. To end the Flush Right command press the Return key ↵ (step 2 of Figure 3-3). Next, insert two blank lines, by pressing Return twice ↵ ↵, placing the cursor on line 4, position 10.

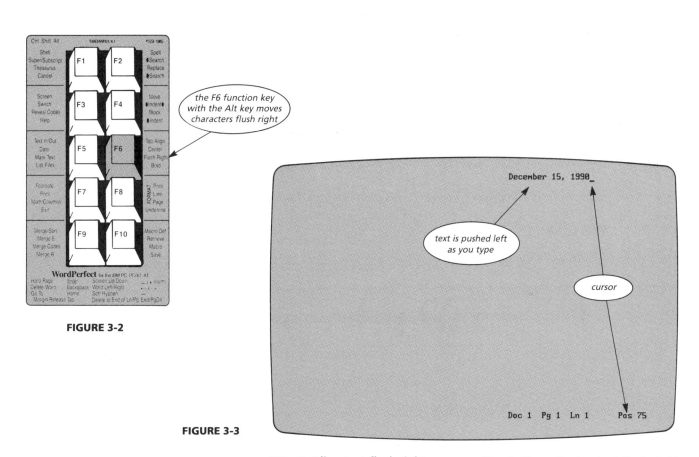

**FIGURE 3-2**

**FIGURE 3-3**

Step 1: Align text flush right    Step 2: Stop aligning text flush right

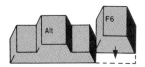

Now, view the code that is inserted when you align text flush right. Press Alt-F3 (step 1 of Figure 3-3). Figure 3-4 shows how the screen is divided. The lower screen reveals the codes that were embedded in your document. The first code you see is **[A]**, followed by the date. The capital [A] signified the *beginning* of a Flush Right command. The A stands for text *aligned to the right*. After the date, notice a lowercase **[a]**, which signifies the end of a Flush Right command. After the [a] code is the [HRt] code, which indicates the hard return you pressed after typing the date. Then you see two more hard returns that inserted two blank lines. To exit the reveal codes screen and return to your typing screen, press the spacebar.

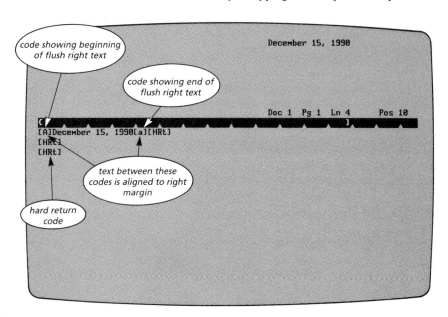

**FIGURE 3-4**

Step 1: View reveal codes          Step 2: Exit reveal codes

*space*

# CENTERING TEXT

**C**enter Text is a useful command and one that is commonly used, such as when you wish to center a heading. In Projects 1 and 2, you learned that the margins in WordPerfect are preset at (or default to) position 10 at the left and position 74 at the right. Instead of figuring the middle of the text by hand, as you would with typewriting, when you invoke the center function in WordPerfect, the program does all the figuring automatically.

Look at the template next to the F6 key. You see the word Center in green. While holding down the Shift key, press the F6 key (step 1 of Figure 3-5). The status line indicates you are at position 42, which is the middle position between the margins of 10 and 74. Before you begin typing, note that the title in Figure 3-1 is in capital (uppercase) letters. To capitalize your title, press the Caps Lock key (step 2 of Figure 3-5). Look at the status line. Figure 3-5 shows that the letters Pos are now POS. This is your indication that anything you type now will be in uppercase letters. The Caps Lock key is a *toggle* key, which means you turn it off the same way you turn it on. In other words, you press it once to activate the capitalization function and press it again to turn it off. For practice you may want to press the Caps Lock key a few times.

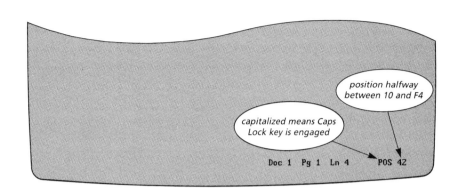

**FIGURE 3-5**

| Step 1: Center text | Step 2: Capitalize text | Step 3: Stop centering text |

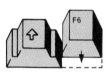  

When you are ready to continue with the project, be sure you see POS on the status line, indicating that type will be in uppercase letters. Type the words LICENSING AGREEMENT and as you do, notice that the text is automatically centered. To end the centering of text, press the Return key ↵ (step 3 in Figure 3-5). To insert a blank line, press the Return key one more time ↵, placing the cursor on line 6, position 10.

Now, to see the codes that are embedded when you use the centering function, hold down the Alt key and press the F3 key (step 1 of Figure 3-6). Figure 3-6 shows the [HRt] code that you inserted before you centered the text.

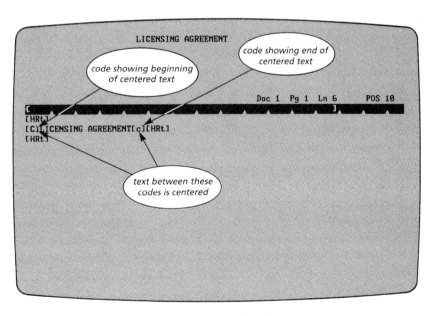

**FIGURE 3-6**

| Step 1: View reveal codes | Step 2: Exit reveal codes | Step 3: Stop capitalizing text |

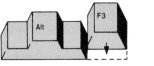  

*space*

On the line where you centered text, you see the code **[C]**, indicating the beginning of centering. At the end of the text is the code **[c]** followed by another [HRt] code, indicating the end of centering. (Because centering is ended by pressing a hard return, which embeds the [c] code, if you were to look at the codes before you inserted the hard return, you would not see the [c] code.) In addition to the [HRt] after the [c] code you also see another [HRt] code, which inserted the blank line. To exit from the reveal codes, press the spacebar (step 2 in Figure 3-6). You are returned to your document. To turn off the capitalizing function, press the Caps Lock key (step 3 of Figure 3-6) and notice on the status line that POS is again Pos.

## BOLDFACING TEXT

*C*ontinue by typing the words You should, and then press the spacebar. The cursor is on line 6, position 21. Note that in Figure 3-1 the word "carefully" is in darker, bolder type. When letters are presented this way in a document, they are said to be **boldfaced** or in boldface type. Look at the template next to the F6 key. You see the word Bold in black. Press the F6 key (step 1 of Figure 3-7) and as you press it look at the position number. If you have a monochrome monitor, the number itself becomes bolder. If you have a color monitor, the number changes to a different color. For practice, press the F6 key several times while watching the position number on the status line.

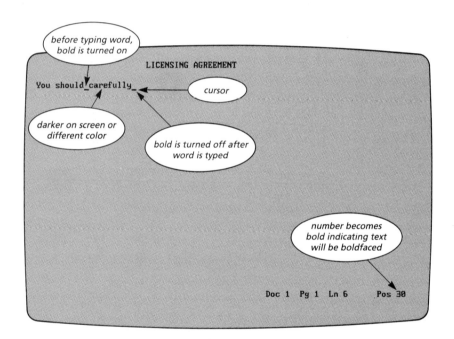

**FIGURE 3-7**

Step 1: Boldface text        Step 2: Stop boldfacing text

Be sure that the Bold command is on, and type the next word in Figure 3-1, which is the word carefully. As shown in Figure 3-7 the cursor is on line 6, position 30. Because you only want one word boldfaced, press F6 again to turn off the Bold command (step 2 of Figure 3-7). To view the codes that are inserted when typing in boldface mode, press Alt-F3 (step 1 of Figure 3-8). Figure 3-8 illustrates that preceding the word carefully is the code **[B]**, indicating the beginning of boldfacing. At the end of the word carefully is the code **[b]**, indicating the end of boldfacing. When the document is printed, the printer reads the codes, and only the typing between the boldface codes will be in boldface. To exit from the reveal codes press the spacebar (step 2 of Figure 3-8), and you are returned to your document.

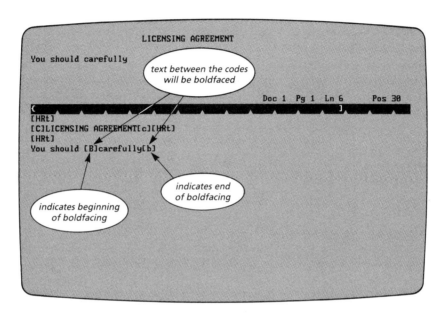

**FIGURE 3-8**

**Step 1: View reveal codes**          **Step 2: Exit reveal codes**

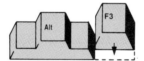

To continue, press the spacebar one time and type these words:

read the following terms and conditions. Your use of this program package indicates your acceptance of them. If you do Then press the spacebar. The cursor is now on line 8, position 27.

## UNDERLINING TEXT

A t times, you may want your type to be underscored with a line. You would then want to use the **underline** function. Look at the template next to the F8 key. Note the word Underline in black. Press the F8 key (step 1 of Figure 3-9). The position number on the status line is underlined, indicating that any text you type now will be underlined. (If you have a color monitor, the color of the number will change.) For practice, press the F8 key several times, so that you can see how your monitor indicates that the words or letters you type will be underlined. Before you begin typing, be sure that the underline command is on. Type the word not. Then, before typing or even spacing, press the F8 key again and notice on the status line that the underline command is off (step 2 of Figure 3-9). The cursor is at position 30.

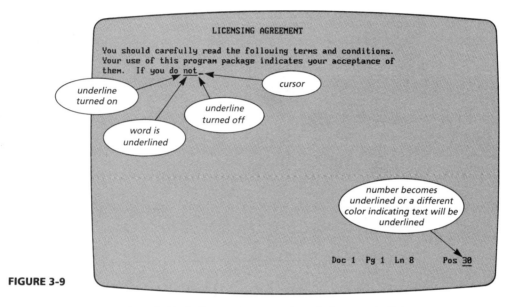

**FIGURE 3-9**

**Step 1: Underline text**    **Step 2: Stop underlining text**

To view the codes used for underlining, press Alt-F3 (step 1 of Figure 3-10). Figure 3-10 shows in the lower screen that before the word not is the code **[U]**, indicating the beginning of underlining. After the word not is the code **[u]**, indicating the end of underlining. To exit from the reveal codes, press the spacebar, and you are back to your document.

To finish typing the paragraph, press the spacebar and, with the cursor at position 31, type these words:

agree with them, you should not use this software package. Instead, you should return the package and your money will be returned to you.

Next, press the return ↵ key twice, placing the cursor on line 12, position 10. Now type the second paragraph of Figure 3-1. Beginning on line 12, position 10, type these words:

PerSoft Inc. provides this program and licenses you to use it.

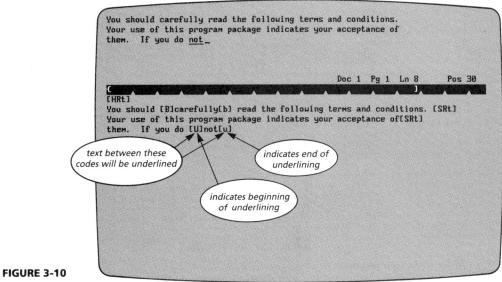

**FIGURE 3-10**

**Step 1: View reveal codes**         **Step 2: Exit reveal codes**

After typing the period, press the spacebar twice, placing the cursor on line 12, position 74. Since the next word is to be underlined, press the F8 key (step 1 of Figure 3-11). Before you type, let's see how the codes appear. Press Alt-F3 (step 2 of Figure 3-11). The lower screen shows both the underline codes together, with only the cursor between them. Press the spacebar to exit from the reveal codes (step 3 of Figure 3-11), and type the word You.

**FIGURE 3-11**

**Step 1: Underline text**      **Step 2: View reveal codes**      **Step 3: Exit reveal codes**

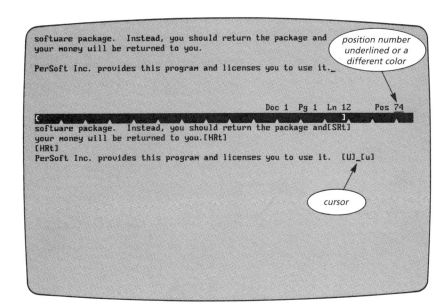

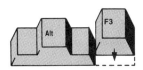

Before you turn off the underline command, look at the reveal codes again by pressing Alt-F3 (step 1 of Figure 3-12). Your screen will look like the one in Figure 3-12. Notice how the lowercase **[u]** code moved to the right and the word you typed appears between the codes. In addition, notice that because the Underline command is still turned on, the cursor is to the left of the [u] code. Press the spacebar to exit from the reveal codes (step 2 of Figure 3-12).

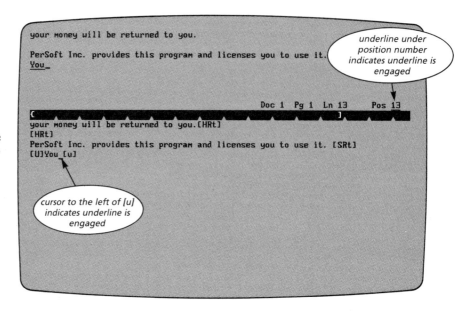

**FIGURE 3-12**

**Step 1: View reveal codes**     **Step 2: Exit reveal codes**

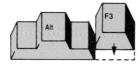 

Press the F8 key to turn off the Underline command (step 1 of Figure 3-13). View the codes again by pressing Alt-F3 (step 2 of Figure 3-13). By turning off the Underline command, you have moved the cursor to the right of the [u] code. Press the spacebar to exit the reveal codes (step 3 of Figure 3-13).

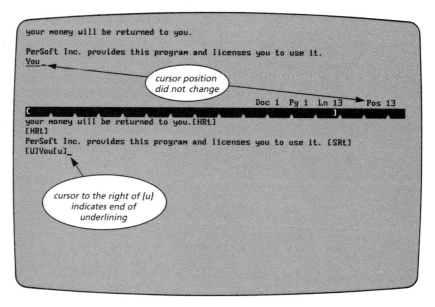

**FIGURE 3-13**

**Step 1: Stop underlining text**    **Step 2: View reveal codes**    **Step 3: Exit reveal codes**

 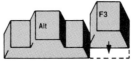

# INSERTING TEXT

ometimes you may wish to insert text between existing text. WordPerfect defaults to the **Insert Text** mode, which means that as you type, text will be inserted wherever the cursor is located.

Press the spacebar to put the cursor on line 13, position 14. Type these words:

assume responsibility for the selection of this program to achieve your intended results. PerSoft Inc. assumes no responsibility for the results you obtain from the use of this package.

When you finish, the cursor is on line 16, position 18. Compare what you typed to Figure 3-1. You see that you omitted the word software before the last word, package. Press the Left Arrow ← key to move the cursor to the left to position it under the p in the word package. Type the word software and as you do, notice that the word is inserted into the text and the word package is moved to the right (Figure 3-14). Finally, press the spacebar once to insert a space between the last two words of the paragraph.

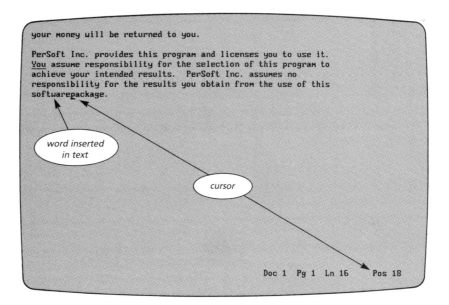

**FIGURE 3-14**

## USING THE BACKSPACE KEY TO CORRECT ERRORS

**A**s you know, if you make a mistake in typing a word, you can press the Backspace key to delete the error. At other times you can use the Backspace key to correct other errors such as hard returns and spacing. For example, you may accidentally press the Return/Enter key ↵, thereby splitting lines of text on the screen. With the cursor still under the p in package, press the Return key ↵. Figure 3-15 shows how this splits the line. Press the Backspace key. Figure 3-16 shows how the word "package" returns to line 16.

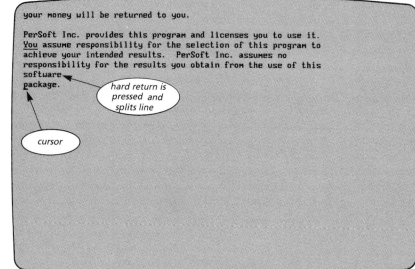

**FIGURE 3-15**

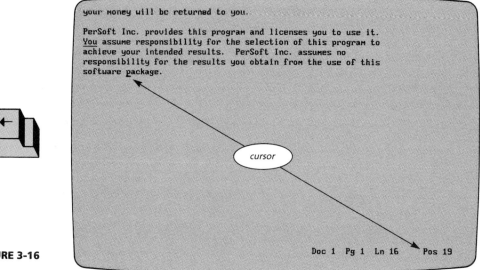

**FIGURE 3-16**

You can also use the Backspace key if you press the spacebar in error. Press the Spacebar two times (step 1 of Figure 3-17). To delete these extra spaces, press the Backspace key two times (step 2 of Figure 3-17) to return the word "package" to its original position.

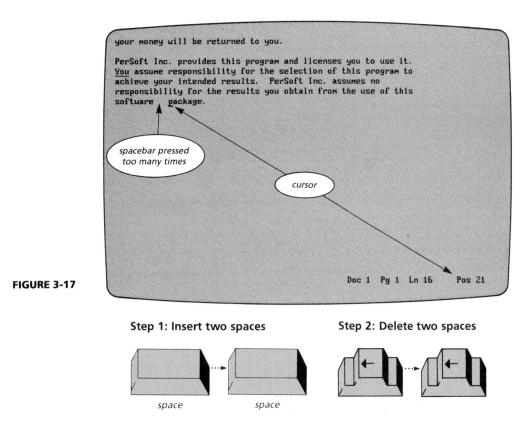

**FIGURE 3-17**

**Step 1: Insert two spaces**     **Step 2: Delete two spaces**

Because you wish to end the paragraph, press Home, then Right Arrow →, placing the cursor to the right of the period, on line 16, position 27. To end the paragraph, press Return ↵. To insert a blank line press Return ↵ again, placing the cursor on line 18, position 10.

## USING THE TYPEOVER COMMAND

s explained earlier, WordPerfect defaults to the Insert mode. However, if you wish to type over existing text instead of using the insert function, you must turn on the Typeover command. The Insert key is a toggle key, which means you turn it off the same way you turn it on.

Beginning at position 10 on line 18 type the word License. Comparing the word with the one in Figure 3-1 you note that it should have been typed in capital letters rather than upper and lowercase letters. One way to do this is to delete the word and then retype it completely. However, you can also use the **Typeover** mode to accomplish this.

Move the cursor to the left under the i in License as shown in Figure 3-18. Before you begin typing press the Caps Lock key, then press the Insert key (step 1 of Figure 3-18). At the bottom left corner of your screen you see the word "Typeover." It means that anything you type will type over existing text. Type the letters ICENSE and as you do notice how the lowercase letters become uppercase letters. When finished, press the Insert key to turn the Typeover command off. The word "Typeover" in the left corner of the screen disappears. Press the Caps Lock key to change from uppercase to lowercase typing (step 2 of Figure 3-18). Press the Return ↵ key to move the cursor to line 19, then press the Return ↵ key again to insert a blank line and move the cursor to line 20, position 10.

Type the words You may perform the following functions: followed by a hard return ↵. To insert a blank line press the hard return ↵ again, placing the cursor on line 22, position 10.

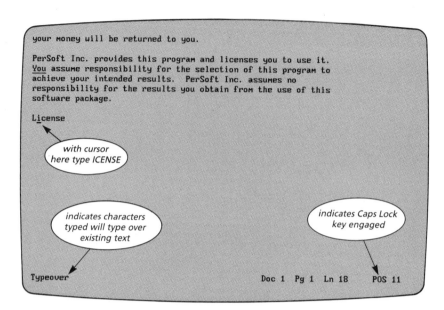

**FIGURE 3-18**   **Step 1: Type over text with capitalized letters**

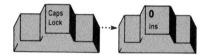

**Step 2: Return to Insert mode and stop capitalizing text**

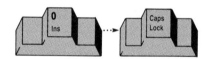

# USING THE INDENT KEY

Without actually changing the margin settings you may wish to change the left margin temporarily so that lines wrap to a specific position setting, making a wider margin, as shown in Figure 3-19. To accomplish this you must use the →Indent key, which is the F4 key. Look at the template next to the F4 key. You see the word →Indent in black. When you use the Indent key you will notice that the cursor always moves to where the Tabs are set. In WordPerfect the tabs setting defaults to every fifth position, or 0, 5, 10, 15, 20, and so on.

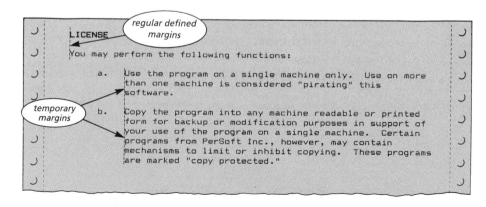

**FIGURE 3-19**

With the cursor at position 10, press the F4 key. The cursor moves to position 15, which is where the first tab is found to the right of the margin. At position 15 type a. then press the F4 key again. As shown in Figure 3-20, the cursor moves to position 20, which is now the new temporary left margin. All text typed will wrap around to position 20.

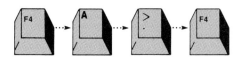

**FIGURE 3-20**

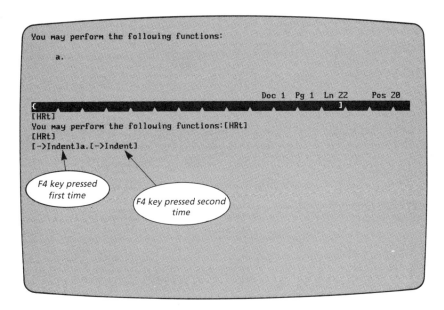

To view the code that is embedded into the text when you press the Indent key, press Alt-F3. Figure 3-21 shows the reveal codes screen. You see the first [→Indent] code, then the letter a. Next you see the second [→Indent] code, which will change the left margin temporarily. Press the spacebar to exit from the reveal codes (step 2 of Figure 3-21).

**FIGURE 3-21**

Step 1: View reveal codes          Step 2: Exit reveal codes

space

Beginning on line 22, position 20 type these lines:

Use the program on a single machine only. Use on more than one machine is considered "pirating" this software.

At the end of the first line when you begin typing the word than, notice that the word wraps to the next line, to position 20, which is the new temporary margin. After typing the word software, end indenting by pressing the Return key. The cursor moves to line 25, position 10, which is the default left margin.

To insert a blank line, press Return ↵ to move the cursor to line 26, position 10 (step 1 of Figure 3-22). Since you need to indent the next paragraph, press the F4 key and type b. then press the F4 key again (step 2 of Figure 3-22). With the cursor on position 20, type this paragraph:

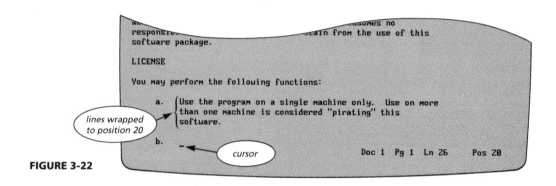

**FIGURE 3-22**

**Step 1: Return to default margin**

**Step 2: Create temporary margin**

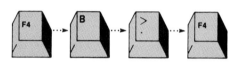

Copy the program into any machine readable or printed form for backup or modification purposes in support of your use of the program on a single machine. Certain programs from PerSoft Inc., however, may contain mechanisms to limit or inhibit copying. These programs are marked "copy protected."

When you have finished typing the paragraph the cursor will be on line 31, position 48. Press the Return key ↵ to end the indenting for this paragraph. Press the Return key ↵ again to insert a blank line, placing the cursor on line 33, position 10 (step 1 of Figure 3-23).

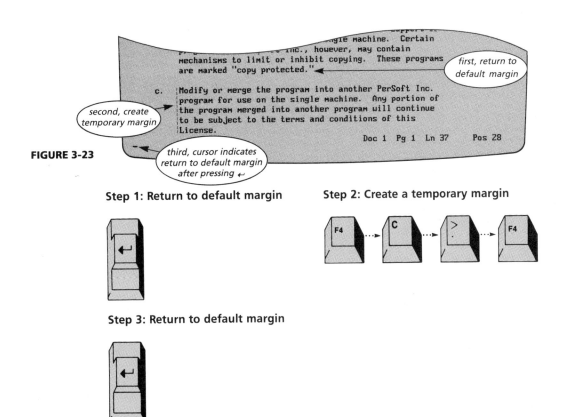

**FIGURE 3-23**

Step 1: Return to default margin          Step 2: Create a temporary margin

Step 3: Return to default margin

Before typing the last indented paragraph, press the F4 key and type c. then press the F4 key again (step 2 of Figure 3-23). Beginning on position 20, type this paragraph:

Modify or merge the program into another PerSoft Inc. program for use on the single machine. Any portion of the program merged into another program will continue to be subject to the terms and conditions of this License.

Figure 3-23 shows that after you type the paragraph, the cursor is on line 37, position 28.

To end indenting the paragraph press the Return key ↵ (step 3 of Figure 3-23), then press the Return key ↵ again to insert a blank line.

With the cursor on Ln 39 Pos 10 type these words:

You MAY NOT use, copy, modify, or transfer the program, in whole or in part, except as

Then press the spacebar, placing the cursor on line 40, position 32.

# BOLDFACING AND UNDERLINING AT THE SAME TIME

*T*o emphasize important words in a document, you may wish to use boldface as well as underlining. Remember how to underline text: Press the F8 key. To boldface text, press the F6 key (step 1 of Figure 3-24). Type the words: expressly permitted. Figure 3-24 shows how your screen will look with the words both boldfaced and underlined (if you have a color screen, the words to be boldfaced and/or underlined appear in different colors). Before you resume typing you must turn off the Boldface and Underline commands. Press F8 to turn off the Underline, then press F6 to turn off the Boldface (step 2 of Figure 3-24).

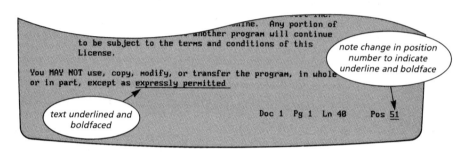

**FIGURE 3-24**

**Step 1: Underline and Boldface text**        **Step 2: Stop underlining and boldfacing**

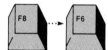        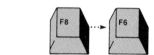

To view the codes in this document, press Alt-F3 (step 1 of Figure 3-25). Figure 3-25 shows both the underline [U][u] and boldface [B][b] codes at the beginning and end of the two words. Press the spacebar to exit from the reveal codes (step 2 of Figure 3-25).

Press the spacebar to insert a space after the word permitted and continue typing:

in this Licensing Agreement. PerSoft Inc. also reserves the right to do the following:

To end the paragraph press the Return key ↵ followed by another Return ↵ to insert a blank line. The cursor should now be on line 44, position 10.

# USING THE LEFT/RIGHT INDENT KEY

*I*f you wish to define wider left and right margins temporarily, you can use the **Left/Right Indent** key. The Left/Right Indent key can be used for long quotes that will be indented from both the left and right margins. The left/right indent moves to where the tabs are currently set. When you use the left/right indent, the right margin will move in the same number of spaces as the left margin.

Look at the template next to the F4 key. You see the word →**Indent**← in green. Press Shift-F4 (step 1 of Figure 3-26). To see the embedded code, press Alt-F3 (step 2 of Figure 3-26). In the lower screen shown in Figure 3-26 notice the code [→**Indent**←], indicating that any text that follows will be indented from both the left and right margins. To exit from the reveal codes, press the spacebar (step 3 of Figure 3-26).

Now type the left/right indented paragraph:

> Withdraw your license if this software package is used for any illegal or immoral purpose which, in the sole judgment of PerSoft Inc., may damage the reputation of PerSoft Inc.

When you finish typing this paragraph, the cursor is on line 47, position 27. To end the Left/Right Indent command, press the Return key ↵, then press the Return key ↵ again to insert a blank line, placing the cursor on line 49, position 10.

Beginning on line 49, position 10, type the last paragraph of the licensing agreement:

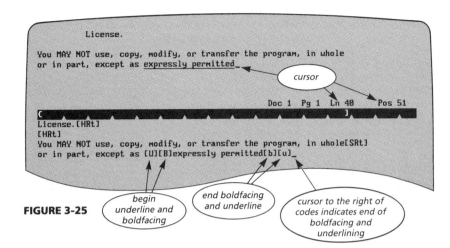

**FIGURE 3-25**

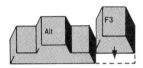

**Step 1: View reveal codes**

**Step 2: Exit reveal codes**

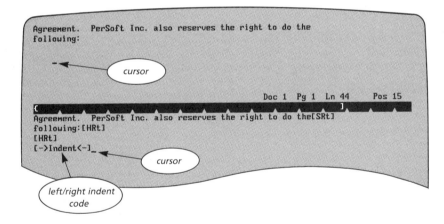

**FIGURE 3-26**

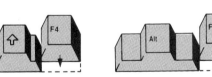

**Step 1: Indent text**     **Step 2: View reveal codes**

**Step 3: Exit reveal codes**

If you transfer possession of any copy, modification, or merged portion of the program to another person, YOUR LICENSE IS AUTOMATICALLY TERMINATED.

The entire document is now typed.

## SAVING A FILE TO THE DISK

t is necessary to save the document to disk so that it can be retrieved for printing or modification later. To save, follow the procedure you learned in Projects 1 and 2. Save this document under the name LICENSE.

## UNDERLINING AND BOLDFACING EXISTING TEXT

t the beginning of Project 3 you were told that you would be creating the document in Figure 3-1. If you compare the document in Figure 3-1 with your completed document as shown in Figure 3-27, you will notice the following differences:

1. In the title, the words LICEN-SING AGREEMENT are not underlined in Figure 3-27.
2. Farther down, the word LICENSE is not in boldface type.
3. The words MAY NOT are not underlined.
4. The last five words of the agreement are not in boldface type.

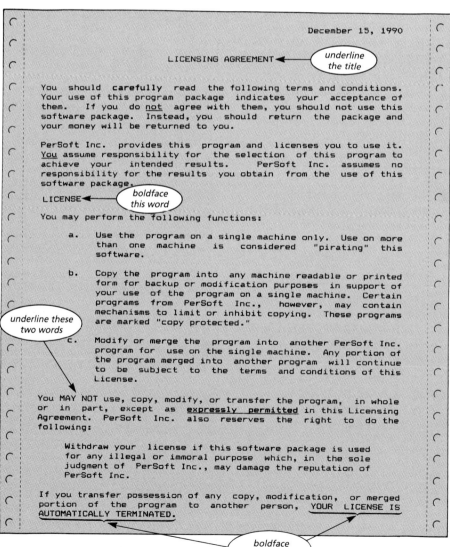

**FIGURE 3-27**

The comparison of the two figures shows that sometimes you need to boldface or underline *existing* text. It is not necessary to delete the text and retype it in boldface or underline mode. Move the cursor to the top of the document by pressing Home, Home, Up Arrow ↑. As the cursor moves to the top of the document, the word "Repositioning" appears in the lower left corner of the screen, advising you that the cursor is in the process of moving.

Move the cursor down so that it is under the L in LICENSING AGREEMENT. The cursor will be on line 4, position 33.

As we learned in Project 2, the block function highlights specified text, thereby isolating that text from the rest of the document. Once the desired text is highlighted you can perform the requested function. Here we use the **block** function to underline and then boldface a block of text.

Look at the template next to the F4 key. You see the word Block in blue. Press Alt-F4 (step 1 of Figure 3-28). The "Block on" message begins blinking in the lower left corner of the screen. To highlight or block the words LICENSING AGREEMENT, move the cursor to the right one character at a time with the Right Arrow → key, or move the cursor more quickly by pressing the Home key followed by the Right Arrow key → (step 2 of Figure 3-28). When the cursor is on position 52 just to the right of the letter T in AGREEMENT, the two words are blocked. You have now isolated these words from the rest of the document and can underline them. As noted on the template, the F8 key is used for underlining. Press the F8 key (step 3 of Figure 3-28). When you do, notice that the "Block on" message turns off on the screen and at the same time the block of text is underlined.

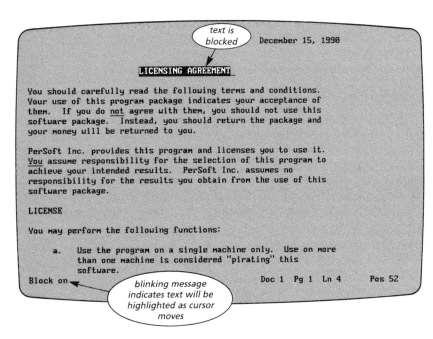

**FIGURE 3-28**

**Step 1: Initiate block mode**      **Step 2: Select text to be blocked**      **Step 3: Underline blocked text**

Move the cursor down to line 18, position 10 so that it is under the L in the word LICENSE. This is existing text you wish to boldface. The same method that was used to underline existing text is used to boldface existing text. Press Alt-F4 (step 1 of Figure 3-29). With the "Block on" message flashing in the lower left corner of your screen, move the cursor to the right to highlight the word LICENSE (step 2 of Figure 3-29). When the word is highlighted, note that the word Bold is in black next to the F6 key, and press the F6 key (step 3 of Figure 3-29). The blocked text is turned off and the word LICENSE is boldfaced.

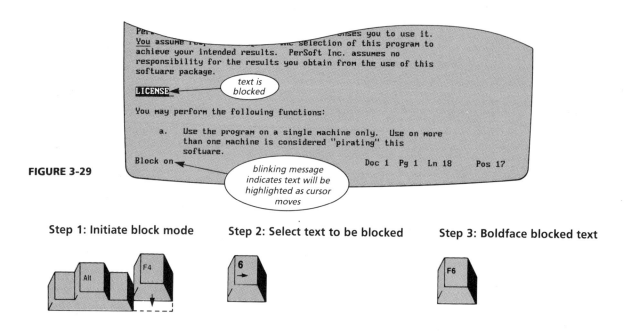

**FIGURE 3-29**

**Step 1: Initiate block mode**   **Step 2: Select text to be blocked**   **Step 3: Boldface blocked text**

Move the cursor down to line 39 of your document, then to position 14. The cursor should be under the M in the word MAY. To block the words MAY NOT, press Alt-F4 (step 1 of Figure 3-30). With the message "Block on" flashing, move the cursor to the right to highlight the words MAY NOT (step 2 of Figure 3-30). When the words are highlighted, press the F8 key (step 3 of Figure 3-30). The block is turned off and the words are underlined.

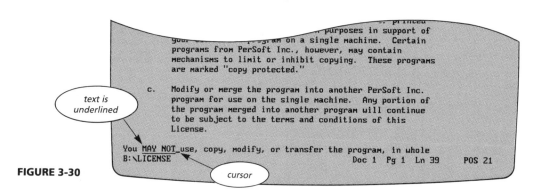

**FIGURE 3-30**

**Step 1: Initiate block mode**   **Step 2: Select text to be blocked**   **Step 3: Underline blocked text**

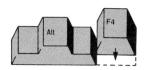

Move the cursor down to line 50. To move to the right, while holding down the Ctrl key, press the Right Arrow → until the cursor is under the letter Y in the word YOUR. The cursor should be at position 52. To highlight the last five words of the document, press Alt-F4 (step 1 of Figure 3-31). With the message "Block on" flashing, move the cursor to highlight the last five words of the document, YOUR LICENSE IS AUTOMATICALLY TERMINATED (step 2 of Figure 3-31). With the desired text highlighted, press the F6 key (step 3 of Figure 3-31). "Block on" is turned off and the text is placed in boldface mode.

**FIGURE 3-31**

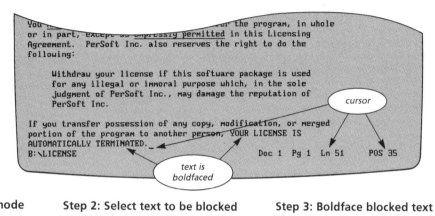

Step 1: Initiate block mode     Step 2: Select text to be blocked     Step 3: Boldface blocked text

To view your last command in the reveal codes, press Alt-F3 (step 1 of Figure 3-32). In the lower screen the **[B]** code (beginning boldface) was placed before the Y and the **[b]** code (ending boldface) was placed after the period. When the document is printed, all type between those codes will be printed in boldface. To exit the reveal codes, press the spacebar (step 2 of Figure 3-32).

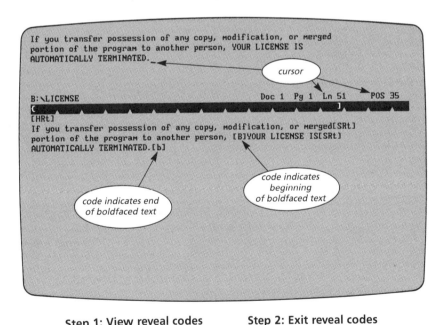

**FIGURE 3-32**

Step 1: View reveal codes     Step 2: Exit reveal codes

## SAVING AND REPLACING A DOCUMENT

When you finished typing this document, you saved it to your disk. But after saving it, you made several changes to the document on your screen. Those changes have not been saved to the disk. If there were a power failure or if you turned off the computer, the revised document in the main memory would be lost. Therefore, you must save the changes to the disk, replacing the old text with the new text. When you instruct the computer to replace the old document with the new one, the entire document will be saved, including any changes or additions.

To **save and replace** your document, press the F10 key (step 1 of Figure 3-33). Notice the message "Document to be Saved:" in the lower left corner of the screen, along with the name you previously gave your document. Once you have named a document, it is not necessary to type the name each time you wish to save and replace. Since that is the name you wish to keep, you only need to press the Enter ↵ key (step 2 of Figure 3-33). When you do, the message "Replace B:\LICENSE? (Y/N) N" appears on the screen (Figure 3-34). Since you want to replace the old document with the new one, type the letter Y for yes. You will hear drive B whirring and see the drive B light go on, indicating that the document is being saved to the diskette and that the new version is replacing the old version.

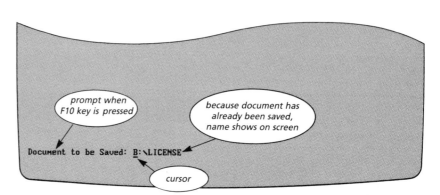

**FIGURE 3-33**  **Step 1: Save and replace document**  **Step 2: Accept existing document name**

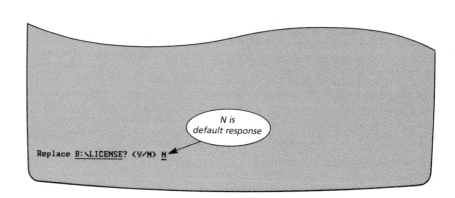

**FIGURE 3-34**

## PRINTING A DOCUMENT

Now you can print the document in its final form. Be sure the printer has paper in place and that the printer is turned on and ready to print.

From Project 1, remember that in order to print the document you must invoke the print function. Press Shift-F7. Figure 3-35 shows the print menu you see at the bottom of the screen.

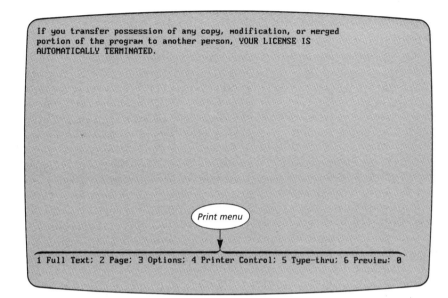

**FIGURE 3-35**

Because you wish to print the complete or full text of this document, press the number 1 for full text, and the printer will begin printing your document. The printed document is illustrated in Figure 3-36.

```
                                                    December 15, 1990
*WPC

                        LICENSING AGREEMENT

You should carefully read the following terms and conditions.
Your use of this program package indicates your acceptance of
them.  If you do not agree with them, you should not use this
software package.  Instead, you should return the package and
your money will be returned to you.*WPC

PerSoft Inc. provides this program and licenses you to use it.
You assume responsibility for the selection of this program to
achieve your intended results.  PerSoft Inc. assumes no
responsibility for the results you obtain from the use of this
software package.*WPC

LICENSE

You may perform the following functions:
*WPC
     a.    Use the program on a single machine only.  Use on more
           than one machine is considered "pirating" this
           software.

     b.    Copy the program into any machine readable or printed
           form for backup or modification purposes in support of
           your use of the program on a single machine.  Certain
           programs from PerSoft Inc., however, may contain
           mechanisms to limit or inhibit copying.  These programs
           are marked "copy protected."                      *WPC

     c.    Modify or merge the program into another PerSoft Inc.
           program for use on the single machine.  Any portion of
           the program merged into another program will continue
           to be subject to the terms and conditions of this
           License.                                           *WPC

You MAY NOT use, copy, modify, or transfer the program, in whole
or in part, except as expressly permitted in this Licensing
Agreement.  PerSoft Inc. also reserves the right to do the
following:*WPC

     Withdraw your license if this software package is used
     for any illegal or immoral purpose which, in the sole
     judgment of PerSoft Inc., may damage the reputation of
     PerSoft Inc.                                             *WPC


If you transfer possession of any copy, modification, or merged
portion of the program to another person, YOUR LICENSE IS
AUTOMATICALLY TERMINATED.
```

**FIGURE 3-36**

# EXITING PROJECT 3

*I*n order to exit this document press the F7 key (step 1 of Figure 3-37). The message "Save Document? (Y/N) Y" appears in the lower left corner of the screen.

Remember that you have already saved this document in its new form to the disk, so it is not necessary to save it again. Look at the right corner of the screen in Figure 3-37. Notice the message "(Text was not modified)." That message is your assurance that everything in your document has been saved. If that message were completed it would say "Text was not modified since you last saved to disk." If you are ever exiting a document you wish to save and you do not see the "(Text was not modified)" message, be sure to save and replace as you exit.

Since you do see the message and are assured that your document has been saved in its entirety, you can answer the prompt by pressing the letter N for no (step 2 of Figure 3-37). The screen then displays the prompt "Exit WP? (Y/N) N" as shown in Figure 3-38. Since you do wish to exit the program, type the letter Y as you have done in Projects 1 and 2 to return to the DOS prompt.

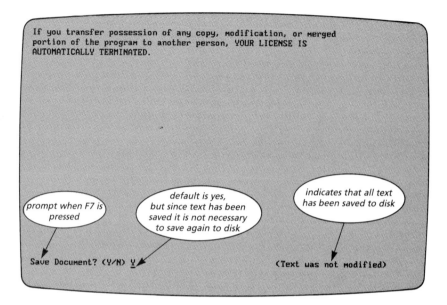

**FIGURE 3-37**   **Step 1: Exit the document**   **Step 2: Respond to prompt**

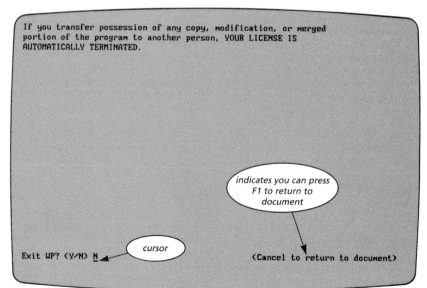

**FIGURE 3-38**

# PROJECT SUMMARY

*I*n Project 3 you learned how to arrange text flush right and centered, how to boldface and underline text, and how to indent text. You saved the document to disk, then returned to existing text and boldfaced and underlined some key words. Then you saved the revised document to the disk, replacing the first version. You printed the document, making a hard copy of the text. Throughout the project, you practiced viewing the reveal codes screen to become familiar with the various codes that are embedded as you create a document.

The following is a list of the keystroke sequence we used in Project 3:

**SUMMARY OF KEYSTROKES—Project 3**

| STEPS | KEY(S) PRESSED | STEPS | KEY(S) PRESSED |
|---|---|---|---|
| 1 | b: [at the A> prompt] | 35 | [space] |
| 2 | ↵ | 36 | [F8] |
| 3 | a:wp [at the B> prompt] | 37 | You |
| 4 | ↵ | 38 | [F8] |
| 5 | ↵ [at first introductory screen] | 39 | [space] |
| 6 | ↵ [only if you see a second introductory screen] | 40 | assume responsibility for the selection of this program to achieve your intended results. PerSoft Inc. assumes no responsibility for the results you obtain from the use of this software package. |
| 7 | [Alt-F6] | | |
| 8 | December 15, 1990 | | |
| 9 | ↵ | 41 | ↵ |
| 10 | ↵ | 42 | ↵ |
| 11 | ↵ | 43 | [Caps Lock] |
| 12 | [Shift-F6] | 44 | LICENSE |
| 13 | [Caps Lock] | 45 | [Caps Lock] |
| 14 | LICENSING AGREEMENT | 46 | ↵ |
| 15 | [Caps Lock] | 47 | ↵ |
| 16 | ↵ | 48 | You may perform the following functions: |
| 17 | ↵ | 49 | ↵ |
| 18 | You should | 50 | ↵ |
| 19 | [space] | 51 | [F4] |
| 20 | [F6] | 52 | a. |
| 21 | carefully | 53 | [F4] |
| 22 | [F6] | 54 | Use the program on a single machine only. Use on more than one machine is considered "pirating" this software. |
| 23 | [space] | | |
| 24 | read the following terms and conditions. Your use of this program package indicates your acceptance of them. If you do | 55 | ↵ |
| | | 56 | ↵ |
| 25 | [space] | 57 | [F4] |
| 26 | [F8] | 58 | b. |
| 27 | not | 59 | [F4] |
| 28 | [F8] | 60 | Copy the program into any machine readable or printed form for backup or modification purposes in support of your use of the program on a single machine. Certain programs from PerSoft Inc., however, may contain mechanisms to limit or inhibit copying. These programs are marked "copy protected." |
| 29 | [space] | | |
| 30 | agree with them, you should not use this software package. Instead, you should return the package and your money will be returned to you. | | |
| 31 | ↵ | 61 | ↵ |
| 32 | ↵ | 62 | ↵ |
| 33 | PerSoft Inc. provides this program and licenses you to use it. | 63 | [F4] |
| 34 | [space] | | |

**SUMMARY OF KEYSTROKES—Project 3 (continued)**

| STEPS | KEY(S) PRESSED | STEPS | KEY(S) PRESSED |
|---|---|---|---|
| 64 | c. | 93 | YOUR LICENSE IS AUTOMATICALLY TERMINATED. |
| 65 | [F4] | 94 | [Caps Lock] |
| 66 | Modify or merge the program into another PerSoft Inc. program for use on the single machine. Any portion of the program merged into another program will continue to be subject to the terms and conditions of this License. | 95 | [F10] |
| | | 96 | license |
| | | 97 | ← [wait for document to be saved] |
| | | 98 | [Home][Home]↑ |
| | | 99 | [move cursor to line 4, position 33 under the L in LICENSING AGREEMENT] |
| 67 | ← | 100 | [Alt-F4] |
| 68 | ← | 101 | [→ to highlight or block LICENSING AGREEMENT] |
| 69 | You | 102 | [F8] |
| 70 | [space] | 103 | [move cursor down to line 18, position 10 under the L in LICENSE] |
| 71 | [Caps Lock] | | |
| 72 | MAY NOT | 104 | [Alt-F4] |
| 73 | [Caps Lock] | 105 | [→ to highlight or block LICENSE] |
| 74 | [space] | 106 | [F6] |
| 75 | use, copy, modify, or transfer the program, in whole or in part, except as | 107 | [move cursor to line 39, position 14 under the M in MAY NOT] |
| 76 | [space] | 108 | [Alt-F4] |
| 77 | [F8] | 109 | [→ to highlight or block MAY NOT] |
| 78 | [F6] | 110 | [F8] |
| 79 | expressly permitted | 111 | [press cursor keys to move cursor to line 50, position 52 under the Y in YOUR] |
| 80 | [F8] | | |
| 81 | [F6] | 112 | [Alt-F4] |
| 82 | [space] | 113 | [press cursor keys to highlight the words YOUR LICENSE IS AUTOMATICALLY TERMINATED.] |
| 83 | in this Licensing Agreement. PerSoft Inc. also reserves the right to do the following: | | |
| | | 114 | [F6] |
| 84 | ← | 115 | [F10] |
| 85 | ← | 116 | ← |
| 86 | [Shift-F4] | 117 | Y [wait for document to be saved] |
| 87 | Withdraw your license if this software package is used for any illegal or immoral purpose which, in the sole judgment of PerSoft Inc., may damage the reputation of PerSoft Inc. | 118 | [Shift-F7] |
| | | 119 | 1 |
| | | 120 | [F7] |
| | | 121 | N |
| 88 | ← | 122 | Y |
| 89 | ← | 123 | [remove disk from drive A if you see prompt "Insert COMMAND.COM disk in drive A and strike any key when ready"] |
| 90 | If you transfer possession of any copy, modification, or merged portion of the program to another person, | | |
| | | 124 | [put DOS disk into drive A] |
| 91 | [space] | 125 | [press any key] |
| 92 | [Caps Lock] | 126 | [at B> remove disks from both drives] |

The following list summarizes the material covered in Project 3:

1. The term **flush right** describes text that is aligned to the right margin. The embedded codes are **[A]** and **[a]**.
2. The **Center Text** command centers text between the margins. The embedded codes are **[C]** and **[c]**.
3. **Boldfaced text** appears darker or bolder. The embedded codes are **[B]** and **[b]**.
4. The **underline** function is used to underline text. The embedded codes are **[U]** and **[u]**.
5. When you **insert** text, existing text is moved to the right.
6. Use the **Typeover** command to type over existing text by pressing the Insert key.

7. The **Indent** key sets a temporary left margin. The embedded code is [→**Indent**]. The temporary margin is removed with a hard return.

8. Use the **Left/Right Indent** key to set temporary left and right margins. The embedded code is [→**Indent**←]. Temporary margins are removed with a hard return.

9. Use the **block** function to highlight text, to isolate it from the rest of the document so that you can underline or boldface it.

10. If you have **saved** a document to disk and then made changes in it on the screen, you must **replace** the old document with the new version by saving it again to disk.

# STUDENT ASSIGNMENTS

## STUDENT ASSIGNMENT 1: True/False

**Instructions:**    Circle T if the statement is true and F if the statement if false.

T  F  1. To use the flush right function you would use the Shift-F6 keys.

T  F  2. The paired codes to indicate boldfacing are [B] and [b].

T  F  3. The Indent key moves the cursor to the next tab setting.

T  F  4. To turn off the block function you could press the Exit (F7) key.

T  F  5. With the Insert key turned on, the message "Typeover" appears on the screen.

T  F  6. The command Alt-F6 can be used to cause boldface characters.

T  F  7. Pressing the Indent key temporarily changes the left margin until a hard return is pressed.

T  F  8. The Ctrl-F4 keys are used to turn on the block function.

T  F  9. The left/right indent function is invoked with the Shift-F4 keys.

T  F  10. To exit a document you can use the F1 (Cancel) key.

## STUDENT ASSIGNMENT 2: Multiple Choice

**Instructions:**    Circle the correct response.

1. When the F6 key is pressed
   a. the position number changes appearance
   b. the codes [B] and [b] are embedded into the document
   c. boldface typing will occur until the F6 key is pressed again, turning boldfacing off
   d. all of the above

2. To underline a word in the body of the text
   a. the user must backspace and underline the characters just typed
   b. press the F8 key, type the text to be underlined, then press F8 again
   c. press the F6 key, type the text to be underlined, then press F6 again
   d. press the F8 key, type the text to be underlined, then press the F7 (Exit) key

3. The boldface function can be specified by pressing
   a. the F8 key
   b. the Shift-F8 keys
   c. the F6 key
   d. none of the above

**Student Assignment 2 (continued)**

4. To center a heading on a page,
    a. the space bar must be used to cause spaces to appear to the left
    b. the Shift-F6 keys must be pressed
    c. a hard return must be pressed after the text has been typed
    d. both b and c are correct
5. The F4 or Indent key will do the following:
    a. temporarily change the left margin
    b. temporarily change the left and right margins
    c. move the cursor to the next tab stop setting
    d. both a and c are correct
6. The code(s) that are inserted when the Alt-F6 keys are pressed (followed by a hard return) are
    a. [Flsh Rt]
    b. [A] [a]
    c. [HRt]
    d. [SRt]
7. To invoke Boldfacing mode,
    a. press F6 at the beginning and end of the type to be boldfaced
    b. press F6 at the beginning and a hard return at the end of the type to be boldfaced
    c. press F8 at the beginning and end of the type to be boldfaced
    d. press Shift-F6 at the beginning of typing, and F7 at the end of the type to be boldfaced
8. To underline existing text,
    a. delete existing text, press F8, type text again, press F8
    b. put the cursor at the beginning of the text, press F8, then press the spacebar under the text
    c. block the existing text using the Alt-F4 keys, then press F8
    d. none of the above

## STUDENT ASSIGNMENT 3: Matching

**Instructions:**   Put the appropriate number next to the words in the second column.

| | | |
|---|---|---|
| 1. Underline codes | _____ | [C] [c] |
| 2. Typeover | _____ | Alt-F4 |
| 3. Boldface codes | _____ | F6 |
| 4. Left/Right Indent | _____ | Insert key |
| 5. Center codes | _____ | Shift-F6 |
| 6. Indent key(s) | _____ | [B] [b] |
| 7. Boldface key(s) | _____ | [U] [u] |
| 8. Flush Right code | _____ | F4 |
| 9. Flush Right key(s) | _____ | Shift-F4 |
| 10. Center key(s) | _____ | [A] [a] |
| 11. Block function | _____ | Alt-F6 |

## STUDENT ASSIGNMENT 4: Writing WordPerfect Commands

**Instructions:**   Next to each command, write its effect.

**Command**                           **Effect**

1. Alt-F6          _____
2. F6             _____
3. Shift-F6        _____
4. F8             _____
5. Insert key      _____
6. Caps Lock key    _____
7. F4             _____
8. Shift-F4        _____
9. Alt-F4 (plus cursor keys)   _____
10. F10            _____
11. Shift           _____
12. F7             _____

## STUDENT ASSIGNMENT 5: WordPerfect Commands

**Instructions:**   The heading shown below was typed in capital letters, centered and underlined. Describe in detail each of the keystrokes that were used to produce this heading.

```
REGIONAL OCCUPATIONAL PROGRAM
```

## STUDENT ASSIGNMENT 6: WordPerfect Commands

**Instructions:**   The illustration below is the beginning of a document. After typing it, the user realized that the heading should have been underlined. Explain in detail how this existing text can be underlined without deleting the text.

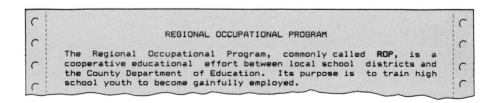

```
                  REGIONAL OCCUPATIONAL PROGRAM

    The Regional Occupational Program, commonly called ROP, is a
    cooperative educational  effort between local school  districts and
    the County Department  of Education.  Its purpose is  to train high
    school youth to become gainfully employed.
```

## STUDENT ASSIGNMENT 7: WordPerfect Commands

**Instructions:** The text in sample A below is typed incorrectly because the margins after each letter should be indented temporarily. The text in sample B is typed correctly. Identify the one function key that made the difference in appearance, and describe in detail where that key should have been used.

```
a.   Copy the program into any machine readable or printed form
for backup or modification purposes in support of your use of the
program on a single machine.  Certain programs from PerSoft Inc.,
however, may contain mechanisms to limit or inhibit copying.
These programs are marked "copy protected."

b.   Modify or merge the program into another PerSoft Inc.
program for use on the single machine.  Any portion of the
program merged into another program will continue to be subject
to the terms and conditions of this License.
```

**Sample A**

```
a.   Copy the program into any machine readable or printed form
     for backup or modification purposes in support of your use
     of the program on a single machine.  Certain programs from
     PerSoft Inc., however, may contain mechanisms to limit or
     inhibit copying.  These programs are marked "copy
     protected."

b.   Modify or merge the program into another PerSoft Inc.
     program for use on the single machine.  Any portion of the
     program merged into another program will continue to be
     subject to the terms and conditions of this License.
```

**Sample B**

## STUDENT ASSIGNMENT 8: WordPerfect Commands

**Instructions:** The text in sample A below is typed normally. The text in the first paragraph of sample B is indented five spaces from both the left and right margins. The text in the second paragraph of sample B is indented ten spaces from both the left and right margins. Describe in detail the keystrokes that were used to make the margins in both the first and second paragraphs of sample B.

```
Copy the program into any machine readable or printed form for
backup or modification purposes in support of your use of the
program on a single machine.  Certain programs from PerSoft Inc.,
however, may contain mechanisms to limit or inhibit copying.
These programs are marked "copy protected."

Modify or merge the program into another PerSoft Inc. program for
use on the single machine.  Any portion of the program merged
into another program will continue to be subject to the terms and
conditions of this License.
```

**Sample A**

> Copy the program into any machine readable or printed form for backup or modification purposes in support of your use of the program on a single machine. Certain programs from PerSoft Inc., however, may contain mechanisms to limit or inhibit copying. These programs are marked "copy protected."
>
> Modify or merge the program into another PerSoft Inc. program for use on the single machine. Any portion of the program merged into another program will continue to be subject to the terms and conditions of this License.

**Sample B**

# STUDENT ASSIGNMENT 9: Creating a Document

**Instructions:**    Create the document below and save it under the name Regional. Then print the document.

### REGIONAL OCCUPATIONAL PROGRAM

The Regional Occupational Program, commonly called ROP, is a cooperative educational effort between local school districts and the County Department of Education. Its purpose is to train high school youth to become gainfully employed.

ROP has served and trained over 95,000 students in some 42 trades since 1988.

ROP plays an important role in the application of basic skills in the world of work, endeavoring to assist the unskilled and undertrained to become gainfully employed. ROP works in cooperation with 1,054 local businesses in the community to provide students on-the-job training. About 500 members of business and industry are involved in an advisory committee role to assure meaningful job skill training, a verified labor market demand, and a high potential for student placement in every course offered through ROP.

Important features of the Regional Occupational Program are:

1.  Students from many schools meet at a centralized classroom. The teacher has a credential in the field being taught plus at least 5 years of directly related work experience.

2.  Students are assigned to business training sites to receive realistic on-the-job skill development. An individualized training plan is developed for each student at each job training site.

3.  Periodically students return to the classroom for additional training and to review progress from an employment point of view.

Courses are offered for three semesters during the year. Enrollment time varies depending on the course topic or trade area. Some programs permit entry on any day, others at the start of each semester.

## STUDENT ASSIGNMENT 10: Correcting a Document

**Instructions:** The document that you created in Student Assignment 9 needs to be changed to look like the document below. Make the following corrections:

1. The characters ROP should appear in boldface type.
2. The heading should be underlined.
3. Add paragraph 4 after paragraph 3 as follows:

   4. There is no tuition charge for any ROP class.

4. Save the new document under the name Regional.2, then print the document.

<u>REGIONAL OCCUPATIONAL PROGRAM</u>

The Regional Occupational Program, commonly called **ROP**, is a cooperative educational effort between local school districts and the County Department of Education. Its purpose is to train high school youth to become gainfully employed.

**ROP** has served and trained over 95,000 students in some 42 trades since 1988.

**ROP** plays an important role in the application of basic skills in the world of work, endeavoring to assist the unskilled and undertrained to become gainfully employed. **ROP** works in cooperation with 1,054 local businesses in the community to provide students on-the-job training. About 500 members of business and industry are involved in an advisory committee role to assure meaningful job skill training, a verified labor market demand, and a high potential for student placement in every course offered through **ROP**.

Important features of the Regional Occupational Program are:

    1.    Students from many schools meet at a centralized classroom. The teacher has a credential in the field being taught plus at least 5 years of directly related work experience.

    2.    Students are assigned to business training sites to receive realistic on-the-job skill development. An individualized training plan is developed for each student at each job training site.

    3.    Periodically students return to the classroom for additional training and to review progress from an employment point of view.

    4.    There is no tuition charge for any **ROP** class.

Courses are offered for three semesters during the year. Enrollment time varies depending on the course topic or trade area. Some programs permit entry on any day, others at the start of each semester.

# PROJECT 4

## Modifying a WordPerfect Document

### Objectives

You will have mastered the material in this project when you can:

- Retrieve a document
- Format a document
- Adjust left and right margins and top and bottom margins
- Justify and unjustify text
- Center text on a page
- Set tabs

## RETRIEVING A DOCUMENT

*I*n many word processing applications, a document must be modified after it has been created. In this project you will make some changes to the memo you created in Project 2. The old memo (Figure 4-1a) contains instructions for corrections to be made. The corrected memo is shown in Figure 4-1b. As you learned in the previous projects, first load WordPerfect into the computer.

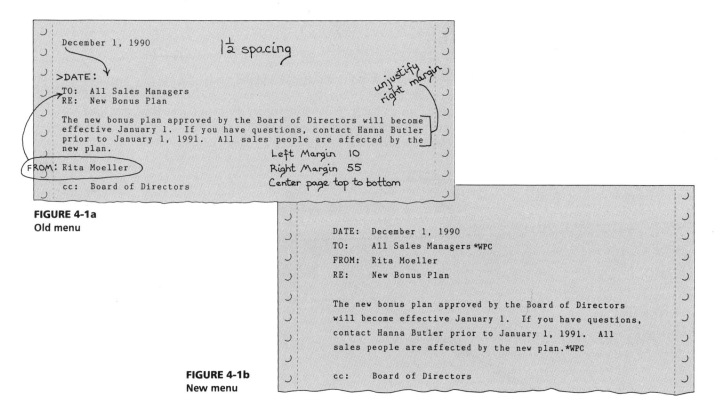

**FIGURE 4-1a**
Old menu

**FIGURE 4-1b**
New menu

In Project 2 you created a document, named it Memo, and saved it. Now you'll retrieve that document and modify it. Look at the template next to the F10 key. The word Retrieve is in green. Press Shift-F10 (step 1 of Figure 4-2). The message "Document to be Retrieved:" appears. Type the name memo, then press Enter ↵ (step 2 of Figure 4-2). The light on drive B goes on, and the memo is retrieved from memory and displayed on the screen.

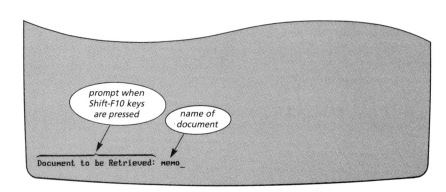

**FIGURE 4-2**

Step 1: Retrieve a document      Step 2: Specify name of document to be retrieved

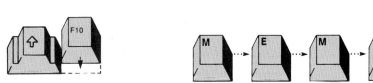

## INSERTING CHANGES INTO TEXT

In a memo's heading, the word DATE: is typed in front of the actual date and the name of the person sending the memo is placed at the top of the document after FROM:. Thus, the first task to modify the old memo is to add the word DATE: in front of the date. With the cursor on line 1, position 10, under the D in December, press the Caps Lock key and type the word DATE:. The date is pushed to the right and the word DATE is inserted (Figure 4-3). With the cursor still under the D in December, press the Tab key. The cursor moves to position 20 (step 1 of Figure 4-4).

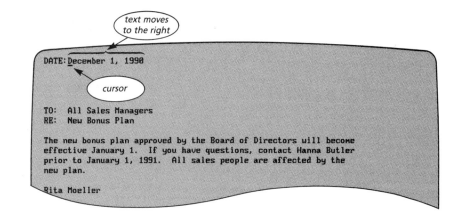

**FIGURE 4-3**

Now, remove the hard returns between the date and the line: TO: All Sales Managers. Press the Down Arrow ↓ to move the cursor to line 2, position 10, then press the Del key four times until the cursor is under the T in TO: on line 2, position 10 (step 2 of Figure 4-4). Press the Down Arrow ↓ to move the cursor under the R in RE: on line 3, position 10, then press Return ↵. You see a blank line inserted, as shown in Figure 4-5. Press the Up Arrow ↑ key to put the cursor on position 10 of line 3, the blank line. With Caps Lock still on, type the word FROM:. To turn off capitalizations, press the Caps Lock key.

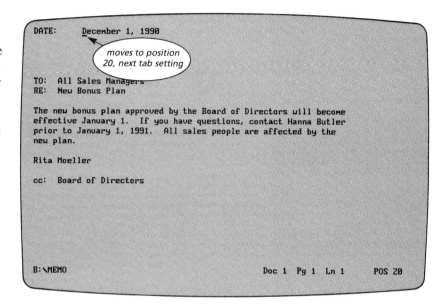

**FIGURE 4-4**

**Step 1: Move cursor to the first tab setting**

**Step 2: Delete 4 lines**

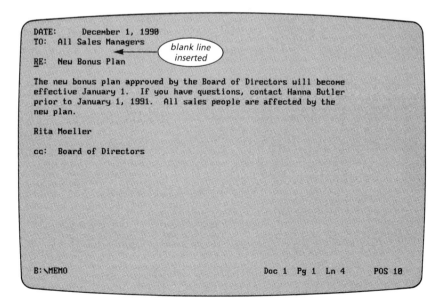

**FIGURE 4-5**

Press the Tab key and type the name Rita Moeller (Figure 4-6). Notice that although you pressed the Tab key only once after each heading, the tabbed lines begin at different positions. Later in this project we will change the tab settings so that they line up.

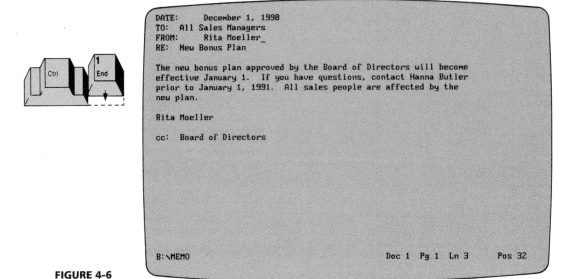

```
DATE:     December 1, 1990
TO:   All Sales Managers
FROM:     Rita Moeller_
RE:   New Bonus Plan

The new bonus plan approved by the Board of Directors will become
effective January 1.  If you have questions, contact Hanna Butler
prior to January 1, 1991.  All sales people are affected by the
new plan.

Rita Moeller

cc:  Board of Directors




B:\MEMO                                    Doc 1  Pg 1  Ln 3      Pos 32
```

**FIGURE 4-6**

It is now necessary to remove the name that was typed at the bottom of the memo. Move the cursor to line 11, position 10. Press Ctl-End (Figure 4-6). The line is deleted. Press the Del key two times. You see the last line of typing move up to line 11.

# DEFAULT SETTINGS

*T*he appearance of the documents in Projects 1 and 2 is governed by a number of default settings established by WordPerfect. In other words, if you do not change or add codes, your document will print with the parameters that have been set. You can, however, change the format of a document either before or after typing it.

# LEFT AND RIGHT MARGINS

*A* normal page of typing paper is 8 1/2" wide by 11" long. The WordPerfect default settings have the length of a line of type almost 6 1/2 inches wide, leaving approximately a 1-inch margin on both the left and right. The length of a line in characters can be easily figured.

Traditionally, typewriters used **pica** or **elite** type. Pica type fits 10 characters into 1 inch of space on a line, and elite type fits 12 characters into that same space. Therefore pica is the larger type and elite is the smaller. Some typewriters can type very small, placing 15 characters within 1 inch of space. When you use a word processor, some of the terminology is different. If you have used different type elements, you may have used the term "typing ball." The term used in word processing is **type font**. Instead of pica or elite, the term used is **10 pitch** (10 characters per inch) or **12 pitch** (12 characters per inch) (Figure 4-7). You could also use a *15 pitch font*. WordPerfect's default is a *10 pitch font*.

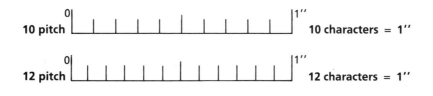

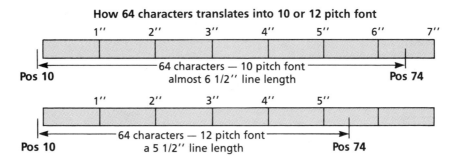

**FIGURE 4-7**

It is important to know which font you are using, because the margin is not set by inches but by characters. The margins default at position 10 on the left and position 74 on the right. If you subtract 10 from 74 you know WordPerfect's default uses 64 characters per line. With 64 characters per line and a default of a 10 pitch font, you can figure that each line of type will be almost 6 1/2 inches long (divide 64 by 10). If you were to leave the margins as they are and change the pitch to a 12 pitch font, divide 12 into 64 and you can see that the length of the line would be about 5 1/2 inches (Figure 4-7).

# TOP AND BOTTOM MARGINS

*F*igure 4-8 shows that a normal piece of paper is 11 inches long. Normal typewriting spacing allows for 6 lines per inch, making 66 lines from the top edge to the bottom edge of the paper. WordPerfect allows for 6 lines or a 1-inch top margin, and 6 lines or a 1-inch bottom margin. If you subtract the 6 lines on top and the 6 lines on the bottom (12 lines) from the total of 66, you know that there are 54 lines available for text. If you double space your typing, you will have 27 lines of type and 27 blank lines.

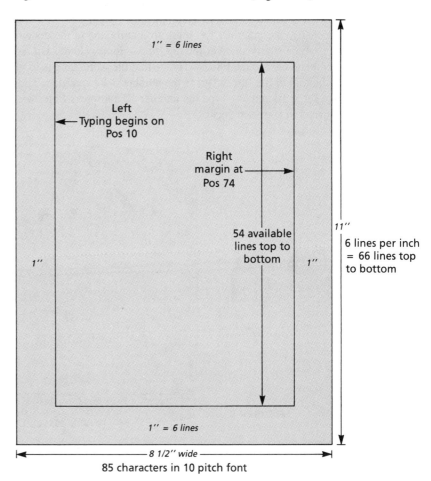

**FIGURE 4-8**
**WordPerfect Default**
**Margins**

# FORMATTING

 ll the default settings we have discussed—pitch, font, lines per inch, line spacing, margin settings, tab settings, or anything that has to do with how the typing will appear on paper—are aspects of **formatting**. Any default setting can be changed by inserting a code, which will be embedded into the particular document on which you are working. You will learn many of the formatting functions in this project. To become familiar with the codes you will refer to the reveal codes screen many times. If you make an error in formatting, refer to the codes and analyze them to decide how they have affected the look of your document.

All the format settings are on the Format key, which is F8, either Ctrl-F8, Alt-F8, or Shift-F8. Next we will change default settings.

# LINE FORMATTING

*T*o change anything having to do with the length of the line, the line spacing, or the tab settings on the line, we must use the **Line Format** key.

## Changing Margin Settings

Look at the memo to be corrected in Figure 4-1a. Notice that the margins are to be changed to 10 on the left and 55 on the right. With 45 characters per line and the default of the 10 pitch font, you can tell that you are going to have a 4 1/2" line.

If you want to change the margins, you must do it at the top of the document, because a code takes effect starting from where it is inserted. To be sure you are at the top, press Home, Home, Up Arrow.

Look at the template next to the F8 key. Notice that the word Line is in green. Press Shift-F8. The menu shown in Figure 4-9 appears at the bottom of the screen. Press the number 3 for margins. The screen changes to the one in Figure 4-10. The default margins are set at 10 and 74. Type the number 10 and press Enter ↵, then type the number 55 and press Enter ↵ again. You are returned to your document.

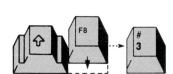

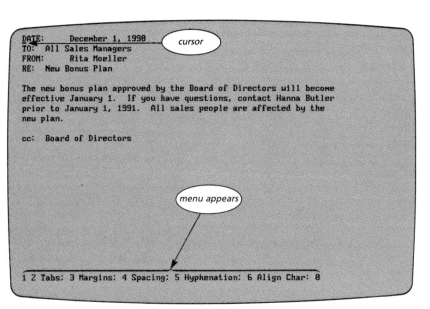

**FIGURE 4-9**

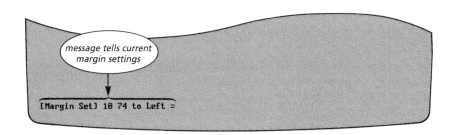

message tells current
margin settings

[Margin Set] 10 74 to Left =

**FIGURE 4-10**

To see that a code for the new margin setting has been embedded into the document, look at the codes using Alt-F3 (Figure 4-11). Notice that the cursor is to the right of the code. Press the Left Arrow ← one time. Notice that an entire code is enclosed within brackets [ ] and that you cannot move the cursor inside the brackets. Also notice, on the bar that separates the two screens, that the right bracket has moved to show the new margin setting. Move the Left Arrow ← and Right Arrow → back and forth and notice how the right bracket moves. When you read a novel, you read from left to right, one line after another. You only understand what you have already read, not what might be coming. It is the same with how the codes work in WordPerfect. Think of the cursor reading left to right, line after line. When the cursor is to the left of the code, it follows the default setting of 10 and 74. When you move the cursor to the right of the code, the cursor in a sense "reads" or "interprets" that code, and the bracket on the bar moves according to what is read.

This code controls the margin until it is replaced by a different code. To see this, press Home, Home, Up Arrow to move the cursor to the top of the document. Press the spacebar to exit the reveal codes. You have decided that a 4 1/2-inch line is too short; you wish to change it to 5 1/2-inches. Because there are 10 characters per inch, you need to have 55 characters on the line. Press Shift-F8. Press the number 3 for margins. Type the number 10 and press Enter ←. Type the number 65 and press Enter ←.

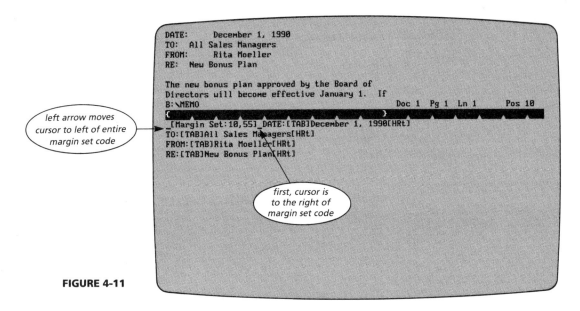

left arrow moves
cursor to left of entire
margin set code

first, cursor is
to the right of
margin set code

**FIGURE 4-11**

As you look at the screen you cannot see any changes to the length of the line. In Project 2 you learned that most problems with WordPerfect can be solved by analyzing the codes. Press Alt-F3. As you see in Figure 4-12 you have two margin setting codes, with the cursor between them. The first code is the new margin setting of 10,65. That code is in effect until it is overridden by a new code. As you see, it is immediately overridden by the old code of 10,55. Therefore, the typing will follow the command of the 10,55 code instead of the 10,65 code. Because you wish to delete the 10,55 code, you wish to delete going *forward*. Press the Delete key once. Be careful when you delete the code. Your tendency may be to press the Delete key many times. But because the margin setting is within brackets, it is only necessary to press the Delete key one time. Then press the spacebar to exit the reveal codes. Figure 4-13 shows how the new margin setting affects the typing.

To emphasize one more time the importance of where you insert a code, move the cursor down to line 8, position 10, under the c in contact. Press Shift-F8. Press the number 3 for margins. Type the number 10 and press Enter ↵. Type the number 30 and press Enter ↵ again. You see now that the code at the top of the memo remains in effect until it is overridden by a new code. Because the new code was inserted later in the document, the new code overrides the old code and will affect typing from where it is inserted *downward*. To view the new code, press Alt-F3 (Figure 4-14). You see the new code on the screen. The cursor is to the right of the code. Press the Backspace key *only one time* to delete the 10,30 code allowing the 10,65 code to take effect again.

After completing this exercise you can understand how important it is to have the cursor in the proper position before you invoke a code. You cannot be at the end of a document, then decide that you want to change the margins of the entire document, without pressing Home, Home, Up Arrow to place the code at the beginning of the document.

Press the spacebar to exit the reveal codes. Press Home, Home, Up Arrow to go to the top of the document.

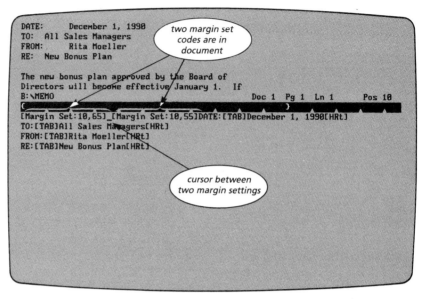

**FIGURE 4-12**

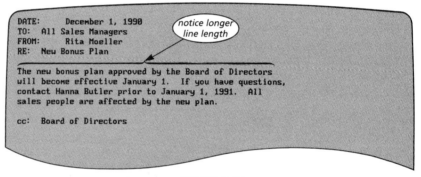

**FIGURE 4-13**

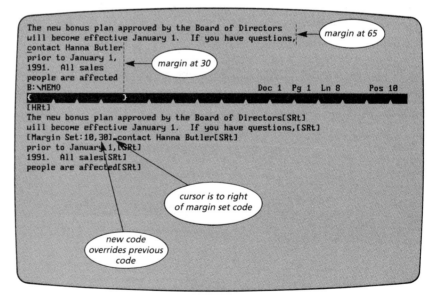

**FIGURE 4-14**

## Changing Tab Settings

So that the first four lines will line up at the tab, you need to add a tab setting at position 17 and delete the tab setting at position 15. Press Shift-F8. Either number 1 or number 2 will choose tabs. Press number 1. Figure 4-15 shows the tab settings on the lower portion of the screen. Type the number 17 and press Enter ↵ (step 1 of Figure 4-16). Notice that there is an L on position 17. To delete the tab setting on position 15, press the Left Arrow two times ← ← to move the cursor under the L on position 15. Press the Delete key one time (step 2 of Figure 4-16). The message on the screen instructs you to press Exit when done. This is how you exit the tab setting screen properly. If you press the Cancel key, you will exit but the changes will not be made. Therefore, press F7 to exit (step 3 of Figure 4-16). Now notice how the tabs have lined up properly, as in Figure 4-17 on the following page.

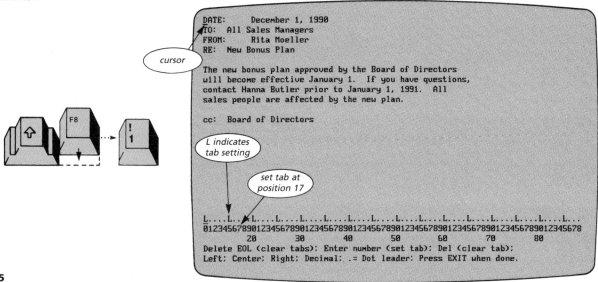

**FIGURE 4-15**

Step 1: Set tab at 17          Step 2: Delete tab at 15                    Step 3: Save tab changes and exit

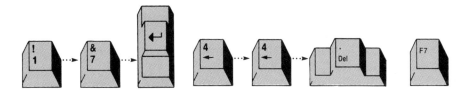

**FIGURE 4-16**

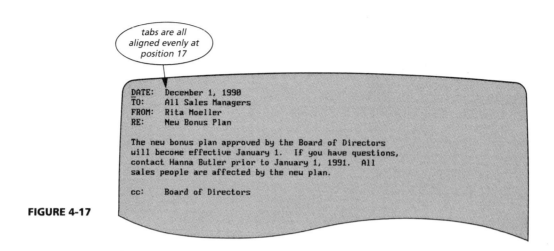

FIGURE 4-17

To view the embedded codes, press Alt-F3 (Figure 4-18). All the tab settings that were present when you inserted the one at position 17 are listed. Remember that codes are within brackets [ ]. Therefore, this is only *one* code. If you were to press the Left Arrow ←, then the Right Arrow → back and forth, you would notice that the cursor cannot move inside the brackets. To exit the reveal codes press the spacebar.

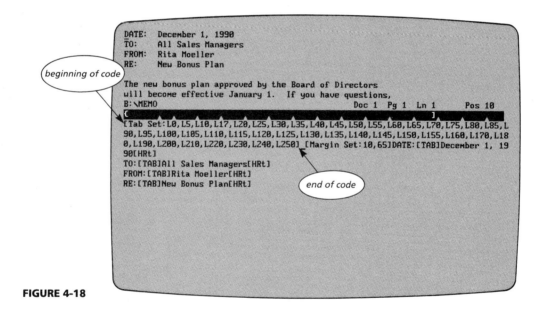

FIGURE 4-18

## Changing the Line Spacing

The next change to make in the memo is to change the line spacing from single space to 1 1/2 spacing. To change the line spacing, you must call up the line format menu. Press Shift-F8 (step 1 of Figure 4-19). At the Line Format menu, press the number 4 (step 2 of Figure 4-19). The prompt on the screen will be "[Spacing Set] 1". Type the number 1.5 and press Enter ← (Figure 4-20). To view the code that was inserted, press Alt-F3 (Figure 4-21).

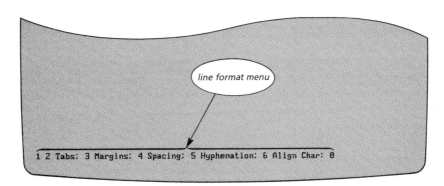

1 2 Tabs; 3 Margins; 4 Spacing; 5 Hyphenation; 6 Align Char: 0

Step 1: View Line Format menu          Step 2: View how spacing is set

**FIGURE 4-19**
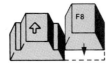

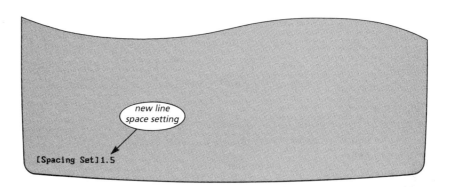

[Spacing Set]1.5

**FIGURE 4-20**

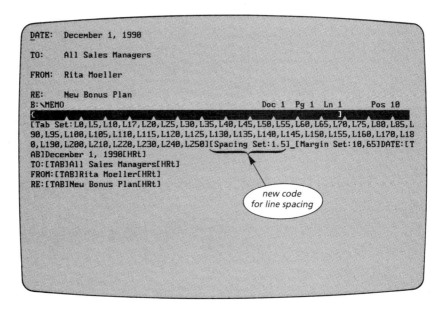

**FIGURE 4-21**

If you ever want to change back to single spacing, you can simply delete the code. WordPerfect would then return to the default, which is single spacing. If you wish to change to double spacing, you must be sure that the cursor *follows* any code you wish to override.

To exit the reveal codes, press the spacebar. The lines on the screen will appear to be double spaced. That is because the screen cannot show 1 1/2 spacing. However, the printer will read the code and print in 1 1/2 spacing. Watching the status line, press the Down Arrow ↓. Figure 4-22 shows how the code is interpreted: the next line is line 2.5. Continue pressing the Down Arrow ↓ and notice that the spacing is indeed 1 1/2 spacing. Press Home, Home, Up Arrow to move the cursor to the top of the document.

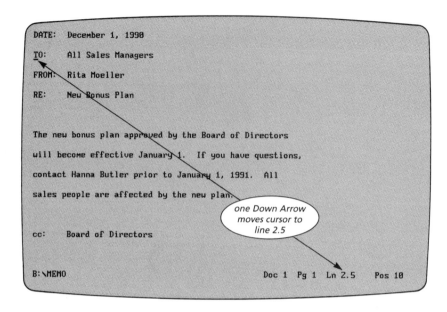

**FIGURE 4-22**

## PREVIEWING

You can **preview** your text exactly as it will be printed. Press Shift-F7 to reveal the Print menu, then press the number 6 for preview and press the number 1 to view the document (step 1 of Figure 4-23). As WordPerfect formats the document for previewing, the message "please wait" appears. Figure 4-23 shows the preview screen identified as Document 3 and shows the word "PREVIEW" in the lower left corner of the screen. This screen shows you exactly how your document will be printed. Notice the 1-inch heading at the top margin. The text has a justified right margin. The screen also shows where the *WPC markings will be printed. To exit the preview screen, press the F7 (Exit) key (step 2 of Figure 4-23).

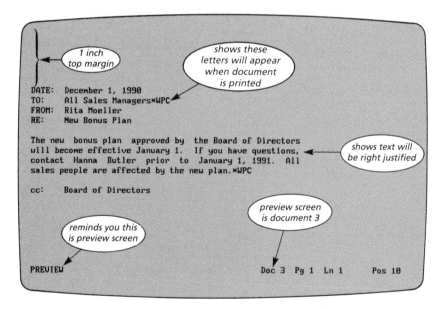

Step 1: Preview the document            Step 2: Exit the preview screen

**FIGURE 4-23**

# PRINT FORMATTING

## Right Justified Text

*T*urning the justification on and off is part of the print formatting process for a document. Look at the template next to the F8 key. You see the words Print Format in red. Press Ctl-F8 (step 1 of Figure 4-24) to view how the document is formatted. Notice that the justification is turned on. Press the number 3 and notice that the justification is now turned off (step 2 of Figure 4-24). Press Enter to exit the print format screen (step 3 of Figure 4-24). To view the code that was inserted, press Alt-F3. Figure 4-25 shows the embedded code that turned the justification off. To exit the reveal codes, press the spacebar.

**FIGURE 4-24**

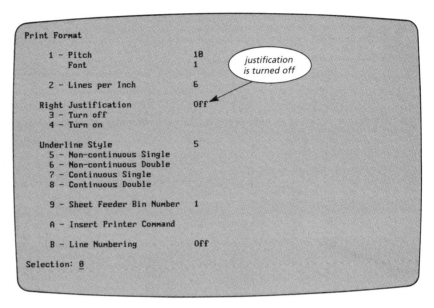

Step 1: View the print format screen

Step 2: Turn off right justification

Step 3: Exit the print format screen

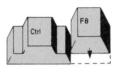

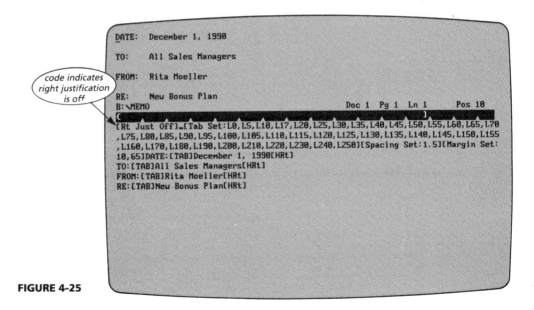

**FIGURE 4-25**

# PAGE FORMATTING

## Centering Page Top to Bottom

**B**ecause your memo is short, when it is printed it will only cover the top portion of the page as shown in Figure 4-1a. To print your document in the center of the paper, as shown in Figure 4-1b, with even margins on the top and the bottom of the page, you must choose the **Center Page Top to Bottom** option from the page format screen.

Press Alt-F8 (step 1 of Figure 4-26). Figure 4-26 shows the page format screen. Press the number 3 and then Enter ↵ to return to your document (steps 2 and 3 of Figure 4-26). To view the inserted code, press Alt-F3. Figure 4-27 shows the code that will tell the printer to center the page, giving it even top and bottom margins. To exit the reveal codes, press the spacebar.

Your document has all the desired changes, as shown in Figure 4-1a. Now you must save the document in its new form, then print the memo on paper.

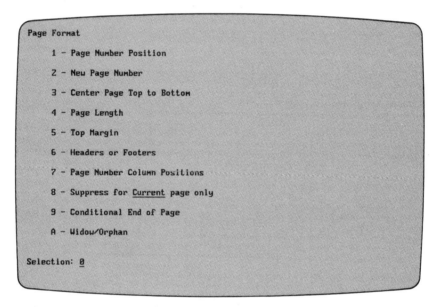

```
Page Format

    1 - Page Number Position

    2 - New Page Number

    3 - Center Page Top to Bottom

    4 - Page Length

    5 - Top Margin

    6 - Headers or Footers

    7 - Page Number Column Positions

    8 - Suppress for Current page only

    9 - Conditional End of Page

    A - Widow/Orphan


Selection: 0
```

**FIGURE 4-26**

**Step 1: View Page Format menu**      **Step 2: Select the Center Page Top to Bottom option**

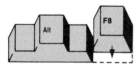      

**Step 3: Return to the document**

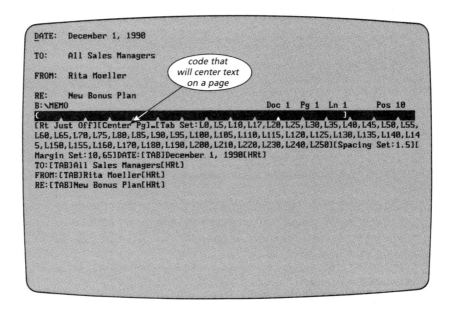

**FIGURE 4-27**

## SAVING, REPLACING, AND PRINTING THE DOCUMENT

hen you finished typing this document in Project 2, you saved the document to your disk. Since that time, you have made several changes to the document on your screen. However, those changes have not been saved to the disk. As you learned in Project 3, it is necessary to save these changes to the disk, replacing the old text with the new text. Keep in mind that you are not just adding but also replacing text. Save and replace your document now as you did in Project 3 (F10, Enter, Y).

The document is now ready to be printed. Be sure that your printer has paper inserted and that the printer is turned on and ready to print. As you have done in previous projects, print the full text of this document. The printed document generated should look like Figure 4-1b.

## OTHER PRINT FORMAT FEATURES

ow that the document has been changed, saved, and printed, we can learn some other print format features. Let's return to the print format screen by pressing Ctrl-F8 (Figure 4-24).

## Pitch

If you wish to change the pitch from 10 to 12 or 15 (Figure 4-28), or the font number, you would press the number 1, then type the preferred pitch followed by the Enter key. Then you'd type the preferred font number followed by the Enter key.

```
This is  a 10 pitch font defined as font #1.  The margins are set
at 10 on the left and 74 on  the right.   There  are 6  lines per
inch.

This is  a 12 pitch font defined as font #1.  The margins are set
at 10 on the left and 74 on  the right.   There  are 6  lines per
inch.

This is  a 15 pitch font defined as font #1.  The margins are set
at 10 on the left and 74 on the right.  Because  the letters are
small, the  computer has  been programmed at 8 lines per inch, so
that there is not too much white space between the lines.
```

**FIGURE 4-28**

## Lines per Inch

If you were using a 15 pitch font where the type is very small, you may wish to have more lines per inch than the default of 6. In the print format screen, you would press number 2, then type the number 8 for 8 lines per inch. WordPerfect will not accept spacing other than 6 or 8, so if you were to type something else, the cursor would not move and when you press Enter, 6 will be inserted automatically.

## Underline Style

If you have some underlined text, you may wish to change the underline style, such as to a double continuous line. On the print format screen, select the desired number, such as number 8 for a continuous double line. Figure 4-29 shows examples of the underline styles available.

```
Non-continuous               Single underlining

Non-continuous               Double underlining

Continuous                   Single underlining

Continuous                   Double underlining
```

**FIGURE 4-29**

# ADVANCED TAB SETTINGS

*H*ere we will learn some of the more advanced tab setting features. You do not want to confuse this lesson with the memo on your screen. WordPerfect has the ability to have two documents in memory and to let you switch quickly back and forth between the two documents. As we learned in Project 1, we can switch to Document 2, while keeping Document 1 as it is. Refer to the template next to the F3 key. You'll see that Shift-F3 will shift documents. Press Shift-F3. Your typing disappears, and you have a blank screen. Notice that the status line indicates document 2. This is a new blank screen; anything you do in this screen will be totally separate from document 1. For practice, press Shift-F3 and notice that you are back in document 1. Press Shift-F3 again and you are in document 2.

Remember that tabs are set by pressing Shift-F8. Press Shift-F8 and then the number 1 for tabs (Figure 4-30). Remember that tab settings are indicated by the letter L.

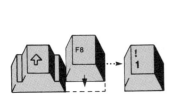
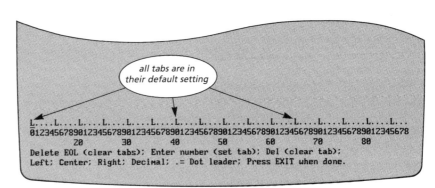

**FIGURE 4-30**

First we need to clear all tab settings. Press Home, Home, Left Arrow to move the cursor to position 0. As the bottom of the screen indicates, "Delete EOL" (Delete End of Line) will clear all tabs. Press Ctrl-End and all tab settings will clear (Figure 4-31).

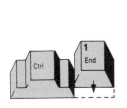
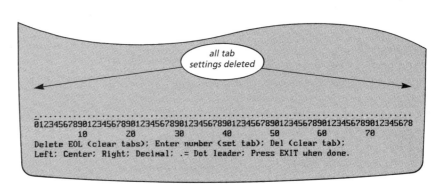

**FIGURE 4-31**

First, let's set the desired tab settings; then their functions will be explained. Type the number 15 and press Enter ↵. You see an L above position 15. Type the number 30 and press Enter ↵. You see an L above position 30. Press the letter c and notice how the L changes to a capital C. Type the number 48 and press Enter ↵. Press the letter r and notice how the L changes to a capital R. Type the number 60 and press Enter ↵. Press the letter d and notice once more how the L changes to a capital D. The screen should now look like the Figure 4-32.

When you set each tab, the default of L appeared first at each setting. Imagine that the tab settings are like anchors. Wherever there is an L, the typing anchors to the *left* and the typing flows to the *right*. When you changed the L at position 30 to C, you were instructing WordPerfect to anchor in the *center*, so the typing will be centered over the tab setting as it does when you use the center function. When you changed the L at position 48 to R, you were instructing WordPerfect to anchor at the right, so the typing flows to the left as it does when you use the flush right function. When you changed the L at position 60 to D, you were instructing WordPerfect to anchor at a decimal point (a period). Figure 4-33 illustrates how each tab setting will be anchored and where the type will flow from the specific tab setting.

To exit from the tab setting screen, press F7. You are returned to the blank screen of document 2. To view the inserted codes, press Alt-F3. Figure 4-34 shows that each tab setting is identified with the proper letter. To exit the codes press the spacebar.

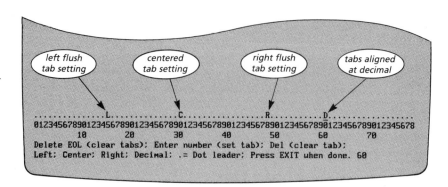

**FIGURE 4-32**

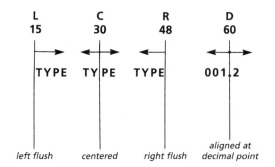

**FIGURE 4-33**

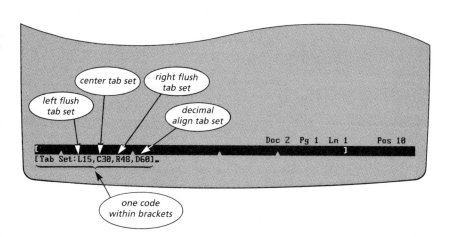

**FIGURE 4-34**

To use each tab setting, first press the Tab key. The cursor stops at the first tab setting, which is 15. The type will flow to the right of the tab setting. Type the two words Now is, and press the Tab key again. The cursor moves to position 30, the next tab setting. This is where the C for center was placed. Type the word Heading. As you do, try to watch the screen and notice how the word centers over position 30. Press the Tab key again and the cursor moves to position 48, the next tab setting. This is where an R was placed for right justified. Type the amount $1,000.00 and as you do notice how the typing anchors at the tab setting and flows to the left of the tab, making the number flush right. For the last setting, press the Tab key, moving the cursor to position 60 where the D was placed, for aligning at the decimal point. In the lower left corner of the screen you see the message "Align Char = ." As you type now, try to watch the screen so you can see how the type anchors at the decimal point and the last two zeros are placed to the right of the decimal. Type the amount $2,000.00. The screen should look like Figure 4-35.

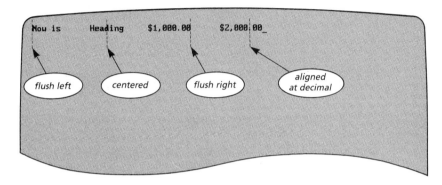

**FIGURE 4-35**

Press the hard return ↵ so you can use each tab setting one more time. The cursor should be on line 2, position 10. Press the Tab key and type these two words: the time. As you do so watch the typing anchor at the left. Press the Tab key again and type the word Head, and the typing centers at the tab setting. Press the Tab key again and type the number 60.00, and notice how the typing anchors at the right. Press the Tab key one more time. Type the number 120.34 and the typing will anchor at the decimal point, putting the 34 to the right of the decimal. Press the hard return two times ↵ ↵, placing the cursor on line 4, position 10.

There is one more tab setting that is also very useful. To use it we must change the present tab settings. As before, press Shift-F8 and the number 1 for tabs. To delete the present settings press Ctrl-End. Type the number 74 and press Enter. An L is placed above position 74. Press the letter r, changing the L to an R. Now type . (a period) and notice how the R is shown in reverse video (Figure 4-36). You know that the R setting will anchor at the right and the text will flow to the left, as in flush

right. By placing the decimal over the R, you are indicating that you want *leader dots* to be inserted automatically from where the cursor is to the tab setting. While you are only placing a period over the R in this particular exercise, you can also place a period over the L (left flush) or D (decimal align) settings. You cannot place a period over the C (center) tab setting.

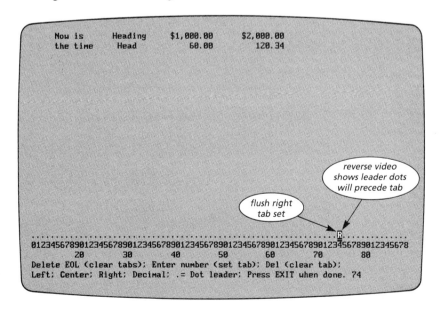

**FIGURE 4-36**

To exit from the tab setting screen, press F7 and you are returned to your document. To demonstrate how this tab setting works, we will type this as if it were part of a program you may be typing. With the cursor on line 4, position 10, type the words Piano Prelude, then press the Tab key. The cursor moves to position 74, which is the tab setting, and as it does, leader dots are inserted from the end of your typing to the tab setting. Now type the name Francis Holt and notice how the type moves to the left of the tab. As it does, it eliminates leader dots where the name is typed (Figure 4-37).

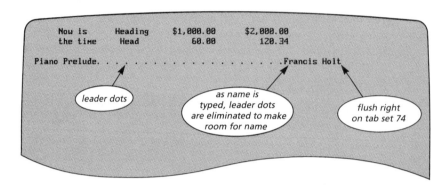

**FIGURE 4-37**

Leader dots can be used as above in programs, or, for example, in a table of contents. The dots lead the reader's eye to the right to follow the line of typing.

Save this document under the name Tabs. Press F10, type Tabs, then press Enter.

# EXITING PROJECT 4

Y ou may remember that document 1 still remains in memory. You will not be able to exit WordPerfect without seeing a reminder that another document remains in memory. Press F7. Press N to the prompt "Save document?". The next prompt is "Exit Doc 2? (Y/N) N." It indicates that MEMO is still in memory in document 1. Type the letter Y to exit document 2 and return to document 1. If you had typed the letter N for no, you would have remained in document 2 and received a blank screen. Then you would have had to use the Shift-F3 function to return to document 1.

Because document 1 has already been saved, it is not necessary to save it again before you exit WordPerfect. Exit Word-Perfect as you have in previous projects (F7, N, Y).

# PROJECT SUMMARY

I n Project 4 you retrieved an existing document and made changes to it. You learned how to change the default margin settings, tab settings, and line spacing, how to justify text, and how to center a short document on the page. You learned about the print format functions of pitch, lines per inch, and underline style. Finally, you practiced advanced tab setting functions and moving back and forth between two documents in memory.

The following is a list of the keystroke sequence we used in Project 4:

## SUMMARY OF KEYSTROKES—Project 4

| STEPS | KEY(S) PRESSED | STEPS | KEY(S) PRESSED | STEPS | KEY(S) PRESSED |
|---|---|---|---|---|---|
| 1 | Shift-F10 | 45 | 30 | 90 | ↵ |
| 2 | memo | 46 | ↵ | 91 | d |
| 3 | ↵ | 47 | Alt-F3 | 92 | F7 |
| 4 | Caps Lock | 48 | Backspace | 93 | TAB |
| 5 | DATE: | 49 | Space | 94 | Now is |
| 6 | TAB | 50 | Home Home ↑ | 95 | TAB |
| 7 | ↓ | 51 | Shift-F8 | 96 | Heading |
| 8 | Del | 52 | 1 | 97 | TAB |
| 9 | Del | 53 | 17 | 98 | $1,000.00 |
| 10 | Del | 54 | ↵ | 99 | TAB |
| 11 | Del | 55 | ← | 100 | $2,000.00 |
| 12 | ↓ | 56 | ← | 101 | ↵ |
| 13 | ↵ | 57 | Del | 102 | TAB |
| 14 | ↑ | 58 | F7 | 103 | the time |
| 15 | FROM: | 59 | Shift-F8 | 104 | TAB |
| 16 | Caps Lock | 60 | 4 | 105 | Head |
| 17 | TAB | 61 | 1.5 | 106 | TAB |
| 18 | Rita Moeller | 62 | ↵ | 107 | 60.00 |
| 19 | [move cursor to line 11, position 10, under R in Rita] | 63 | Home Home ↑ | 108 | TAB |
| | | 64 | Ctrl-F8 | 109 | 120.34 |
| 20 | Ctrl-End | 65 | 3 | 110 | ↵ |
| 21 | Del | 66 | ↵ | 111 | ↵ |
| 22 | Del | 67 | Alt-F8 | 112 | Shift-F8 |
| 23 | Home Home ↑ | 68 | 3 | 113 | 1 |
| 24 | Shift-F8 | 69 | ↵ | 114 | Ctrl-End |
| 25 | 3 | 70 | F10 | 115 | 74 |
| 26 | 10 | 71 | ↵ | 116 | ↵ |
| 27 | ↵ | 72 | y | 117 | r |
| 28 | 55 | 73 | [be sure printer is on] | 118 | . |
| 29 | ↵ | 74 | Shift-F7 | 119 | F7 |
| 30 | Home Home ↑ | 75 | 1 | 120 | Piano Prelude |
| 31 | Shift-F8 | 76 | Shift-F3 | 121 | TAB |
| 32 | 3 | 77 | Shift-F8 | 122 | Francis Holt |
| 33 | 10 | 78 | 1 | 123 | F7 |
| 34 | ↵ | 79 | Home Home ← | 124 | y |
| 35 | 65 | 80 | Ctrl-End | 125 | tabs |
| 36 | ↵ | 81 | 15 | 126 | ↵ |
| 37 | Alt-F3 | 82 | ↵ | 127 | y |
| 38 | Del | 83 | 30 | 128 | F7 |
| 39 | Space | 84 | ↵ | 129 | n |
| 40 | [move cursor to line 8, position 10] | 85 | c | 130 | y |
| | | 86 | 48 | 131 | [if not at the DOS prompt, take WordPerfect disk out of drive A and insert DOS disk] |
| 41 | Shift-F8 | 87 | ↵ | | |
| 42 | 3 | 88 | r | | |
| 43 | 10 | 89 | 60 | 132 | [press any key] |
| 44 | ↵ | | | | |

The following list summarizes the material covered in Project 4:

1. The term **type font** refers to the typeface or print style of a document.
2. Traditionally, typewriters used the terms **pica** or **elite** to describe type size. Pica type fits 10 characters into 1 inch of space on a line; elite type fits 12 characters into 1 inch of space.

**Project Summary (continued)**

3. Instead of pica or elite, the terms used in word processing are **10 pitch font** and **12 pitch font**.
4. **Formatting** is the process of defining how a document will look when printed.
5. The **Line Format** key is used to define tab settings, margins, and line spacing.
6. The **preview** function allows the user to see how a document will look when it is printed.
7. The **Center Page Top to Bottom** option from the page format screen centers the print on a page evenly between the top and bottom of the page.

# STUDENT ASSIGNMENTS

## STUDENT ASSIGNMENT 1: True/False

**Instructions:**    Circle T if the statement is true and F if the statement is false.

T    F    1. On the template, the word Retrieve is in red, meaning the user presses Ctrl-F10 to retrieve a document.
T    F    2. WordPerfect default margin settings are at position 10 on the left and position 74 on the right.
T    F    3. A piece of paper that is 11" long has 60 typing lines from the top edge of the paper to the bottom edge.
T    F    4. To change any of the line format settings, press Shift-F8.
T    F    5. The default letter setting for tabs is the letter L.
T    F    6. When changing the line spacing to 1 1/2 spacing, press Shift-F8, then 4, then type 1.5 and press Enter.
T    F    7. To change the type to be unjustified on the right margin, press the number 3 on the page format screen.
T    F    8. When setting tab stops, if the user changes the L to R, the type will anchor at the right.
T    F    9. When setting tab stops, changing the L to D will cause leader dots to be typed on the screen.
T    F    10. When setting tab stops, changing the L to C will enable type to be centered over the tab stop.

## STUDENT ASSIGNMENT 2: Multiple Choice

**Instructions:**    Circle the correct response.

1. Circle all answers that refer to formatting functions.
    a. Shift-F8
    b. F6
    c. Alt-F8
    d. Ctrl-F8
2. It is possible to invoke leader dots when setting a tab stop by pressing which key?
    a. D for decimal
    b. L for leaders
    c. . (period)
    d. none of the above
3. To change the line spacing to double space, press the following keys:
    a. Alt-F8, 3, 2, Enter
    b. Ctrl-F8, 4, 2, Enter
    c. Shift-F8, 4, 2, Enter
    d. Shift-F8, 3, 2, Enter

4. To turn off right justification, press the following keys:
   a. Ctrl-F8, 3
   b. Alt-F8, 3
   c. Alt-F8, 4
   d. Ctrl-F8, 4
5. The code embedded into the document to signify that right justification has been turned off is:
   a. [Rt Just Off]
   b. [Right Just Off]
   c. [R Justification Off]
   d. [Rt Justification Off]
6. When the tab setting has been changed to one tab stop at position 30, the code embedded into the document shows the following:
   a. [Tab Set]
   b. [Tab Set: 30]
   c. [Tab Set: Pos 30]
   d. [Tab Set: L30]
7. If the user were to change the margins to 15 on the left and 75 on the right, the code embedded into the document would read:
   a. [Margin Set]
   b. [Margin Set: 15,75]
   c. [Margin Set: 15 left, 75 right]
   d. none of the above

## STUDENT ASSIGNMENT 3: Matching

**Instructions:**   Put the appropriate number next to the words in the second column.

1. Margin set                    _____   Shift-F8
2. Top margin line default       _____   Home, Home, Up arrow
3. Default tab set letter         _____   Shift-F8, 3
4. Justification off              _____   Shift-F8, 1 or 2
5. Line format                    _____   Alt-F8, 3
6. Print format                   _____   6 lines
7. Tab set                        _____   L
8. Top of document                _____   Ctrl-F8, 3
9. Line spacing                   _____   Ctrl-F8
10. Center page, top to bottom    _____   Shift-F8, 4

## STUDENT ASSIGNMENT 4: Understanding WordPerfect Commands

**Instructions:**   Next to each command, describe its effect.

| Command | Effect |
| --- | --- |
| Shift-F8, 1 | _____ |
| Shift-F8, 3 | _____ |
| Shift-F8, 4 | _____ |
| Ctrl-F8, 3 | _____ |
| Alt-F8, 3 | _____ |
| Shift-F7, 1 | _____ |

## STUDENT ASSIGNMENT 5: Identifying Default Settings

**Instructions:**   Describe what default means. Then identify the default settings for the following commands.

| Command | Default setting |
| --- | --- |
| Top margin | _____ |
| Bottom margin | _____ |
| Left margin | _____ |
| Right margin | _____ |
| Line spacing | _____ |
| Lines per inch | _____ |
| Pitch | _____ |
| Font | _____ |
| Right justification | _____ |
| Tab settings | _____ |
| Letter tab setting | _____ |
| Lines from top edge of paper to bottom edge | _____ |
| Number of single-spaced text lines | _____ |

## STUDENT ASSIGNMENT 6: Modifying a WordPerfect Document

**Instructions:**   The screen below illustrates a memo that was prepared using WordPerfect. The margins are to be changed to 15 on the left and 75 on the right. The letter is to be centered top to bottom, and the right justification is to be turned off. Explain in detail the steps necessary to perform those changes.

```
DATE:      December 15, 1990
TO:  All Sales Managers
FROM:     Rita Moeller
RE:  New Bonus Plan

The new  bonus plan will become effective January 1.  If you have
questions, contact Hanna Butler.  All  sales people  are affected
by the new plan.
```

## STUDENT ASSIGNMENT 7: Creating a WordPerfect Document

**Instructions:**   Perform the following tasks.

1. Load DOS into main memory.
2. Load WordPerfect into main memory by inserting the WordPerfect diskette into drive A, putting a data disk into drive B, typing b: and pressing Enter. At the B> prompt, type a:wp and press Enter.

Problem 1:
   1. Set the left margin to 12 and the right margin to 50.
   2. Turn the right justification off.
   3. Center the page top to bottom.
   4. Type the letter on the following page.

```
    March 15, 1990

    Ms. Roberta Weitzman
    President, SpaceTek Inc.
    44538 Scroll Avenue
    Monnett, NJ 08773

    Dear Ms. Weitzman:

    This letter confirms our purchase of
    thirteen DF-132 Modular Pin Brackets
    from your company, delivery by April 1.

    James R. McMillan, AirFrame Inc.
```

Problem 2:  Save the document, using the name Weitzman.
Problem 3:  Print the document.

## STUDENT ASSIGNMENT 8: Modifying a WordPerfect Document

**Instructions:**   Perform the following tasks.

1. Load DOS into main memory.
2. Load WordPerfect into main memory by inserting the WordPerfect diskette into drive A, putting a data disk into drive B, typing b: and pressing Enter. At the B> prompt, type a:wp and press Enter.

Problem 1:
   1. Retrieve the document named Weitzman, created in Student Assignment 7.
   2. Change the margins to 10 on the left and 60 on the right (Hint: Either delete the old margin codes or be sure the new margin code is to the right of the old one. The last code governs).
   3. The correct address is 44358 Scroll Street.
   4. Change the purchase to 35 Pin Brackets.
   5. Remove the words "from your company" on line 2 and end the sentence following the word "Brackets."
   6. Insert the words "We expect" in front of the word "delivery" on the second line.
   7. The last name of the sender of the letter is MacMillan, not McMillan.

Problem 2:  Save the document again, replacing the old version with the new version.
Problem 3:  Print the modified document. It should look like the letter below.

```
    March 15, 1990

    Ms. Roberta Weitzman
    President, SpaceTek Inc.
    44358 Scroll Street
    Monnett, NJ 08773

    Dear Ms. Weitzman:

    This letter confirms our purchase of 35 DF-132
    Modular Pin Brackets.  We expect delivery by April
    1.

    James R. MacMillan, AirFrame Inc.
```

## STUDENT ASSIGNMENT 9: Advanced Tab Settings

**Instructions:**  Perform the following tasks.

1. Load DOS into main memory.
2. Load WordPerfect into main memory by inserting the Word-Perfect diskette into drive A, putting a data disk into drive B, typing b: and pressing Enter. At the B> prompt, type a:wp and press Enter.

Problem 1:
  1.  Set margins to 15 on the left and 65 on the right.
  2.  Begin typing on line 7.
  3.  Center and capitalize heading, followed by three hard returns.
  4.  Change line spacing to 2 (double space).
  5.  Clear all tab settings. Place one tab stop at position 65. Change the L to R. Type a . (period) over the R. Exit out of tab setting.
  6.  Type remaining portion of program.

```
                    GRADUATION PROGRAM


      Opening Procession. . . . . . . .Graduating Class

      Flag Ceremony . . . . . . . . . . . . . . . . ROTC

      Greeting. . . . .Vice President of Student Affairs

      Special number. . . . . . . . . .String Quartet

      Remarks . . . . . . . . . . University President

      Song. . . . . . . . . . . . . A Cappella Choir

      Presentation of Diplomas. . . . . .College Deans

      School Song . . . . . . . . . .Graduating Class

                    Recessional


                      *****


          Refreshments served in the foyer


                      *****
```

Problem 2:  Save the document to disk as Program.
Problem 3:  Print the document.

## STUDENT ASSIGNMENT 10: Advanced Tab Settings

**Instructions:**  Perform the following tasks.

1. Load DOS into main memory.
2. Load WordPerfect into main memory by inserting the Word-Perfect diskette into drive A, putting a data disk into drive B, typing b: and pressing Enter. At the B> prompt, type a:wp and press Enter.

```
                        PRICE LIST
      Products      Wholesale Price      Retail Price
    Ladies Skirts        34.00              59.95
    Mens Shirts          13.50              26.95
   Childrens T-Shirts     5.95               9.95
    Hair clips             .25                .49
```

Problem 1:
  1.  Center and capitalize the heading, followed by three hard returns.
  2.  Enter the tab setting screen, clear all current tab stops.
  3.  Enter a C (Center) tab stop at positions 20, 42 and 62.
  4.  Type the first line of headings (Products, Wholesale Price, Retail Price).
  5.  After typing the column headings, press two Hard Returns. Enter the tab setting screen again and change the tab designations on positions 42 and 62 to a D.
  6.  Type the remainder of the price list.

Problem 2:  Save the document to disk, using the name Price.
Problem 3:  Print the document.

## PROJECT 5

## Formatting Functions, File Management, and Macros

### Objectives

You will have mastered the material in this project when you can:

- Invoke the List Files option
- Change page length and insert hard page breaks
- Add headers and footers
- Specify date format and employ the date function
- Create and invoke macros

# FILE MANAGEMENT

**L**oad WordPerfect as you have in the previous projects. In this project you will revise a document to look like Figure 5-1. In Project 4 you retrieved a file using the Shift-F10 (retrieve) function. At the prompt you typed the name of the file to be retrieved. It is possible that you may not remember the name of the file, or perhaps you need to see how many bytes of memory a particular file uses. In these situations and to perform other file management functions, it is not necessary to exit WordPerfect, you can use the **List Files** function.

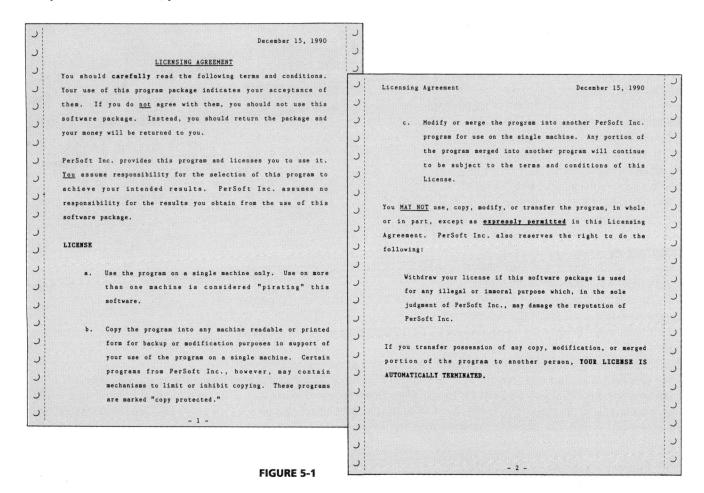

**FIGURE 5-1**

Look at the template next to the F5 key. You see the words List Files in black. Press the F5 key. Figure 5-2 shows that the message "Dir B:\*.*" appears in the lower left corner of your screen. As you learned in the Introduction to DOS, the * is a global character. B:/*.*, therefore, stands for drive b and *all the files* (*) before the period and *all the files* (*) after the period. To accept this default and to see all the files on drive B, press the Enter key. Figure 5-3 shows a screen similar to what your screen will look like. (You may see some other files not shown in Figure 5-3).

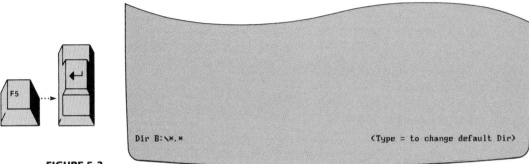

Dir B:\*.*                                                    ⟨Type = to change default Dir⟩

**FIGURE 5-2**

The top left corner shows the date and time you entered when you loaded WordPerfect into main memory. At the top middle is the directory you are currently in. At the top right you are shown the disk space that is still free. As each file is saved, bytes (each character or space is approximately equivalent to one byte) are subtracted from the free disk space. The Current Directory and Parent Directory are reserved if you are using a hard disk. Because you are using diskettes all files on drive B are listed in alphabetical order. After the name of the file, you see a dot or period and then the file extension name, if any. To the right of the file name are the number of bytes used by that particular file, then the date and time that particular file was saved. If you have since saved and then replaced a file, the last date and time of saving is shown. This is one reason why it is so important to enter the date when turning on the computer. Because all files are saved by date, you can often find a particular file you are

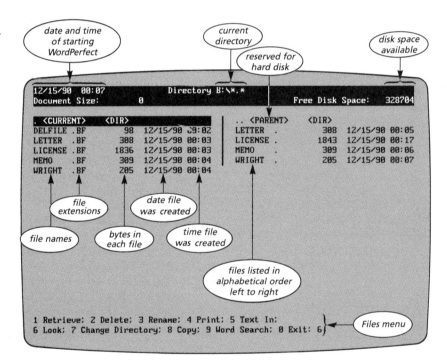

**FIGURE 5-3**

looking for just by knowing when you last saved it. The Files menu at the bottom of the screen shows all the options that are available.

To invoke any of the options, you must highlight a file. To do this, press the Down Arrow ↓ and then the Right Arrow →. Notice how the cursor highlights one file at a time. If you have many files you may have more than one screenful of file names. To view other files you can press PgDn or Home, Down Arrow to move down a screen at a time. To move up a screen at a time, press PgUp or Home, Up Arrow. To move to the last document listed (even if it were several screens down), press Home, Home, Down Arrow. To move to the top of the files listing, press Home, Home, Up Arrow.

Notice that there is a file named MEMO. To go quickly to this file press the letter M (capital or lowercase). Figure 5-4 shows that the menu at the bottom of the screen is replaced by the letter M. When you press a letter, the first file beginning with that letter is highlighted. If you do not wish to type any more letters to view other files, press the spacebar to bring the menu back. (If you press the spacebar too long or press it twice, you will lose the files screen. If that happens, press F5 and then Enter to retrieve it.)

At the files screen, press Home, Home, Up Arrow to move the cursor to the top of the list of files. You now wish to highlight the document you saved as LICENSE. Since there is more than one file that begins with the letter L it will be necessary to type more than just L. Type L (lowercase or capital) (Step 1 in Figure 5-5). Notice how the file LETTER is highlighted and the letter L is shown at the bottom of the screen. Type the letter I and notice in Step 2 of Figure 5-5 how the highlighting moves to the first file that begins with LI. If you had many files, you could continue typing more letters of a file name, or you could move the cursor to the desired file name. Press any of the cursor keys or the spacebar, and the menu is restored (Step 2, Figure 5-5). To exit the List Files menu press the spacebar (Step 3 in Figure 5-5). You can now see that you have a blank screen or a clean work space.

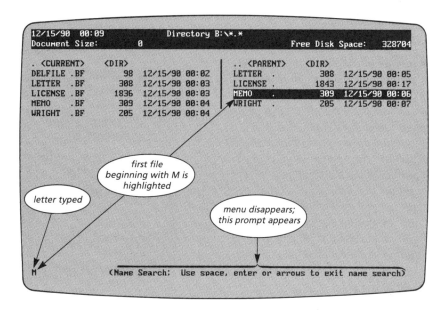

**FIGURE 5-4**

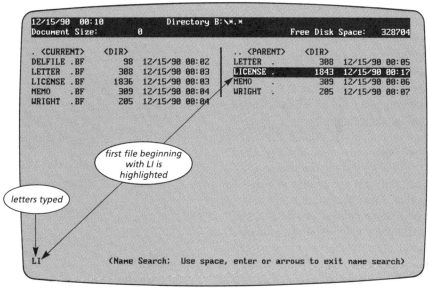

**FIGURE 5-5**

Step 1: Type the first letter of the file name

Step 2: Type the second letter of the file name. To retrieve the menu press the spacebar

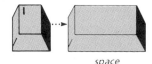

*space*

Step 3: Exit the List Files function

*space*

## Look Function

You will now retrieve a copy of a file from disk and place it into main memory. Note that you have a blank screen on which to retrieve that file. If you did not have a clean work space, and you retrieved a document on the screen, text that was on the screen would be pushed down below the incoming text. Since it might not be visible, you'd think it was gone, but you might find later that you saved two documents together. Remember to *clean the workspace* before you retrieve a new document into memory. The workspace can only be cleared using the Exit (F7) key.

To look at the entire listing of files on drive B, press F5, then Enter ↵. To work on the file named LICENSE, retrieve a copy of that file into the main memory of the computer. The term "copy" is used because the original file remains on the disk, and only a copy of that file is retrieved and placed in main memory. You will be changing that file, but all changes are made to the copy in main memory. To save all the changes you will have to use the Save key and then replace the old file on disk with the new changes that are in main memory.

Type LI and the document LICENSE that you created is highlighted. Press the spacebar to restore the menu. Since there are many files, you would waste time if you retrieved the wrong document into memory only to have to exit out again. WordPerfect includes an option to look at a document that is on the disk without actually retrieving a copy into main memory.

Look at the menu at the bottom of the screen as shown in Figure 5-6. Next to number 6 is the word Look. Press

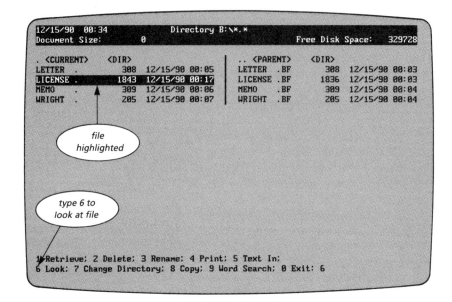

**FIGURE 5-6**

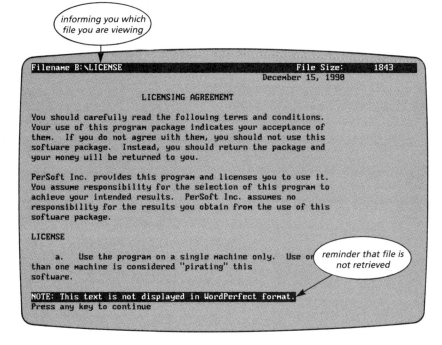

**FIGURE 5-7**

number 6 and the document LICENSE is displayed on your screen. Figure 5-7 shows, however, that you are just viewing the document. The bar at the top of the screen tells you which file you are looking at and how large the file is. At the bottom of the screen the highlighted message warns you that this is not displayed in WordPerfect format, that is, that the document has not been loaded into main memory. The document looks the same as you typed it. But in some documents (such as those that have columns or tabbed numbers) the typing may appear strange. Since the document has not been loaded into main memory you cannot do any editing. You can move the cursor down or even press the PgDn key to view more of the document, but you cannot press any other key or you will exit the look function.

To return to the Files menu press the spacebar. The file you were just viewing remains highlighted in the Files menu.

## Retrieving a Document

Because the highlighted file you just viewed is the file you wish to retrieve, look at the menu at the bottom of the screen. Next to the number 1, notice the word Retrieve. With the file name LICENSE still highlighted, press the number 1. The document named B:\LICENSE, which you typed in Project 3, is retrieved and placed in memory and displayed on your screen.

Press F5 and then Enter ↵. You now see the list files screen again. If you were to highlight a document and then retrieve it by pressing the number 1 you would be retrieving another document on top of the one already in main memory. Press the spacebar, and you are returned to your document still on the screen.

Now that you have the document named LICENSE retrieved and loaded into main memory, you will use this document to learn more formatting features. First, it is necessary to delete a line of type in the document. It may seem that the line is needed in the text, but deleting it rearranges the page breaks so that you can learn more formatting features in this project.

To delete the line of type, press the Down Arrow 19 times to move the cursor to line 20, position 10. Then press Ctrl-End. Press the Delete key two times to delete the blank lines. Press Home, Home, Up Arrow to move the cursor to the top of the document.

# MORE FORMATTING FEATURES

**N**ow that you have deleted the one line, note that the body of the text should be in 1 1/2 spacing instead of single spacing. Since you do not want to change the spacing for the date and heading, press the Down Arrow ↓ five times to place the cursor on line 6, position 10 under the Y in You. To change the line spacing press Shift-F8. Press number 4 for spacing. Type 1.5 and press Enter ↵. Figure 5-8 shows that typing below the code is now in 1 1/2 line spacing.

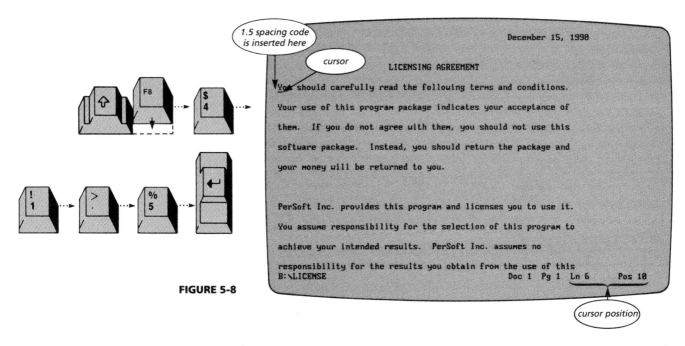

**FIGURE 5-8**

Before printing any document, it is important to view each screen to see if the format and the page breaks make reading easy. To do this, press the Plus ( + ) key on the numeric keypad to move to the bottom of the current screen. To move to the bottom of the next screen press the + key again. The cursor moves to line 37.5. To continue moving to the next screen, press the + key. Notice that the cursor crosses the page break and is on page 2, line 1. To view the code that is embedded when the page breaks, press Alt-F3. The code **[SPg]** is inserted because the page break was invoked by the computer, causing a **soft page break**. To exit the reveal codes, press the spacebar.

The page break comes in an awkward place; the four lines of the paragraph should be kept together. There are three ways in which the document can be formatted to keep these lines together. All three ways will now be demonstrated. When you type other documents in the future, you can decide which way will be most advantageous for each document.

## Changing the Page Length

As discussed in Project 4, WordPerfect defaults to a one-inch margin on the top and bottom of each page; that is why the page breaks at line 54. Knowing this, you can invoke a code that will make the page break at line 57, which is below the four-line paragraph. Remembering that a code is only good going downward from where it is invoked, you must move the cursor above the page break in order to lengthen page 1. Press the Up Arrow ↑ ↑ two times to move the cursor to line 52.5. Look at the template next to the F8 key. You see Page Format in blue. Press Alt-F8. The menu shown in Figure 5-9 appears on the screen.

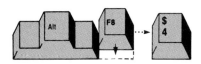

```
Page Format

    1 - Page Number Position

    2 - New Page Number

    3 - Center Page Top to Bottom

    4 - Page Length

    5 - Top Margin

    6 - Headers or Footers

    7 - Page Number Column Positions

    8 - Suppress for Current page only

    9 - Conditional End of Page

    A - Widow/Orphan

Selection: 0
```

**FIGURE 5-9**

Because you wish to **change the page length**, press the number 4. Figure 5-10 shows that option 1 describes the default setting. Option 2 would be chosen if you had a page that would be printed on legal size paper. Since neither one of these options are what you wish to use, press the number 3 for "other." You will still be printing on 8 1/2 × 11-inch paper, which is 66 lines long from top to bottom, so it is not necessary to change the 66. Just press Enter ↵ to accept the 66. The cursor moves underneath the 54. Type the number 57 to change the number of typed lines on the page. Press Enter ↵ and you are returned to the page format screen.

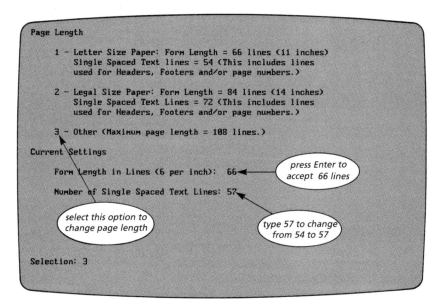

```
Page Length

    1 - Letter Size Paper: Form Length = 66 lines (11 inches)
        Single Spaced Text lines = 54 (This includes lines
        used for Headers, Footers and/or page numbers.)

    2 - Legal Size Paper: Form Length = 84 lines (14 inches)
        Single Spaced Text Lines = 72 (This includes lines
        used for Headers, Footers and/or page numbers.)

    3 - Other (Maximum page length = 108 lines.)
Current Settings

    Form Length in Lines (6 per inch):   66

    Number of Single Spaced Text Lines: 57

Selection: 3
```

*press Enter to accept 66 lines*

*select this option to change page length*

*type 57 to change from 54 to 57*

**FIGURE 5-10**

Press Enter ↵ again and you are returned to your document. Note that the page break is still in the same place. This is because the code has not yet been interpreted by the WordPerfect software, and so the screen has not yet rewritten itself to reflect this code. To view the code that was embedded into the document, press Alt-F3. The embedded code shows that the page has 66 lines and that the typing will be 57 lines long (Figure 5-11). Notice that the [SPg] code still follows the word Licensing. To exit the reveal codes, press the spacebar. As you do, notice that the screen rewrites itself and that the four lines are now above the page break (Figure 5-12). Return to the reveal codes by pressing Alt-F3.

To try another way to keep the four lines together, it is necessary to delete the code that was just inserted into the document. The cursor should be to the right of the page length code. To delete backward, press the Backspace key one time, and the code is deleted. Press the spacebar to exit the reveal codes. As you do, notice that the four lines are split again by a dotted line, indicating the page break. The cursor should still be under the Y in You.

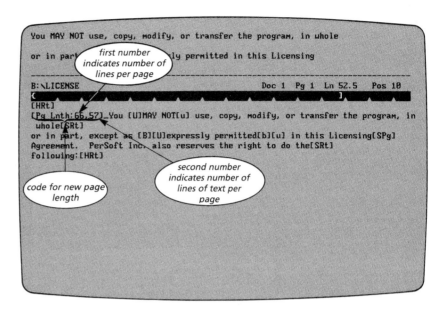

**FIGURE 5-11**

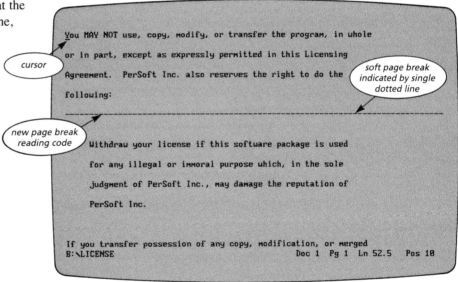

**FIGURE 5-12**

## Hard Page Break

When you see a dotted line across the page, you know that it is a page break invoked by the WordPerfect software as it interprets the page length codes, or the conditional end of page. You have viewed the [SPg] code that is embedded when the computer interprets Page Length commands. There could be times when you wish to invoke a page break code to ensure that no typing can be inserted below a certain point on a page. This is called a **hard page** break. Even if margins or page lengths are redefined, the hard page break will continue to be invoked by the software as long as the code exists.

With the cursor on line 52.5 under the Y in You, press Ctrl-Enter. You can see how the page break has occurred (Figure 5-13), and you can also see that instead of a single dotted line, WordPerfect uses a double dotted line when you invoke a hard page break.

To view the code, press Alt-F3. Notice that above the first line of the paragraph a **[HPg]** code is embedded (Figure 5-14). To delete the hard page break, press the Backspace key. Press the spacebar to exit the codes.

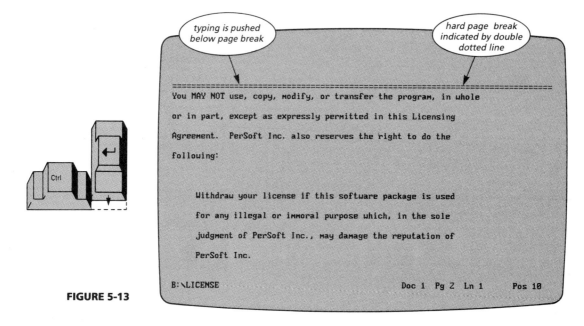

**FIGURE 5-13**

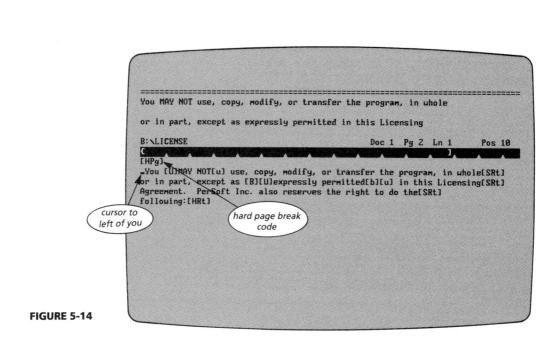

**FIGURE 5-14**

## Conditional End of Page

Another formatting feature, **conditional end of page**, is found on the Page Format key. This feature keeps a specified number of lines together on one page. If the current page is not long enough, it will move all lines specified to the next page. This is helpful if you have a table or graph that must be kept on one page.

The cursor must be *above* the lines to be kept together, so press the Up Arrow ↑ to move the cursor to line 51, which is the blank line before the paragraph. Press Alt-F8. The Page Format menu appears. Press number 9 for conditional end of page. The message "Number of lines to keep together = " appears on the screen. Type the number 4 (because there are four lines you wish to keep together), as shown in Figure 5-15. Press Enter ↵, then press Enter ↵ again to exit the Page Format menu. The lines will reformat after you have looked at the codes.

To view the code that was inserted, press Alt-F3. Figure 5-16 shows the conditional end of page code, **[CndlEOP]**, embedded in your document. Before you exit the codes, notice that the [SPg] code again follows the word Licensing. Press the spacebar to exit the codes. As you do, notice that all four lines have been kept together by being moved down to the next page below the dotted line (see Figure 5-17 on the following page).

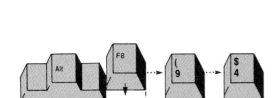

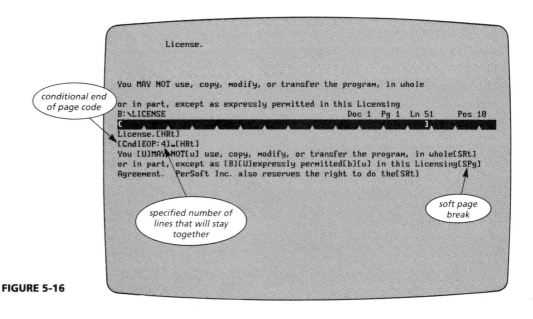

**FIGURE 5-15**

**FIGURE 5-16**

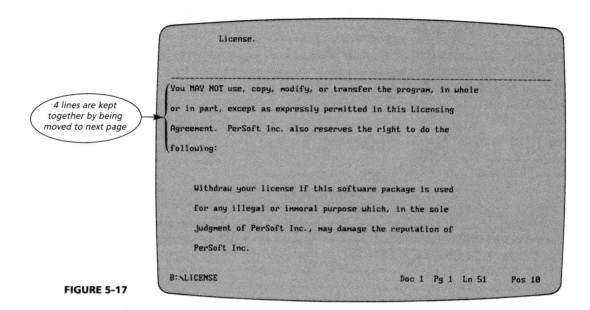

4 lines are kept together by being moved to next page

**FIGURE 5-17**

# HEADERS AND FOOTERS

Whenever your document contains more than one page, you will most likely wish to number the pages. You may also wish to have a heading at the top or bottom of each page, or perhaps both. A heading and page number placed at the top of a page is called a **header**; placed at the bottom of a page, it is called a **footer**. You may have noticed headers and footers in your textbooks. It is not necessary to type headers and footers on each and every page when you compose a document. It can be done once for the entire document.

WordPerfect allows you to have as many as two headers and/or two footers per page, which is helpful if you are typing a document that will have facing pages. Facing pages are normally used in books or magazines. You have probably noticed that in books odd pages are normally on the right side and even pages on the left side, either at the top or bottom of the page. This type of numbering is called facing pages numbering. For our exercise, we will use only one position for the numbering.

After you type headers and footers, a code is embedded and they are held in screens separate from the normal typing screen. When the pages are printed, headers will be printed at the top of each page and footers at the bottom of each page. WordPerfect allows one blank line to be inserted between either the header or footer and the body of the text. The lines required for the headers and/or footers are typed within the 54 lines of typing, leaving the top and bottom margins intact. Headers and footers should always be typed at the beginning of a document. If you have invoked a margin set change, the headers and footers code should follow the margin set code.

## Headers

To move to the top of the document, press Home, Home, Up Arrow ↑. Headers and footers are found on the Page Format key. Press Alt-F8. The Page Format menu that was shown in Figure 5-15 appears on the screen. Press number 6 for headers or footers. Figure 5-18 shows the screen you will see. Look at the menu on the left. You have a choice of header A or B and/or footer A or B. The menu on the right shows the options you can choose for each header or footer.

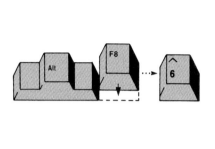

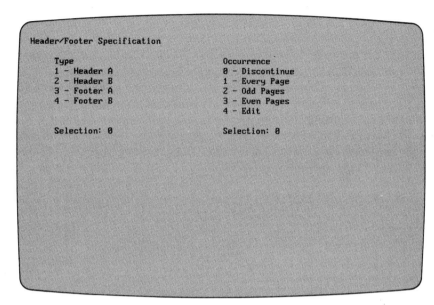

**FIGURE 5-18**

For this document, you will define one header and then one footer. Press the number 1 for header A. The 1 is accepted and the cursor moves to the next column. To place the header on every page type the number 1 again. A totally blank screen with a mini status line appears. This screen is reserved for header A. What you type is held in reserve and will be printed when the document is sent to the printer. Type the words Licensing Agreement. Because you also want the date to appear in the upper right corner, you must add the date flush right. Press Alt-F6. The cursor moves to position 75. Type the date December 15, 1990 (or the current date, if you wish). Because you want an extra blank line between the header and the text, press the hard return ↵ key. Your screen should look like Figure 5-19. As indicated on the screen, press F7 to exit. You are returned to the Page Format menu (Figure 5-15).

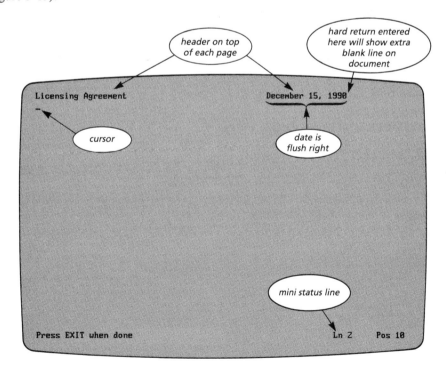

**FIGURE 5-19**

## Footers

Because you also wish to add a footer, press the number 6 for headers or footers. The screen you saw in Figure 5-18 appears again. This time press the number 3 for footer A. Next, press the number 1 for every page. Again you have a blank screen, which is reserved for footer A. The typing will be at the bottom of the page, and you want an extra blank line between the body of the text and the footer, so first press the hard return ↵ key. The cursor should be on line 2, position 10. Because you are going to put in page numbering, which you want centered at the bottom of each page, you must center the typing. Press Shift-F6. The cursor moves to position 42. Type a hyphen (–) followed by the spacebar. At this point you would normally type the number. You need to put in a code that will merge with the status line, so that, for instance, when page 2 is typed, the printer will read the status line and invoke that particular page number. To put in a numbering merge code, hold down the Ctrl key and type the letter B. Press the spacebar and then type another hyphen. The screen should look like Figure 5-20. Press F7 to exit. You are returned to the page format screen.

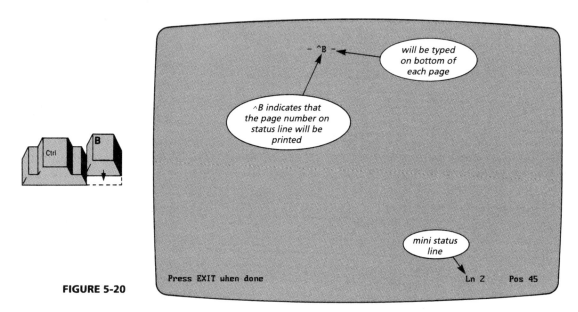

**FIGURE 5-20**

## Suppress for Current Page Only

The codes for headers and footers are being invoked at the top of your document, but you do not wish to have the header typed on the first page, since that page has its own heading. To suppress the header for page 1, which is the current page, press the number 8 for **suppress for current page only**. The menu in Figure 5-21 shows that you can suppress any number of options. You only wish to suppress the header, not the footer, so press the number 5 to turn off header A. Press Enter ↵, then press Enter ↵ again to return to your document.

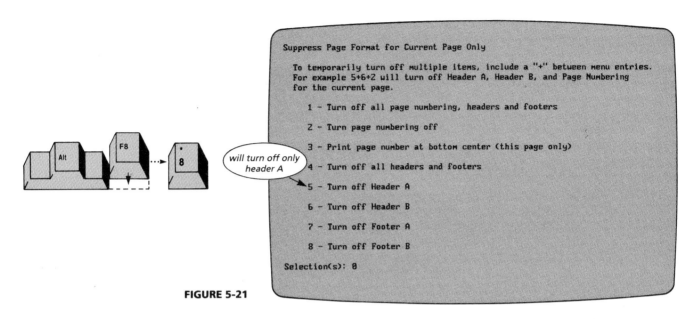

**FIGURE 5-21**

To view the three codes you just invoked, press Alt-F3. Figure 5-22 shows that first you have the header code, then the footer code, and then the suppress code. To exit the reveal codes, press the spacebar.

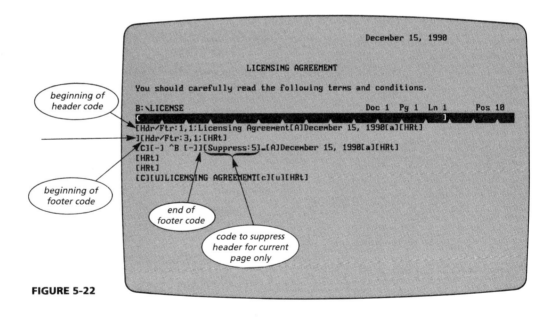

**FIGURE 5-22**

# SAVING AND REPLACING A DOCUMENT

*B*efore you save your document, it is necessary to delete the 1.5 line spacing, since the training version of WordPerfect cannot send that command to the printer. It can, however, accept the command of double spacing. Press the Down Arrow five times to move the cursor to line 6 and then press Alt-F3. In reveal codes the cursor is to the right of the 1.5 spacing code. To delete the code press the backspace key. Press the spacebar to exit reveal codes. To make the document print in double spacing press Shift-F8. Press the number 4 for spacing. Type the number 2 for double spacing, then press Enter ↵.

When you finished typing this document in Project 3, you saved the document to your disk. However, you have now made several changes to the document on your screen, but those changes have not been saved to the disk. As you learned in Projects 3 and 4, it is possible to save these changes to the disk by replacing the old text with the new text. In this case, you want to save both the version made in Project 3 as well as the changes made here in Project 5. Therefore, when you save you will give this document a different name.

To save your document, press the F10 key. At the prompt "Document to be Saved: B:\LICENSE" type the new name license.2 and press Enter. The document is saved to the disk in drive B.

# PRINTING A DOCUMENT

**Y**ou have saved and replaced your document, and it is now ready to be printed. At this point be sure that your printer has paper inserted, and that the printer is on and ready to print.

Press Shift-F7. You will see the Print menu at the bottom of the screen. Because you wish to print the full text of this document, press the number 1 for full text. At this point, the printer begins printing your document. The printed document generated is illustrated in Figure 5-23.

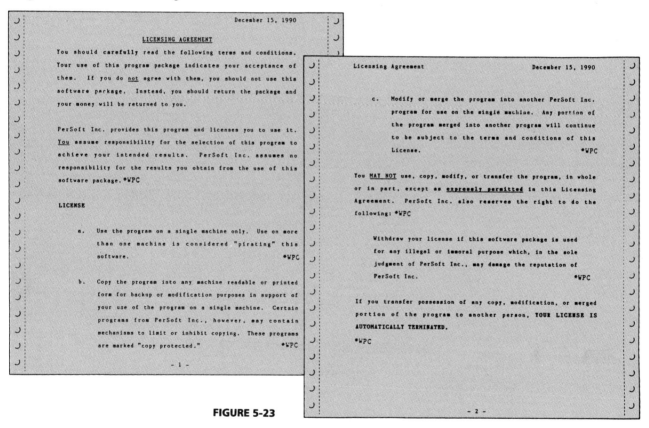

**FIGURE 5-23**

# EXITING A DOCUMENT

**Y**our document has been saved to disk and printed. It is now necessary to exit the document and clear the screen, but not exit the WordPerfect program.

Press the F7 key. At the prompt "Save Document? (Y/N) Y" type the letter N because the document has already been saved. At the prompt "Exit WP? (Y/N) N" type the letter N. The document exits and a clear screen appears.

# DATE FORMAT FUNCTION

**W**hen you first turned on your computer you were prompted to enter the date. It is always important to enter the date, because all files are saved by their date. Another good reason for inserting the date is that you can invoke the date with the F5 key. But when you use F5, the date you invoke will be the date you entered when first turning the machine on.

Look at the template next to the F5 key. Notice the word Date in green. Press Shift-F5. The menu shown in Figure 5-24 appears. Press the number 1 to enter today's date on your blank screen. Press a hard return ↵ to move the cursor to line 2.

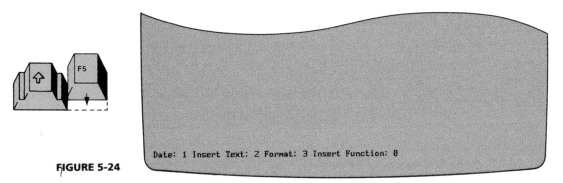

Date: 1 Insert Text; 2 Format; 3 Insert Function: 0

**FIGURE 5-24**

Whatever date you entered when you booted DOS will appear on the screen. For example, if you had entered 12-15-90 you would see December 15, 1990—the same date but in a different form. (If you did not enter a date you will see the system default date.) You can understand why the date appears in the form it does by viewing the **Date Format** menu.

To view the Date Format menu, press Shift-F5 and type the number 2. Figure 5-25 shows what your screen will look like. At the bottom in boldface typing you see "Date Format: 3 1, 4." The numbers are the default characters used. To understand the meaning of each number, look at the menu above. The 3 1, 4 stands for the following: 3 = month (word), 1 = day of the month (a comma is placed after the day because if you were typing it you would include a comma), 4 = year (all four digits). This explains how a date can be displayed or printed in one format when it was inserted in a different format. Press F7 to exit the Date Format menu.

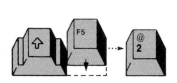

```
Date Format

        Character   Meaning
           1        Day of the month
           2        Month (number)
           3        Month (word)
           4        Year (all four digits)
           5        Year (last two digits)
           6        Day of the week (word)
           7        Hour (24-hour clock)
           8        Hour (12-hour clock)
           9        Minute
           0        am / pm
           %        Include leading zero for numbers less than 10
                       (must directly precede number)

        Examples:  3 1, 4      = December 25, 1984
                   %2/%1/5 (6) = 01/01/85 (Tuesday)
                   8:90        = 10:55am

Date Format: 3 1, 4
```

*format can be changed*

**FIGURE 5-25**

With the Date menu at the bottom of the screen, now press the number 3 for Insert Function. As you can see on the screen, the date is typed again.

To see the difference between 1 Insert Text and 3 Insert Function you need to view the codes. Press Alt-F3. The screen in Figure 5-26 shows that in the upper screen the date appears twice in exactly the same format. But the codes show that two different things happen. The first date is when you inserted text, exactly as if you had typed the date by hand. If you were to save this document and bring it up tomorrow, it would

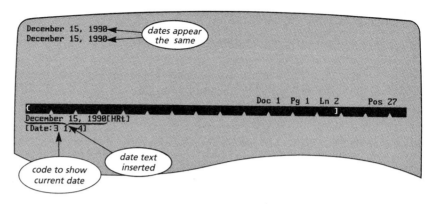

FIGURE 5-26

still have the same typing you see now. The second date is not a date at all in the codes. All you see is the code [3 1, 4]. The code inserts the current month, day, and year, which you entered when turning on the computer. If you were to bring this document up tomorrow, the date that would be invoked by the code would have tomorrow's date on the screen. This is especially useful if you type a letter today, but will be printing it out at some time in the future. Press the spacebar to exit the reveal codes.

# MACROS

P robably the single most time-saving feature of WordPerfect is its capability of using macros. Simply stated, a **macro** stores frequently used keystrokes that make up phrases, paragraphs, or commands, so that instead of having to press a sequence of keystrokes each time, you only have to press a few keys. If any typing or string of commands is used frequently, you can make a macro of those keystrokes. You will learn how to create two macros, and then whenever keystrokes become repetitive, you can create and then invoke your own macros.

You have just learned how to invoke a date function. You will now learn how to put those keystrokes into main memory in a macro.

Press a hard return ↵ to move to a clean line. To define a macro look at the template next to the F10 key. You see the words Macro Def in red. Press Ctrl-F10. The prompt "Define Macro:" appears on your screen (step 1 of Figure 5-27). First, you must name the macro. You can use letters of the alphabet or a word or abbreviation to name a macro. To save time, you should make the name short and representative of what the macro does. In this case hold down the Alt key and press the letter D for date (step 2 of Figure 5-27). The prompt "Macro Def" begins flashing in the lower left corner of the screen (Figure 5-28). Any and all keys you press now will be stored in sequence until you turn the macro define

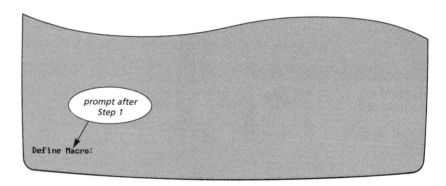

Step 1: Invoke macro function

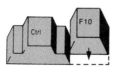

Step 2: Ready the software to receive the macro

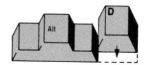

FIGURE 5-27

off. Recalling what we did before to retrieve the current date, press Shift-F5. When you receive the Date menu press the number 3 (step 1 of Figure 5-28). The current date appears on the screen.

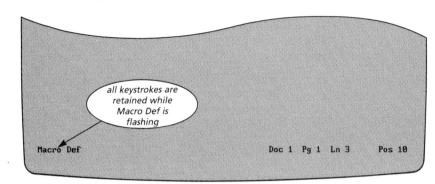

**FIGURE 5-28**

Step 1: Type the macro          Step 2: Save the macro and escape from macro define mode

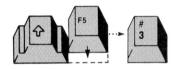          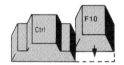

Turn off the macro define the same way you turned it on, by pressing Ctrl-F10 (step 2 of Figure 5-28). The light on drive B goes on, indicating that the macro is being saved to the disk. The prompt then stops flashing. Press a hard return ↵ to put the cursor on a clean line. To invoke the macro, press Alt-D. Immediately you see the date on the screen.

When you use this macro, the date will be inserted wherever the cursor is. To make the date flush right, press Alt-F6. When the cursor is flush right, press Alt-D. The date types out flush right. Press a hard return ↵ to move the cursor to a clean line. To center the date press Shift-F6. With the cursor centered, press Alt-D. Press a hard return. The date types out centered.

Because the macro has the code of 3 1, 4, no matter on which date you invoke the macro, the current date will appear on the screen in the form of month (word), day, and year (all four digits).

To learn the second way to invoke a macro it is best to clear the screen. Press F7 then the letter N to not save the document, then the letter N again to not exit WordPerfect.

The second macro you will learn is the ending of a letter. This is a sequence of keystrokes that is often repeated. To define a macro, press Ctrl-F10. Name the macro by typing the letters SY (for sincerely yours), and press Enter ↵. When "Macro Def" begins flashing, press the Tab key eight times, moving the cursor to position 50. (If you go too far or make a mistake, backspace and correct the error.) When the cursor is on position 50 type the phrase Sincerely yours, then press a hard return ↵. Press a hard return three more times ↵ ↵ ↵. Press the Tab key eight times to move to position 50. Type the name Francis Morris and press a hard return ↵. Press the Tab key eight times to move to position 50 again. Type the word Manager and press hard return. All your keystrokes are now defined. To turn off the macro define, press Ctrl-F10. The light on drive B goes on, indicating that the macro is being saved to the disk.

To invoke the macro this time, look at the template next to the F10 key. Notice the word Macro in blue. Press Alt-F10. The prompt "Macro:" appears. Type the letters SY and press Enter ↵. The macro is invoked and the typing appears on the screen.

To view how WordPerfect lists the macros, look at the List Files menu. Press F5 and then Enter ← (step 1 of Figure 5-29). Notice that the macro files have the extension of .MAC for macro (Figure 5-29). Do not try to retrieve the macro files from this screen. If you do try to retrieve a macro file from the List Files menu, you will receive the message "ERROR: Invalid file name". Press the spacebar to exit from this screen (step 2 of Figure 5-29).

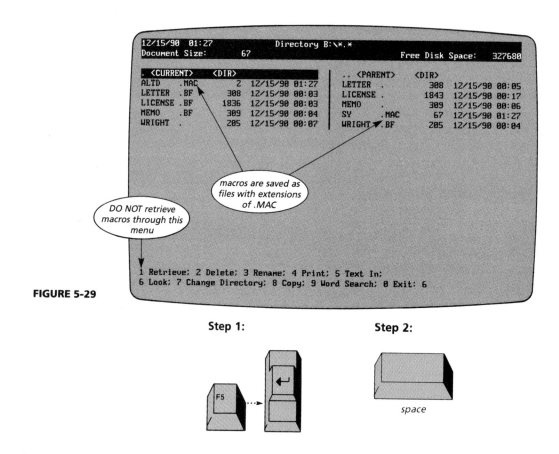

FIGURE 5-29

Step 1:

Step 2:

space

# EXITING WORDPERFECT

s you have done before, exit this document and WordPerfect. It is not necessary to save this document because the macros have already been saved to disk.

# PROJECT SUMMARY

n Project 5 you learned about file management with the List File options. You retrieved the document you typed in Project 3 and practiced more formatting features on that document. You changed the page length, put in a conditional end of page, and used a hard page break. You added a header and a footer to the document. After you saved, replaced, and exited the document, you learned about the date format and how to create macros.

The following is a list of the keystroke sequence we used in Project 5:

**SUMMARY OF KEYSTROKES—Project 5**

| STEPS | KEY(S) PRESSED | STEPS | KEY(S) PRESSED | STEPS | KEY(S) PRESSED |
|---|---|---|---|---|---|
| 1 | F5 | 52 | 1 | 103 | ← |
| 2 | ← | 53 | 1 | 104 | Ctrl-F10 |
| 3 | LI | 54 | Licensing Agreement | 105 | Alt-D |
| 4 | Space | 55 | Alt-F6 | 106 | Shift-F5 |
| 5 | 1 | 56 | December 15, 1990 | 107 | 3 |
| 6 | [↓ 19 times to line 20, position 10] | 57 | ← | 108 | Ctrl-F10 |
| 7 | Ctrl-End | 58 | F7 | 109 | ← |
| 8 | Del | 59 | 6 | 110 | Alt-D |
| 9 | Del | 60 | 3 | 111 | Alt-F6 |
| 10 | Home Home ↑ | 61 | 1 | 112 | Alt-D |
| 11 | ↓ | 62 | ← | 113 | ← |
| 12 | ↓ | 63 | Shift-F6 | 114 | Shift-F6 |
| 13 | ↓ | 64 | - | 115 | Alt-D |
| 14 | ↓ | 65 | Space | 116 | ← |
| 15 | ↓ | 66 | Ctrl-B | 117 | F7 |
| 16 | Shift-F8 | 67 | Space | 118 | N |
| 17 | 4 | 68 | - | 119 | N |
| 18 | 1.5 | 69 | F7 | 120 | Ctrl-F10 |
| 19 | ← | 70 | 8 | 121 | SY |
| 20 | + (on numeric keypad) | 71 | 5 | 122 | ← |
| 21 | + | 72 | ← | 123 | Tab [8 times to move cursor to position 50] |
| 22 | + | 73 | ← | 124 | Sincerely yours, |
| 23 | ↑ | 74 | ↓ | 125 | ← |
| 24 | ↑ (to line 52.5) | 75 | ↓ | 126 | ← |
| 25 | Alt-F8 | 76 | ↓ | 127 | ← |
| 26 | 4 | 77 | ↓ | 128 | ← |
| 27 | 3 | 78 | ↓ | 129 | Tab [8 times to move cursor to position 50] |
| 28 | ← | 79 | Alt-F3 | 130 | Francis Morris |
| 29 | 57 | 80 | Backspace [delete spacing code] | 131 | ← |
| 30 | ← | 81 | Space | 132 | Tab [8 times to move cursor to position 50] |
| 31 | ← | 82 | Shift-F8 | 133 | Manager |
| 32 | Alt-F3 [view codes] | 83 | 4 | 134 | ← |
| 33 | Space | 84 | 2 | 135 | Ctrl-F10 |
| 34 | Alt-F3 | 85 | ← | 136 | ← |
| 35 | Backspace [delete code] | 86 | F10 | 137 | ← |
| 36 | Space | 87 | license.2 | 138 | Alt-F10 |
| 37 | Ctrl-Enter | 88 | ← | 139 | SY |
| 38 | Alt-F3 | 89 | Shift-F7 | 140 | ← |
| 39 | Backspace [delete code] | 90 | 1 | 141 | F5 |
| 40 | Space | 91 | F7 | 142 | ← |
| 41 | ↑ (to Ln 51) | 92 | N | 143 | Space |
| 42 | Alt-F8 | 93 | N | 144 | F7 |
| 43 | 9 | 94 | Shift-F5 | 145 | N |
| 44 | 4 | 95 | 1 | 146 | Y |
| 45 | ← | 96 | ← | 147 | [if not at a DOS prompt, take WP disk out and put DOS disk in drive A] |
| 46 | ← | 97 | Shift-F5 | | |
| 47 | Alt-F3 [view codes] | 98 | 2 | 148 | ← |
| 48 | Space | 99 | F7 | | |
| 49 | Home Home ↑ | 100 | 3 | | |
| 50 | Alt-F8 | 101 | Alt-F3 | | |
| 51 | 6 | 102 | Space | | |

## Project Summary (continued)

The following list summarizes the material covered in Project 5:

1. **File Management** is done through the **List Files** menu. After a file is highlighted, it can be retrieved, renamed, printed, looked at, or copied under another name or to another directory. A word search can also be done through the List Files menu.
2. A **soft page break** is one invoked by the software. The embedded code is **[SPg]**.
3. **Changing the page length** is a page format function that can be used to shorten or lengthen the number of lines on a page.
4. A **hard page break** is invoked by the user to prevent typing from being inserted past a certain point on the page. The embedded code is **[HPg]**.
5. The **conditional end of page** feature keeps a specified number of lines together on one page. The embedded code is **[CndlEOP]**.
6. A **header** is typing found at the top of every page. Headers only have to be typed one time, then they are held in reserve to be printed on top of every page. Headers can consist of several lines of type, or perhaps just a code so the printer will print the current page number.
7. A **footer** is typing found at the bottom of every page. Footers only have to be typed one time, then they are held in reserve to be printed on the bottom of every page. Footers can consist of several lines of type, or perhaps just a code so the printer will print the current page number.
8. The **suppress for current page only** function can instruct the printer *not* to print a combination of page numbering or headers and footers on specified pages.
9. The **date format** function allows you to place a code in a document, so that the current date (or the date entered when loading DOS into the computer) will always be present in a document. Any combination of date formats can be used, such as day of month first, month as a word, and year in all four digits.
10. A **macro** is defined and invoked by the user to replace a sequence of keystrokes that is used frequently. When a macro is defined, all keystrokes are stored under one short name and can be invoked quickly by pressing just a few keys.

# STUDENT ASSIGNMENTS

## STUDENT ASSIGNMENT 1: True/False

**Instructions:**    Circle T if the statement is true and F if the statement is false.

T   F    1. Headers and footers are found on the Shift-F8 keys.
T   F    2. To delete a file from the List Files menu, highlight the file, press the number 2, and respond Y for yes.
T   F    3. WordPerfect lets you define two headers and two footers.
T   F    4. WordPerfect defaults at 50 single lines of type per page.
T   F    5. To list the files on the default drive, press F5 and Enter.
T   F    6. To suppress a header/footer for the current page only, choose option 8 in the Page Format menu.
T   F    7. To access the Macro Define option, press Alt-F8.
T   F    8. The date function is found by pressing Shift-F5.
T   F    9. Each time a document is saved, the name must be retyped.
T   F   10. To cause a hard page break, press the Scroll Lock/Break key.

## STUDENT ASSIGNMENT 2: Multiple Choice

**Instructions:**   Circle the correct response.

1. It is possible to delete a file by
   a. highlighting the file in List Files and pressing the Cancel key.
   b. highlighting the file in List Files and pressing the 2 key, then Y.
   c. highlighting the file in List Files and pressing the Exit key.
   d. pressing Ctrl-F5.
2. When defining headers and footers, WordPerfect allows for
   a. one header and one footer.
   b. two headers and one footer.
   c. either two headers or two footers but not both.
   d. two headers and/or two footers.
3. The Date format and function can be found on the following key(s):
   a. F5
   b. Ctrl-F5
   c. Alt-F5
   d. Shift-F5
4. To invoke a macro,
   a. define the macro with Ctrl-F10
   b. while "Macro Def" is flashing, press all keys to be stored.
   c. call up the macro through either Alt-F10 or Alt-(letter).
   d. all of the above
5. When defining a conditional end of page,
   a. press Alt-F8, 9 and all lines will be kept together until you press a hard return.
   b. press Alt-F8, 9, and designate how many lines are to be kept together.
   c. press Ctrl-F8, 2, and designate how many lines to an inch.
   d. none of the above
6. By pressing Ctrl-Enter, a hard page break occurs. The code embedded in the document for a hard page break is:
   a. [HPg]
   b. [HPgBrk]
   c. [Hard Page]
   d. [Page Brk]
7. In the List Files function, feature 6 will
   a. retrieve the document into memory.
   b. allow the user to look at the entire document, without retrieving it into memory.
   c. not allow the user to do any editing in the document.
   d. both b and c
8. "Suppress for current page only" will
   a. allow the user to cancel all headers and/or footers.
   b. allow the user to cancel specific headers.
   c. allow the user to cancel specific footers.
   d. all of the above

## STUDENT ASSIGNMENT 3: Matching

**Instructions:** Put the appropriate number next to the words in the second column.

1. Delete a file            _____ Alt-F8, 4, 3
2. Conditional end of page    _____ Ctrl-Enter
3. Macro define           _____ 2 on List Files menu
4. Look option on List
     Files menu            _____ Shift-F5, 3
5. Date format            _____ 6 on List Files menu
6. Hard page break        _____ Alt-F8, 9
7. Retrieve a file         _____ 1 on List Files menu
8. Change page length     _____ Ctrl-F10
9. Define a header         _____ Shift-F5, 2
10. Insert date function     _____ Alt-F8, 6, 1, 1

## STUDENT ASSIGNMENT 4: Understanding WordPerfect Commands

**Instructions:** Next to each command, describe its effect.

| Command | Effect |
| --- | --- |
| Alt-F8, 9 | _____ |
| Ctrl-F10 | _____ |
| Ctrl-Enter | _____ |
| Alt-F8, 4 | _____ |
| F5, Enter | _____ |
| 1 on List Files menu | _____ |
| 2 on List Files menu | _____ |
| 6 on List Files menu | _____ |
| Alt-F8, 8 | _____ |
| Alt-F8, 6 | _____ |

## STUDENT ASSIGNMENT 5: Describing a Footer

**Instructions:** At the bottom of the following document is a footer created on WordPerfect. Describe in detail how that footer was created.

The Regional Occupational Program, commonly called ROP, is a cooperative educational effort between local school districts and the County Department of Education. Its purpose is to train high school youth to become gainfully employed.

ROP has served and trained over 95,000 students in some 42 trades since 1988.

ROP plays an important role in the application of basic skills in the world of work, endeavoring to assist the unskilled and under-trained to become gainfully employed. ROP works in cooperation with 1,054 local businesses in the community to provide students on-the-job training. About 500 members of business and industry are involved in an advisory committee role to assure meaningful job skill training, a verified labor market demand, and a high potential for student placement in every course offered through ROP.

Important features of the Regional Occupational Program are:

1. Students from many schools meet at a centralized classroom. The teacher has a credential in the field being taught plus at least 5 years of directly related work experience.

2. Students are assigned to business training sites to receive realistic on-the-job skill development. An individualized training plan is developed for each student at each job training site.

3. Periodically students return to the classroom for additional training and to review progress from an employment point of view.

Courses are offered three semesters during the year. Enrollment time varies depending on the course topic or trade area. Some programs permit entry on any day, others at the start of each semester.

– 1 –

## STUDENT ASSIGNMENT 6:
## Identifying the List Files Menu

**Instructions:** Look at this screen of a List Files menu. Circle the following areas and place the identifying number within the circle.

1. Amount of free disk space
2. Columns with names of files
3. Columns with names of extensions
4. Number of bytes used for files
5. Dates files were made
6. Directory of files

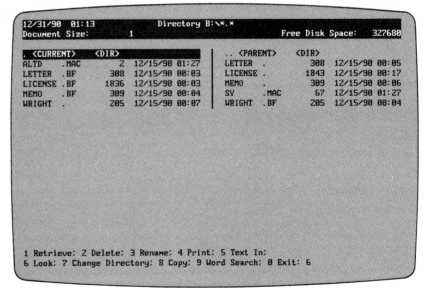

## STUDENT ASSIGNMENT 7: Identifying Codes

**Instructions:** This screen shows several codes. Circle the entire code and identify it with the appropriate number from the list below.

1. Margin setting
2. Header
3. Tab setting
4. Date function
5. Suppress for current page only
6. Hard page break
7. Page length
8. Conditional end of page

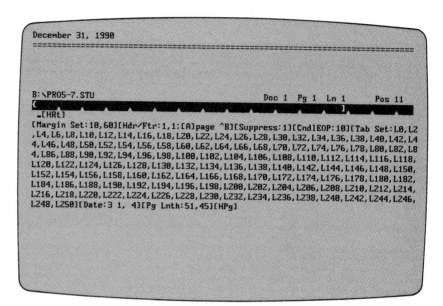

```
December 31, 1990
=====================================================================

B:\PRO5-7.STU                                   Doc 1  Pg 1  Ln 1      Pos 11
[                                                                   ]
 _[HRt]
[Margin Set:10,60][Hdr/Ftr:1,1:[A]page ^B][Suppress:1][CndlEOP:10][Tab Set:L0,L2
,L4,L6,L8,L10,L12,L14,L16,L18,L20,L22,L24,L26,L28,L30,L32,L34,L36,L38,L40,L42,L4
4,L46,L48,L50,L52,L54,L56,L58,L60,L62,L64,L66,L68,L70,L72,L74,L76,L78,L80,L82,L8
4,L86,L88,L90,L92,L94,L96,L98,L100,L102,L104,L106,L108,L110,L112,L114,L116,L118,
L120,L122,L124,L126,L128,L130,L132,L134,L136,L138,L140,L142,L144,L146,L148,L150,
L152,L154,L156,L158,L160,L162,L164,L166,L168,L170,L172,L174,L176,L178,L180,L182,
L184,L186,L188,L190,L192,L194,L196,L198,L200,L202,L204,L206,L208,L210,L212,L214,
L216,L218,L220,L222,L224,L226,L228,L230,L232,L234,L236,L238,L240,L242,L244,L246,
L248,L250][Date:3 1, 4][Pg Lnth:51,45][HPg]
```

## STUDENT ASSIGNMENT 8: Making a Macro

**Instructions:** This heading will be used frequently.

```
      Robert B. Jones
      Attorney
      Jones, Richards, and Smith
      534 Harrison Blvd.
      Salt Lake City, UT 84106
```

Problem 1: Define the heading as a macro. Define the name as HEAD.
Problem 2: Practice retrieving the heading with Alt-F10.
Problem 3: Print the page of typing.

## STUDENT ASSIGNMENT 9: Making a Macro

**Instructions:** Here is an ending that will be used frequently.

Problem 1: Define the ending as a macro. Define the name by using Alt-M.

Problem 2: Practice retrieving the ending with Alt-M.

Problem 3: Print the page of typing.

```
      Sincerely yours,


      Robert B. Jones
      Attorney
      Jones, Richards, and Smith

      RBJ/rg
```

## STUDENT ASSIGNMENT 10: Modifying a Document

**Instructions:**   Perform the following tasks.

1. Load DOS into main memory.
2. Load WordPerfect into main memory by inserting the WordPerfect diskette into drive A, putting a data disk into drive B, typing b: and pressing Enter. At the B> prompt, type a:wp and press Enter.

Problem 1:
1. Retrieve the file named Regional.
2. Change the margins to 15 on the left and 75 on the right.
3. Delete all existing tabs. Set tab stops at every third interval, beginning with position 0.
4. Change the line spacing to 2
5. Create a footer as follows:
   Regional Occupational Program (flush left)
   Page number (flush right)
6. Suppress the footer for the first page only.

Problem 2: Save the new document to disk under the new name of Regional.3.

Problem 3: Print the revised document; it should look like the document below.

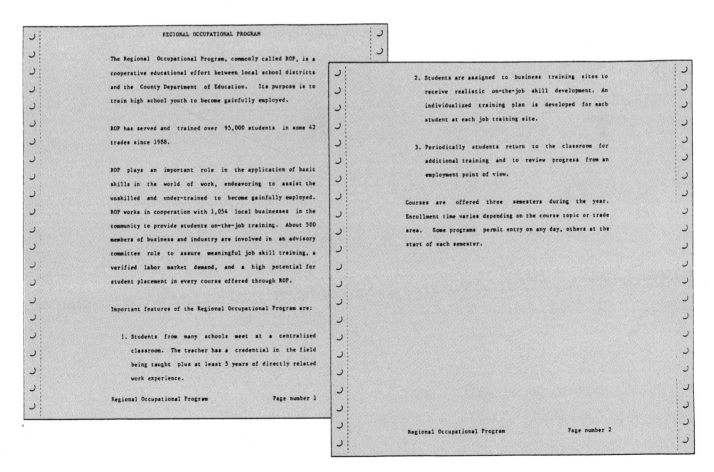

# PROJECT 6

## Advanced WordPerfect Features

## Objectives

You will have mastered the material in this project when you can:

■ Search and reverse search the text of a document
■ Employ the search and replace function
■ Practice using the thesaurus and speller demonstration example

**B**oot up and load WordPerfect into main memory. Retrieve License.2, the document you saved in Project 5, by pressing Shift-F10. Type the name License.2 and press Enter ↵. The document appears on the screen.

Let's assume that we must modify this document because PerSoft Inc. has been acquired by a company called UMC Corp. The modified document to be prepared is shown in Figure 6-1. Six changes must be made to the existing licensing agreement so that it can be used for the new company's products:

1. Remove the double spacing.
2. Emphasize the fact that the company assumes no responsibility.
3. Change the word License to License Agreement in section c.
4. Replace all occurrences of the name PerSoft Inc. with the name UMC Corp.
5. Switch the order of the first and second paragraphs.
6. Switch the order of the two sentences in section a.

**FIGURE 6-1**

```
                                                    December 15, 1990
   *WPC

                    LICENSING AGREEMENT

   UMC Corp. provides this program and licenses you to use it. You
   assume responsibility for the selection of this program to
   achieve your intended results. UMC Corp. assumes absolutely no
   responsibility for the results you obtain from the use of this
   software package.*WPC

   You should carefully read the following terms and conditions.
   Your use of this program package indicates your acceptance of
   them. If you do not agree with them, you should not use this
   software package. Instead, you should return the package and
   your money will be returned to you.*WPC

   LICENSE

        a.   Use on more than one machine is considered "pirating"
             this software. Use the program on a single machine
             only.                                           *WPC

        b.   Copy the program into any machine readable or printed
             form for backup or modification purposes in support of
             your use of the program on a single machine. Certain
             programs from UMC Corp., however, may contain
             mechanisms to limit or inhibit copying. These programs
             are marked "copy protected."                    *WPC

        c.   Modify or merge the program into another UMC Corp.
             program for use on the single machine. Any portion of
             the program merged into another program will continue
             to be subject to the terms and conditions of this
             License Agreement.                              *WPC

   You MAY NOT use, copy, modify, or transfer the program, in whole
   or in part, except as expressly permitted in this Licensing
   Agreement. UMC Corp. also reserves the right to do the
   following:*WPC

        Withdraw your license if this software package is used
        for any illegal or immoral purpose which, in the sole
        judgment of UMC Corp., may damage the reputation of UMC
        Corp.                                               *WPC

   If you transfer possession of any copy, modification, or merged
   portion of the program to another person, YOUR LICENSE IS
   AUTOMATICALLY TERMINATED.
   *WPC

                             - 1 -
```

# SEARCH FUNCTIONS

## Searching for Codes

**B**efore you begin manipulating text in the license, you decide that you do not want the document double spaced. Knowing that a code was inserted, you can **search** or look for that code among the reveal codes. But instead of manually searching for it, you can issue a command in WordPerfect to have the program search for you. A search can be conducted within or outside the reveal codes screen. In this case, let's search in reveal codes, so press Alt-F3. Look at the template next to the F2 key. Notice the word Search in black. Press the F2 key. The message " →Srch:" appears on your screen. Notice that the arrow is pointing forward, indicating a forward search. To search for a code, you must invoke it the way you invoked the original code. Recall that double spacing is invoked by pressing Shift-F8 and the number 4 for the spacing option. Thus, press Shift-F8 and 4. Figure 6-2 shows that your screen now displays the search command followed by the invoked code **[Spacing Set]**. To invoke the search press F2. Your tendency will be to press the Enter key. But if you do that a [HRt] code will be inserted, and you will need to backspace to delete the [HRt] code. As you press the F2 key, notice that the cursor moves to the right of the first code it finds (Figure 6-3 on the following page).

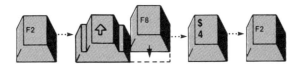

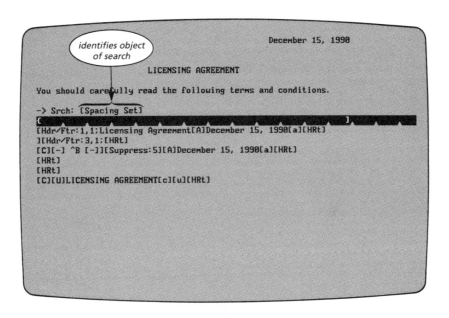

**FIGURE 6-2**

To delete the code press the Backspace key (step 1 of Figure 6-3). Because there may be more than one spacing code, you want to continue the search. Press the F2 key (step 2 of Figure 6-3), and notice that the words "Spacing Set" appear again to remind you that you are searching for spacing set codes. Press F2 again to continue the search. Because you have another spacing set code, the cursor will stop at that code. Press the Backspace key to delete the code.

To be sure there are no more spacing set codes, press the F2 key again. The words "Spacing Set" will appear again to remind you that you are searching for spacing set codes. Press the F2 key again to continue the search. When the prompt "* Not Found *" appears you are assured that all spacing codes have been deleted. Press the spacebar to exit the reveal codes screen.

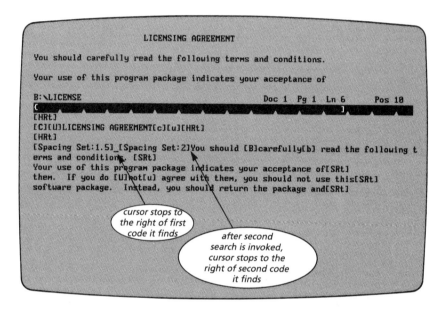

**FIGURE 6-3**

Step 1: Delete the code

Step 2: Continue to search for the code then backspace to delete

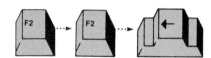

## Forward Search

Move the cursor to the top of the document by pressing Home, Home, Up Arrow.

In the second paragraph of the document you wish to emphasize the fact that the company assumes no responsibility. You can do this by searching for the word assumes and inserting the word absolutely, so the phrase will read: assumes absolutely no responsibility. To search forward for the word "assumes", press the F2 key. The last command to search for, spacing set codes, is still within brackets next to the search forward prompt. But you do not wish to use that command. Type the word assumes, because that is the object of your search (step 1 of Figure 6-4). The code "Spacing Set" is deleted and the word assumes appears next to the Srch: command. To begin the search, press the F2 key (step 2 of Figure 6-4). The cursor moves immediately to the right of the word. Press the spacebar and type the word absolutely.

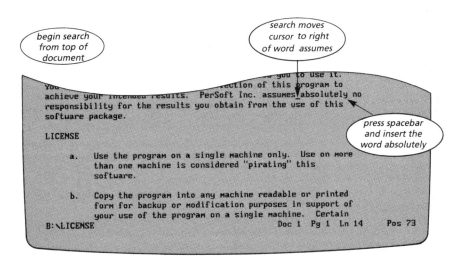

**FIGURE 6-4**

**Step 1: Specify the object of the search**

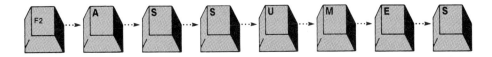

**Step 2: Begin the search**

## Reverse Search

Move the cursor to the bottom of the document by pressing Home, Home, Down Arrow. At the end of section c is the word License, which you want to change to License Agreement. You may search backward with the Reverse Search key, which is Shift-F2. Press Shift-F2, and you will see the message "←Srch:" at the bottom left corner of the screen. Notice that the arrow points in the reverse direction, indicating that the search will be going backward from the cursor position. Type the word license in all lowercase letters. This causes WordPerfect to search for a word in lowercase, uppercase, or a combination of the two. If, however, you type in uppercase or upper and lowercase letters, WordPerfect will look only for those exact characters. Press the F2 key to begin the search. The cursor stops at the first license it finds, even though it is in uppercase letters. This is not the one you wish to change. To continue the search backward through the document, press Shift-F2, then press F2 again. The cursor stops again at the word license but it is still not the one you desire. To continue, press Shift-F2, then the F2 key. The cursor stops at the desired spot. Press the spacebar and type the word Agreement. The period moves to the right as the word is inserted into the text (Figure 6-5).

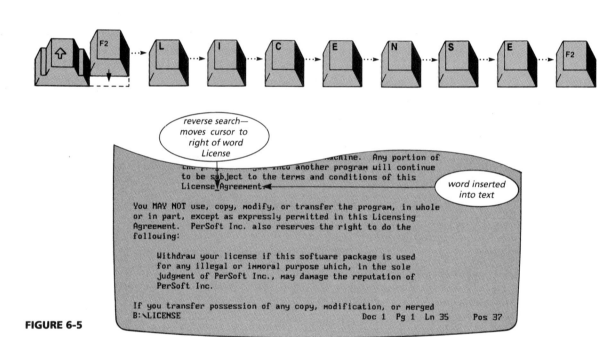

**FIGURE 6-5**

## Search and Replace

Move the cursor to the top of the document by pressing Home, Home, Up Arrow.

WordPerfect provides commands that allow you to search the document for specific characters and, after finding these characters, automatically replace them with other characters. This series of commands is called **Search and Replace**.

Recall that we are changing the document named License because the company for which the document was prepared, PerSoft Inc., has been acquired by a company called UMC Corp. Look at the template next to the F2 key. Notice the word Replace in blue. Press Alt-F2. A prompt message appears asking if you want to confirm each occurrence of the change. Type the letter Y for yes. You are prompted with "→Srch:". Type the name PerSoft Inc. (Figure 6-6). Press F2 to produce the prompt "Replace with:" (Figure 6-7). Type the name UMC Corp., then press the F2 key again. The cursor stops at the first occurrence of PerSoft Inc. and prompts "Confirm? (Y/N) N" (Figure 6-8); you may see the message "please wait" prior to seeing the prompt. Type the letter Y to change the name. The name will change and the cursor will move to the next occurrence of the name PerSoft Inc. and prompt again "Confirm? (Y/N) N". Type Y and the process will repeat itself. At each occurrence of the name, to confirm type Y until the prompt no longer appears at the lower left corner of the screen. That is your indication that there are no more occurrences of the name PerSoft Inc.

As you can see, you also could have typed N to not confirm each change. The WordPerfect software would have automatically made each change without stopping at each occurrence. You must be sure, however, that you do wish to change all occurrences of the searched-for word. For instance, you may have typed U.S. throughout a document and decided to change all occurrences of U.S. to United States. But you may have typed U.S. Grant for Ulysses S. Grant, in which case, had you not confirmed each change, his name would be changed to United States Grant. If you are *sure* all occurrences should be changed, there is no need to confirm.

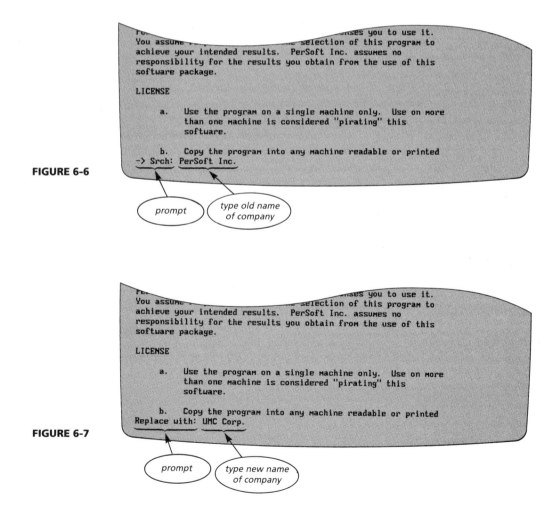

**FIGURE 6-6**

**FIGURE 6-7**

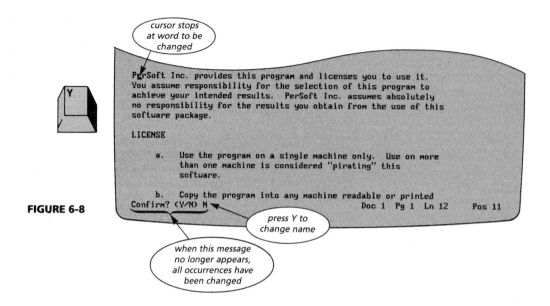

**FIGURE 6-8**

# MOVING TEXT WITHIN A DOCUMENT

## Cut and Paste a Paragraph

*T*o move the cursor to the top of the document, press Home, Home, Up Arrow.

There are times when you wish to move text from one place in a document to another place. This is called **cut and paste**. Recall that you want to reverse paragraphs one and two. To **move** an entire paragraph, first you must move the cursor to the beginning of the paragraph. Press the Down Arrow to move to line 6, position 10 so that the cursor is under the Y in You in the first paragraph. Look at the template next to the F4 key. Notice the word Move in red. Press Ctrl-F4 (step 1 of Figure 6-9). The menu shown in Figure 6-9 gives you three options to move text, then three options to retrieve text. Notice the options to move a sentence, paragraph, or page. Type the number 2 for paragraph (step 2 of Figure 6-9). Figure 6-10 on the opposite page shows how the entire paragraph following the cursor is highlighted, indicating the text to be cut and pasted elsewhere. The figure also shows that at the bottom of the screen, you are given the options to cut, copy, or delete the highlighted text. Press the number 1 to cut the text for placement elsewhere (step 1 of Figure 6-10). The text of the highlighted first paragraph is cut and the second paragraph moves up to be in the first paragraph's position. Although the text of the first paragraph has been deleted from the screen, it has not been deleted from memory. Imagine that the text has been placed on a clipboard, and will be held there until the cursor has been moved to the desired new position, at which time you will retrieve the text from the clipboard.

Press the Down Arrow ↓ to move the cursor to line 12, position 10 so that it is under the L in License. When the text is retrieved, this text will be moved down to make room for the incoming paragraph. Now, to retrieve the text that was cut, press Ctrl-F4. The Move menu appears again. This time use the retrieve option on the menu to retrieve the text on the clipboard. Because number 5 indicates text, press the number 5 (step 2 of Figure 6-10). The cut text is inserted in place and text at the cursor is moved down.

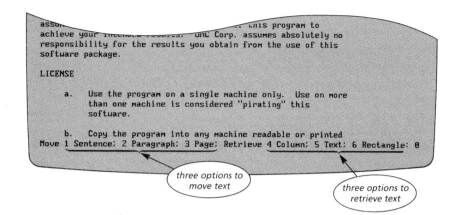

**FIGURE 6-9**

three options to move text

three options to retrieve text

Step 1: View the Move menu

Step 2: Identify text to be moved

**Step 1: Cut highlighted text**

**Step 2: Move cursor to line 12, position 10 and retrieve the cut text**

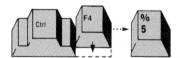

copy leaves text on screen and holds it off screen as if it were on a clipboard

**FIGURE 6-10**

cursor

LICENSING AGREEMENT

December 15, 1990

paragraph is highlighted

cut removes highlighted text and holds it off screen as if it were on a clipboard

## Cut and Paste a Block

Sometimes you may wish to move a specific block of text rather than a whole sentence, paragraph, or page. To illustrate this, you will reverse the two sentences of section a. Move the cursor down to line 20, position 63 so that it is under the U in the word Use (if you only inserted one space between the sentences, the cursor would be on position 62).

As you have learned, to turn the block on press Alt-F4 and notice the message "Block on" flashing in the lower left corner of the screen. To highlight the sentence you can either move the cursor to the right one character at a time or press the Down Arrow key two times ↓ ↓ to highlight the entire sentence, as shown in Figure 6-11. Using the block function you can be exact about the text you wish to cut and paste. To move the highlighted or blocked text press Ctrl-F4. The prompt asks you to cut or copy the block (Figure 6-12). Press number 1 to cut the block (step 1 of Figure 6-12). The text is deleted and placed on the "clipboard." Move the cursor to line 20, position 20 under the U in Use. To retrieve the text from the "clipboard," press Ctrl-F4, then the number 5 (step 2 of Figure 6-12). Figure 6-13 shows no spaces between the first and second sentence. If you have spaces between the first and second sentence, it is not necessary to add any more. However, if you have no spaces, move the cursor down one line and to the right, under the U in Use. Press the spacebar two times to insert the two needed spaces. Press the Down Arrow key two times ↓ ↓ to reformat the text.

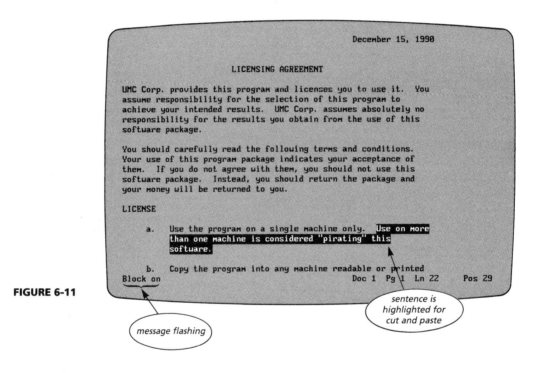

**FIGURE 6-11**

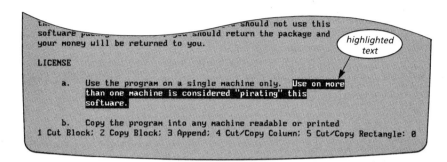

**FIGURE 6-12**

Step 1: View the Move menu; cut the block and move it to the clipboard

Step 2: Move cursor to line 20, position 20; retrieve and insert cut text

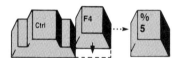

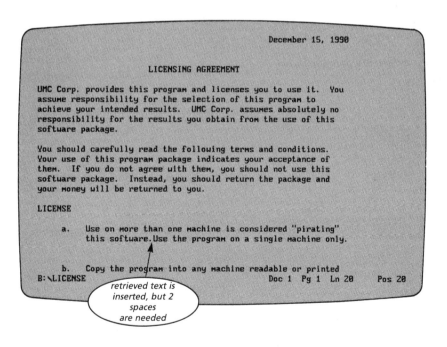

**FIGURE 6-13**

## SAVING THE DOCUMENT UNDER A NEW NAME

**N**ow that the document has been changed, you decide that you wish to leave the document as it is on the disk, saved as it was in Project 5. You also wish to save this new version of the document. Therefore, as you save this document, you must give it another name. Look at the template by the F10 key. Notice the word Save in black. Press the F10 key. At the prompt "Document to be Saved:" type License.3 and press the Enter ↵ key. The document is saved under the new name.

## PRINTING A DOCUMENT

**N**ow that you have saved your document, it is ready to be printed. At this point be sure that your printer has paper inserted and that the printer is on and ready to print.

    Press Shift-F7. You will see the Print menu at the bottom of the screen. Press number 1 for full text. At this point the printer will begin printing your document. The printed document generated is illustrated in Figure 6-14.

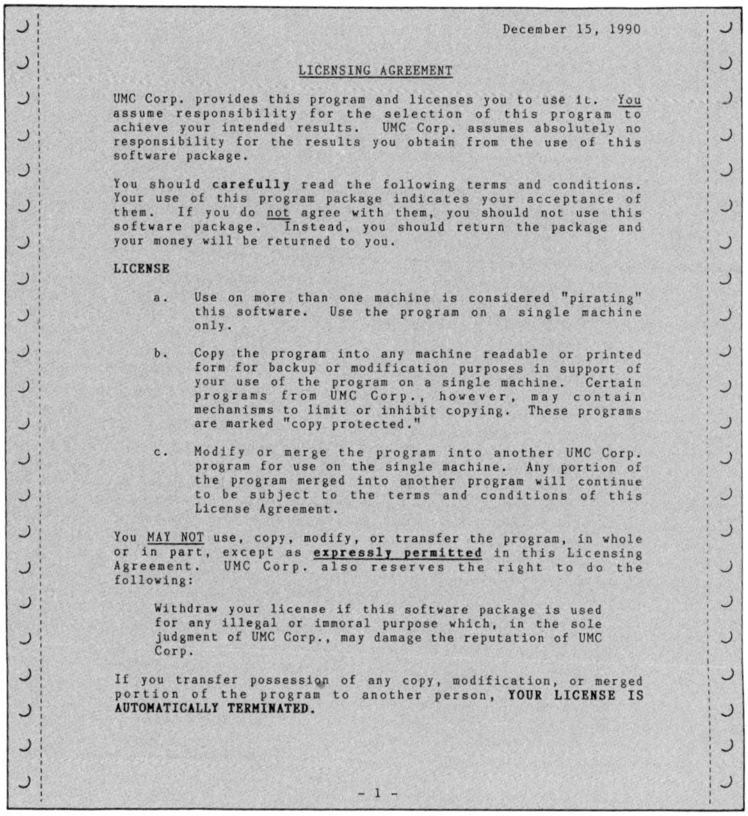

**FIGURE 6-14**

# EXITING A DOCUMENT

**Y**our document has been saved to disk and printed. It is now necessary to exit the document and clear the screen, but not exit the WordPerfect program.

Press the F7 key. At the prompt "Save Document? (Y/N) Y" type N because the document has already been saved. At the prompt "Exit WP? (Y/N) N" type N. The document is exited and a clear screen appears.

# THESAURUS/SPELLER USING THE README.WP FILE

**B**ecause of space restrictions on the disk containing the training version of WordPerfect, you are unable to use the thesaurus or speller on the documents you have created yourself. WordPerfect has, however, provided a sample sentence for the thesaurus and a sample paragraph for the speller. By practicing with these samples, you will learn the most valuable functions of the WordPerfect thesaurus and speller.

To use the sample thesaurus and speller it is necessary to retrieve the sample document WordPerfect has prepared. Press Shift-F10. At the prompt of "Document to be Retrieved:" type a:readme.wp and press Enter ↵. The screen shown in Figure 6-15 explains about the specially designed thesaurus and speller and gives you instructions on how to use them.

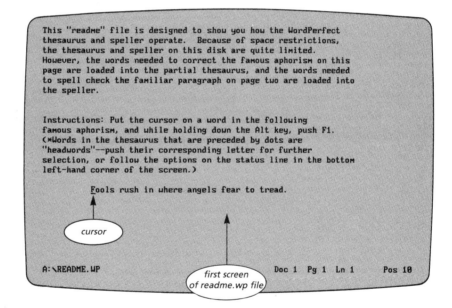

**FIGURE 6-15**

## Thesaurus

A thesaurus is a collection of words and their synonyms and antonyms. We'll use the WordPerfect **thesaurus** to choose different words for the famous saying shown. The words that you can use in this special version of the thesaurus are in boldface typing on your screen.

Move the cursor down to line 17, position 20 under the F in Fools. Look at the template next to the F1 key. Notice the word Thesaurus in blue. Press Alt-F1. Figure 6-16 shows the list of nouns (n), verbs (v), and antonyms (ant) that relate to the word Fools. A letter of the alphabet is next to each word in the first column, which will facilitate choosing a replacement for the word Fools. The words with dots are called **headwords**. If you wish to see other possible choices you can look up a word using one of the headwords. Press the number 3. The prompt "Word:" appears in the lower left corner of the screen. Type the word idiot and press Enter ↵.

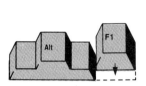

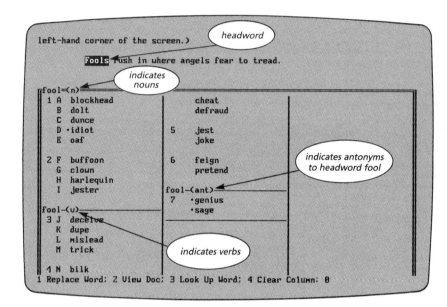

**FIGURE 6-16**

The screen will look like Figure 6-17. Notice that the second column shows the word idiot as the headword, giving synonyms and an antonym. The letter choices have moved from the first column to the second column. To look for more choices, press the number 3 again, then type the word simpleton and press Enter ↵.

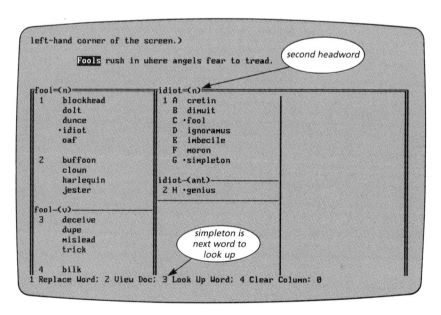

**FIGURE 6-17**

Figure 6-18 shows that the third column is now headed by the word simpleton and that the letters for choices have moved to the third column. Because you do not wish to use any of the words in columns two or three, press the Left Arrow ← to move the letter choices to the middle column. Instead of moving the cursor again to the left, notice that option number 4 is to clear a column. Type the number 4 and notice how the simpleton list is moved from column three to column two and that the letter choices are by the words in column two. Type the number 4 again and the letter choices are moved to column one (step 1 of Figure 6-19). Notice that the word clown is next to the letter G. To replace the word Fools with Clown press the number 1. The prompt "Press letter for word" appears on the screen. Press the letter G and notice that the word Fools is replaced by the word Clown. Type an s to make clown plural (step 2 of Figure 6-18). Because the word you are replacing, Fools, begins with a capital letter, the lowercase c in clown in the thesaurus will become uppercase when inserted into the document.

**Step 1: Clear columns**

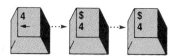

**Step 2: Replace the word Fools with the word Clowns and add the letter s**

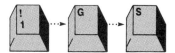

**FIGURE 6-18**

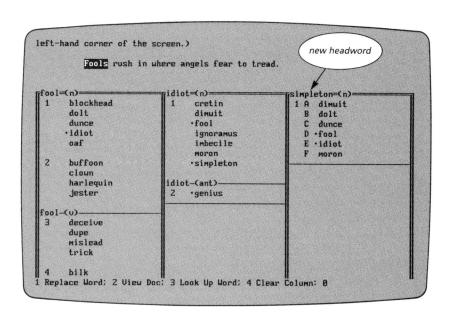

Continue practicing with the thesaurus. Press the Right Arrow → to move to the word angels. Press Alt-F1. Synonyms and an antonym appear on the screen (Figure 6-19).

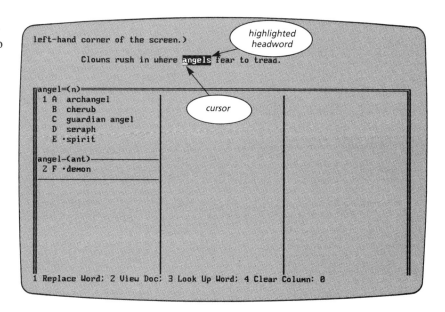

**FIGURE 6-19**

Press the number 1 to replace the word. Type the letter c and notice how angels changes to guardian angel. Type an s to make angel plural. Figure 6-20 shows how the corrected sentence appears.

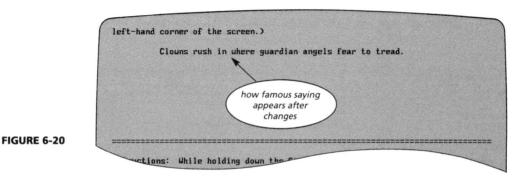

**FIGURE 6-20**

## Speller

Many word processing programs include a **speller**, a feature that checks the spelling of words you have typed. To demonstrate the WordPerfect speller press the PgDn key to move the cursor to page 2, line 1, position 10. Figure 6-21 shows the practice paragraph provided by the training version of WordPerfect. You can see that there are misspelled words in the paragraph.

Look at the template next to the F2 key. Notice the word Spell in red. Press Ctrl-F2. Figure 6-22 shows the menu at the bottom of the screen. Since you only want to use the speller on page 2, press the number 2 for Page.

Each word on the page will be matched against the words in the speller. If a word is not recognized it will be highlighted. Then a menu will appear from which you can make a choice of what you wish to do with that particular highlighted word.

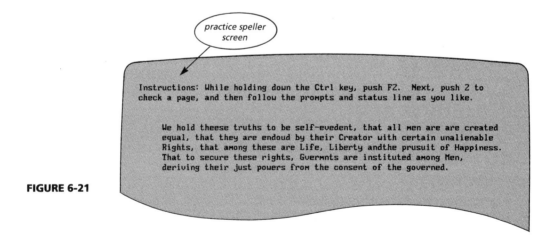

**FIGURE 6-21**

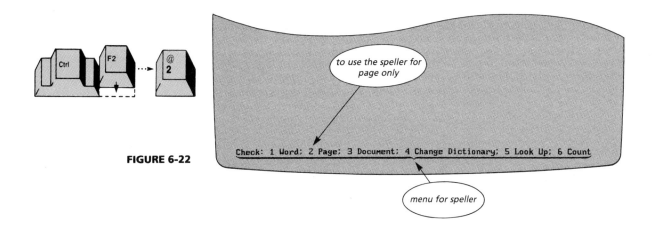

**FIGURE 6-22**

The first word to be highlighted is F2 (see Figure 6-23). Look at the menu. Words that mix letters and numbers are not recognized. If you were to press number 4, the cursor would move to the word F2 so that you could make a manual correction. Choosing number 3 on the menu allows you to ignore all words in your document that contain both numbers and letters. Because the word F2 is correct in this paragraph you simply wish to skip over it without changing it. Press number 1. The speller skips over F2 and highlights the next word it does not recognize.

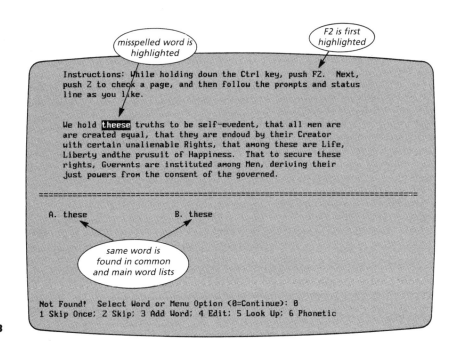

**FIGURE 6-23**

The next word to be highlighted is the misspelled word theese. When the WordPerfect speller does not recognize a word, it scans two lists: a *common* word list and a *main* word list. For speed's sake, WordPerfect first checks the common word list, then the main word list. Thus, it is possible that the correct spelling may be listed twice, as shown in Figure 6-23. In other words, you can choose either A or B and the misspelling will be corrected. Press the letter A, then notice on the screen how the misspelling is corrected and evedent, the next misspelled word, is highlighted. Two choices again appear. Press the letter A to correct the word.

Next you see that the same two words were typed together. The speller recognizes double words and gives you the menu shown in Figure 6-24. There are times when you purposely type two words together, such as in the sentence "I had had enough." In that case you would skip over the double words. In the case shown on the screen, the second are is not needed, so press the number 3. The second are is deleted and the next word to be highlighted as misspelled is endoud. Press the letter A to correct the word.

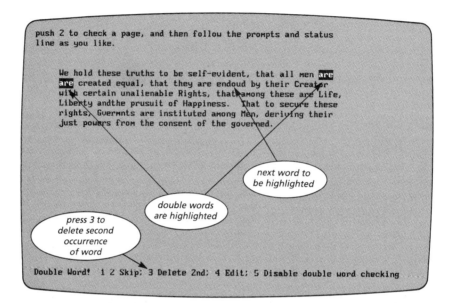

**FIGURE 6-24**

Next to be highlighted are the words andthe, which were typed with no space in between. The speller recognizes this as a misspelling but cannot find it in either the common or main word lists. Since you know what the problem is, you can correct the error. Press the number 4 and the cursor moves to the beginning of the misspelled word. Press the Right Arrow → three times to move the cursor under the t in the. Press the spacebar to insert a space between the words (Figure 6-25). As noted on the screen, press Enter ↵ when done. The speller recognizes the two words as correct and moves on to highlight the word prusuit. Press the letter A to correct the word.

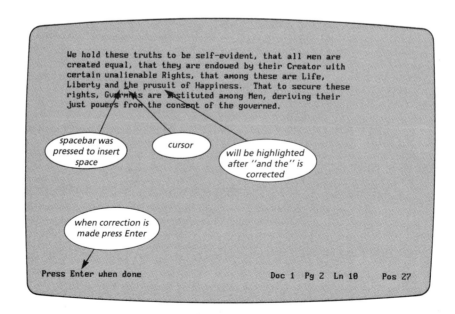

**FIGURE 6-25**

The next word that the speller does not recognize is Gvermnts (see Figure 6-26). Although the word governments is in the speller, there are not enough vowels in the misspelling for the speller to recognize it and give you an option on the lower screen. If you were not sure how to spell this word and were typing on a typewriter, you would probably go to the dictionary and look up the word. In WordPerfect you can also *look up* a misspelled word. Look at the menu at the bottom of the screen. Press the number 5 for Look Up. The prompt "Word pattern:" appears on the screen. Type the word gov*ts. Because you know the word begins with gov and ends with ts, but you may not be sure what is in between, you place the asterisk (*) between the beginning and the end. As you learned in *Introduction to DOS*, the asterisk is a global command. Using it in the look-up function causes WordPerfect to look in its dictionary for all words that begin with gov and end with ts, no matter how many letters are in between. If you were to type g*s it would look for all words that begin with g and end with s. You can see there would probably be many more words given as an option if you were to type g*s. If you are not sure how a word ends, you could also type gov* and the speller would look for all the words that begin with gov no matter what the ending. Using the question mark can also help, but the question mark can only stand in the place of one character. For instance, the word pattern could be gover?ments and the speller would find the n where the question mark is. Since the asterisk stands for one or more characters, it is better to use the asterisk.

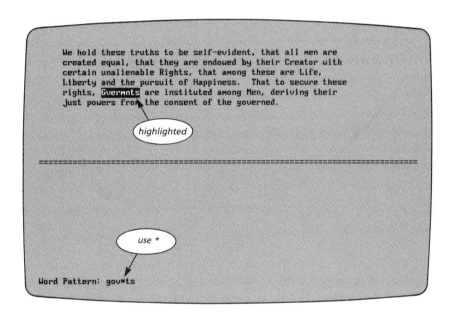

**FIGURE 6-26**

With gov*ts on the screen as the word pattern, press the Enter ↵ key. The word governments is shown under the letter A. Press the letter A and the word is spelled correctly in the document. Because the word you are replacing begins with a capital letter, the lowercase g in government in the speller will become uppercase when inserted into the document.

Since there are no more misspelled words, the speller reviews the menu shown in Figure 6-27 on the following page. WordPerfect automatically counts the number of words on the page. If you had checked the spelling for the entire document, the number of words in the entire document would have been counted.

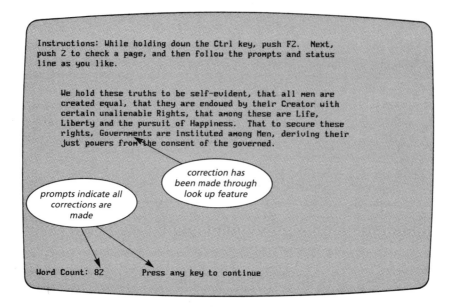

**FIGURE 6-27**

Press the spacebar to continue. The original menu appears again and shows that you have the option to look up a word directly from the speller without having it highlighted in a document. The option is number 5, the same option you use when checking the spelling of a word. To exit from the speller, press the spacebar. You are returned to your document.

It is important to remember that all corrections that you made to your document with the speller have been made only in the memory of the computer and have not been saved to disk. Immediately after checking the spelling of a document, save and replace the corrected version to the disk.

## Exiting the Thesaurus/Speller

If you wish to save the changes you made when using the thesaurus and the speller on your document you must exit by saving and replacing, as you have done in previous projects. If you wish to leave this thesaurus/speller document as it originally was so that you can practice again, you must exit without saving the changes to disk. To do this, press the F7 key. At the prompt "Save Document? (Y/N) Y" press the letter N for no. At the prompt "Exit WP? (Y/N) N" type Y for yes. You have exited the document without replacing the misspellings.

## PROJECT SUMMARY

In Project 6, you learned how to use the search function, the reverse search function, search and replace, and the move function. You used these functions to make changes to your document. In addition, you learned how to use the Word-Perfect thesaurus and speller to change words in your document and to correct misspelled words.

The following is a list of keystroke sequences we used in Project 6:

## SUMMARY OF KEYSTROKES—Project 6

| STEPS | KEY(S) PRESSED | STEPS | KEY(S) PRESSED | STEPS | KEY(S) PRESSED |
|---|---|---|---|---|---|
| 1 | [Be in WP at a blank screen] | 43 | Home Home ↑ | 81 | 3 |
| 2 | Shift-F10 | 44 | [↓ to line 6, position 10, under Y in You] | 82 | simpleton |
| 3 | License.2 | | | 83 | ↵ |
| 4 | ↵ | 45 | Ctrl-F4 | 84 | ↵ |
| 5 | Alt-F3 | 46 | 2 | 85 | 4 |
| 6 | F2 | 47 | 1 | 86 | 4 |
| 7 | Shift-F8 | 48 | [↓ to line 12, position 10 under L in License] | 87 | 1 |
| 8 | 4 | | | 88 | G |
| 9 | F2 | 49 | Ctrl-F4 | 89 | s |
| 10 | Backspace | 50 | 5 | 90 | [→ to the word angels] |
| 11 | F2 | 51 | [↓ then → to line 20, position 63 under U in Use] | 91 | Alt-F1 |
| 12 | F2 | | | 92 | 1 |
| 13 | Backspace | 52 | Alt-F4 | 93 | c |
| 14 | F2 | 53 | ↓ | 94 | s |
| 15 | F2 ["Not Found" should appear on screen] | 54 | ↓ | 95 | PgDn |
| | | 55 | Ctrl-F4 | 96 | Ctrl-F2 |
| 16 | Space | 56 | 1 | 97 | 2 |
| 17 | Home Home ↑ | 57 | [← to line 20, position 20 under U in Use] | 98 | 1 |
| 18 | F2 | | | 99 | A |
| 19 | assumes | 58 | Ctrl-F4 | 100 | A |
| 20 | F2 | 59 | 5 | 101 | 3 |
| 21 | Space | 60 | [↓ then → to U in Use] | 102 | A |
| 22 | absolutely | 61 | Space | 103 | 4 |
| 23 | Home Home ↓ | 62 | Space | 104 | → |
| 24 | Shift-F2 | 63 | ↓ | 105 | → |
| 25 | license | 64 | ↓ | 106 | → |
| 26 | F2 | 65 | F10 | 107 | Space |
| 27 | Shift-F2 | 66 | License.3 | 108 | ↵ |
| 28 | F2 | 67 | ↵ | 109 | A |
| 29 | Shift-F2 | 68 | Shift-F7 | 110 | 5 |
| 30 | F2 | 69 | 1 | 111 | gov*ts |
| 31 | Space | 70 | F7 | 112 | ↵ |
| 32 | Agreement | 71 | N | 113 | A |
| 33 | Home Home ↑ | 72 | N | 114 | Space |
| 34 | Alt-F2 | 73 | Shift-F10 | 115 | Space |
| 35 | Y | 74 | a:readme.wp | 116 | F7 |
| 36 | PerSoft Inc. | 75 | ↵ | 117 | N |
| 37 | F2 | 76 | [↓ then → to line 17, position 20 under F in Fools] | 118 | Y |
| 38 | UMC Corp. | | | 119 | [take WordPerfect disk out of Drive A and place DOS disk in Drive A] |
| 39 | F2 | 77 | Alt-F1 | | |
| 40 | Y | 78 | 3 | | |
| 41 | Y | 79 | idiot | | |
| 42 | [continue to type "Y" to change each occurrence of PerSoft Inc. to UMC Corp] | 80 | ↵ | 120 | ↵ |

The following list summarizes the material covered in Project 6:

1. The **search** function allows you to find a character, a code, or a string of text within a document.
2. **Search and replace**, also known as a global search and replace, allows you to look for every occurrence of a specified character, code, or string of text and either delete them or replace them with another specified code or text.
3. The **move** function allows you to highlight a specific block of text, then cut or copy the text, move it to another part of the document or to another document, and retrieve the cut or copied text.
4. The **thesaurus** allows you to point to a specific word, then invoke a search for possible replacement words. The thesaurus displays not only synonyms but also antonyms for the marked word. Use **headword** to look up other words in the thesaurus.
5. The **speller** provided in the full version of WordPerfect has a dictionary of more than 115,000 words with which it checks the spelling of the words in a document. You can add up to 20,000 words to the speller.


# STUDENT ASSIGNMENTS

## STUDENT ASSIGNMENT 1: True/False

**Instructions:**   Circle T if the statement is true and F if the statement if false.

T  F  1. When you invoke the search function, the cursor stops to the left of what you are searching for.
T  F  2. A reverse search is invoked by pressing Shift-F2, typing what is to be searched for, then pressing F2.
T  F  3. The search feature cannot search for codes embedded in the document.
T  F  4. When moving text, either cut or copy a block of text.
T  F  5. The move function is invoked through Ctrl-F4.
T  F  6. Alt-F1 will access the thesaurus.
T  F  7. The reveal codes function can be accessed through Alt-F4.
T  F  8. The speller will only spell words that are typed on the screen; it cannot look up words.


## STUDENT ASSIGNMENT 2: Multiple Choice

**Instructions:**   Circle the correct response.

1. The move function can
   a. move paragraphs
   b. move sentences
   c. move specific blocks of text
   d. all of the above
2. When invoking the search function and the desired code or words are defined, the user must
   a. press Enter
   b. press F2
   c. press Alt-F2
   d. press Shift-F2
3. When using the speller the user can
   a. look up a word by giving the word pattern
   b. skip over words whose spelling is not to be changed
   c. add words to the dictionary
   d. all of the above

## STUDENT ASSIGNMENT 3: Matching

**Instructions:**   Put the appropriate number next to the words in the second column.

| | | | | |
|---|---|---|---|---|
| 1. Ctrl-F2 | _____ Reverse Search | 5. Alt-F3 | _____ | Speller |
| 2. Ctrl-F4 | _____ Search | 6. F2 | _____ | Reveal codes |
| 3. Alt-F1 | _____ Speller, Look Up | 7. Shift-F2 | _____ | Thesaurus |
| 4. Ctrl-F2, 5 | _____ Move function | 8. Alt-F2 | _____ | Search and Replace |

## STUDENT ASSIGNMENT 4: Moving text

**Instructions:**   In the paragraph below, it is necessary to move the second sentence in the paragraph to be the first sentence. Describe in detail the steps to accomplish this.

> Students from many schools meet at a centralized classroom. The teacher has a credential in the field being taught plus at least 5 years of directly related work experience.

## STUDENT ASSIGNMENT 5: Using Search and Replace

**Instructions:**   Perform the following tasks.

1. Load DOS into main memory.
2. Load WordPerfect into main memory by inserting the WordPerfect diskette into drive A, putting a data disk into drive B, typing b: and pressing Enter. At the B> prompt, type a:wp and press the Enter key.

Problem 1:

1. Create the resume as shown at the right. The titles in the left column should be in boldface type. (Hint: Don't forget the Indent [F4] key, or the hanging indent function [F4, Shift-Tab]).
2. Save the document under the name Cook.
3. Print the document.

```
                           JEREMY L. COOK
                         2311 No. Hickorey Street
                           Anaheim, CA 33245
                            (714) 555-6712

EDUCATION        CA State University, Fullerton
                 Management Science Major, BS June 1984

                 Anaheim, CA High School
                 Major Area of Study - College Preparation

                 University of CA, Los Angeles
                 Graduate Business Courses

EMPLOYMENT       Farmers East, Inc., Garden Grove, CA
                 August 1988 - present
                     Chief Accountant
                         Designed complete computer accounting
                             system
                         Responsible for 42 employees within the
                             accounting department
                         Corporation has gross revenues in excess
                             of $150 million per annum
                         Entire accounting operation reports to
                             me

                 Peterson Manufacturing, Inc.
                 Fountain Valley, CA
                 June 1984 - August 1988
                     Senior Accountant
                         Responsible for all accounts payable for
                             $300 million company
                         Supervised 21 junior accountants
                         Received most valuable employee - 1987

OTHER SKILLS     Computer Programmer - COBOL, BASIC

PERSONAL DATA    Married, one child
                 Age: 25
                 Good health

REFERENCES       Available upon request
```

## Student Assignment 5 (continued)

Problem 2:
1. Beginning at the top of the document, search for all designations of CA and replace them with California. (Hint: Type Y to confirm).
2. Save the document as Cook.2.
3. Print the document.

```
                         JEREMY L. COOK
                       2311 No. Hickorey Street
                       Anaheim, California 33245
                            (714) 555-6712

   EDUCATION        California State University, Fullerton
                    Management Science Major, BS June 1984

                    Anaheim, California High School
                    Major Area of Study - College Preparation

                    University of California, Los Angeles
                    Graduate Business Courses

   EMPLOYMENT       Farmers East, Inc., Garden Grove, California
                    August 1988 - present
                         Chief Accountant
                              Designed complete computer accounting
                                 system
                              Responsible for 42 employees within the
                                 accounting department
                              Corporation has gross revenues in excess
                                 of $150 million per annum
                              Entire accounting operation reports to
                                 me

                    Peterson Manufacturing, Inc.
                    Fountain Valley, California
                    June 1984 - August 1988
                         Senior Accountant
                              Responsible for all accounts payable for
                                 $300 million company
                              Supervised 21 junior accountants
                              Received most valuable employee - 1987

   OTHER SKILLS     Computer Programmer - COBOL, BASIC

   PERSONAL DATA    Married, one child
                    Age: 25
                    Good health

   REFERENCES       Available upon request
```

## STUDENT ASSIGNMENT 6: Modifying a Document with the Move Function

**Instructions:**    Perform the following tasks:

1. Load DOS into main memory.
2. Load WordPerfect into main memory by inserting the WordPerfect diskette into drive A, putting a data disk into drive B, typing b: and pressing Enter. At the B> prompt, type a:wp and press the Enter key.

Problem 1:
1. Retrieve the document named Cook.2 created in Student Assignment 5.
2. Using the block function, move the whole section of type under EDUCATION to be second after the heading EMPLOYMENT as shown below.

```
                        JEREMY L. COOK
                      2311 No. Hickorey Street
                      Anaheim, California 33245
                          (714) 555-6712

EMPLOYMENT       Farmers East, Inc., Garden Grove, California
                 August 1988 - present
                     Chief Accountant
                         Designed complete computer accounting
                             system
                         Responsible for 42 employees within the
                             accounting department
                         Corporation has gross revenues in excess
                             of $150 million per annum
                         Entire accounting operation reports to
                             me

                 Peterson Manufacturing, Inc.
                 Fountain Valley, California
                 June 1984 - August 1988
                     Senior Accountant
                         Responsible for all accounts payable for
                             $300 million company
                         Supervised 21 junior accountants
                         Received most valuable employee - 1987

EDUCATION        California State University, Fullerton
                 Management Science Major, BS June 1984

                 Anaheim, California High School
                 Major Area of Study - College Preparation

                 University of California, Los Angeles
                 Graduate Business Courses

OTHER SKILLS     Computer Programmer - COBOL, BASIC

PERSONAL DATA    Married, one child
                 Age: 25
                 Good health

REFERENCES       Available upon request
```

Problem 2:  Save the document to disk as Cook.3.

Problem 3:  Print the revised document.

## STUDENT ASSIGNMENT 7: Using the Speller

**Instructions:**  Perform the following tasks:

1. Load DOS into main memory.
2. Load WordPerfect into main memory by inserting the WordPerfect diskette into drive A, putting a data disk into drive B, typing b: and pressing Enter. At the B > prompt, type a:wp and press the Enter key.

Problem 1:  Create the document exactly as written below, even the spelling errors.

Problem 2:  Save the document to disk as Speller.

Problem 3:  Print the document.

Problem 4:  Invoke the speller and correct any misspellings.

Problem 5:  Save the corrected document to disk as Speller.1.

Problem 6:  Print the revised document.

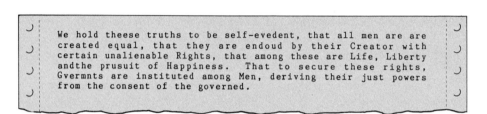

We hold theese truths to be self-evedent, that all men are are created equal, that they are endoud by their Creator with certain unalienable Rights, that among these are Life, Liberty andthe prusuit of Happiness.  That to secure these rights, Gvermnts are instituted among Men, deriving their just powers from the consent of the governed.

## STUDENT ASSIGNMENT 8: Using the Thesaurus

**Instructions:**  Perform the following tasks:

1. Load DOS into main memory.
2. Load WordPerfect into main memory by inserting the WordPerfect diskette into drive A, putting a data disk into drive B, typing b: and pressing Enter. At the B > prompt, type a:wp and press the Enter key.

Problem 1:  Type the sentence: Fools that rush to step on me.

Problem 2:  Position the cursor under the word Fools. Invoke the Thesaurus. Press the Print Screen option to print a hard copy of the screen as shown below.

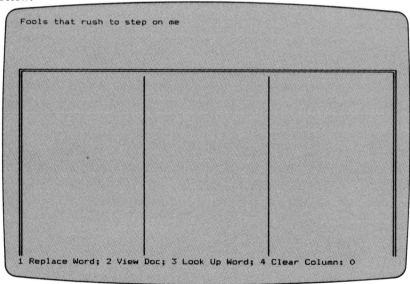

Fools that rush to step on me

1 Replace Word; 2 View Doc; 3 Look Up Word; 4 Clear Column: 0

Problem 3:  Repeat the process in problem 2 for the words rush and step, making a print screen hard copy.

# WordPerfect Index

(*) Asterisk character, WP 126, 167
(*)WPC
  printing documents and, WP 16
Alt key, **WP 4**
Antonyms, in thesaurus, WP 162–163
Arrow keys, WP 35–42
  ctrl key and, WP 38–39
  home key and, WP 36–38, 40–42

Backspace key, **WP 5**, 50, 76–77
Black template color code, **WP 6**
Block, **WP 55**
  cut and paste, WP 158–159
Block function (Alt-F4), **WP 85**
Blue template color code, **WP 6**
Boldface, **WP 70**
  codes for, WP 71
  color monitor and, WP 31
  text, WP 70–71, WP 84–87
  underline and, WP 82
Bytes, and file size, WP 126

Cancel key (F1), WP 10
Capital letters, WP 4
Caps Lock key, WP 68
Centering, WP 70, 116–117
Center Page Top to Bottom option,
  in page format menu, **WP 112**
Clearing
  tabs, WP 115
  workspace, WP 128
Codes
  boldface, WP 71
  centering text, WP 70
  conditional end of page, WP 133
  date format, WP 140
  deleting, WP 152
  effect on printing, WP 30
  flush right, WP 68
  footers, WP 137
  hard page break, WP 132
  hard return, WP 12
  indent, WP 79
  Left/Right Indent key (Shift-F4), WP 83
  placement of, WP 106
  reveal, **WP 12–13**
  searching for, WP 151–152
  soft page break, WP 129
  soft return, WP 32
  suppress, WP 137
  tab, WP 32
  underlining, WP 72
Color monitor, and boldfacing, WP 31
Commands, and enter key, WP 4
Common word list, in speller, WP 165
Conditional end of page, **WP 133**, 134
Correcting errors, and backspace key, WP 76–77
Ctrl key, **WP 4**, 38–39
Ctrl-Backspace, deleting words with, WP 54
Ctrl-Home, go to function and, WP 46–48
Current directory, and hard disk, WP 126
Cursor, **WP 8**, 35
Cursor movement, WP 17–19
  by word, WP 38
  end key and, WP 40
  esc key and, WP 48–49
  go to function and, WP 46–48
  margins and, WP 41
  status line and, WP 18

Cut and paste, **WP 156**–159
Date Format function, **WP 139**–140
Decimal tab setting, WP 116–117
Default setting, **WP 6**
  font, WP 102
  formatting, WP 104
  insert text mode, WP 75
  margins, WP 28
Delete key, use of, WP 51
Deleting
  with backspace key, WP 50
  block, WP 55–56
  with delete key, WP 51
  margin codes, WP 106
  tab settings, WP 117
  text, WP 50–56
  word, WP 54
Disk space, WP 126
Document
  creating, WP 10–11
  exiting, WP 90, 138, 161
  moving to end, WP 36–38
  moving to top, WP 36–38
  naming, WP 15
  printing, WP 15–16, 88–89, 113, 138, 160
  replacing, WP 113, 137–138
  retrieving, WP 99–100, 129
  switching, WP 18, 115
  typing, WP 29–30
DOS disk, inserting, WP 20
Down Arrow key, **WP 5**

Elite type, **WP 102**
End key, and cursor movement, WP 40
Enter key, **WP 4** (See also Return key)
Esc key, **WP 48**
Exiting
  document, WP 90, 138, 161
  reveal codes, WP 13, 32
  WordPerfect, WP 18–19

F10 key, saving documents, WP 32–34
F4 key, block marking, WP 55
Facing pages, WP 134
File(s)
  highlighting, WP 126
  listing, WP 128
  size, WP 126
File management, WP 125–129
  look function and, WP 128
Flush left tab setting, **WP 116**
Flush right, **WP 67**–68
  tab setting, WP 116–117
Font, default, WP 102
Footers, **WP 134**, WP 136–137
Formatting, **WP 104**
  line, WP 104–110
  page, WP 112–113, 129–134
  print, WP 110–111, 113–114
Forward search key (F2), WP 153
Function keys, WP 3, **WP 5**

Global character, WP 126, 167
Go to function, WP 46–48
Green template color code, **WP 6**

Hard disk
  current directory and, WP 126
  parent directory and, WP 126

Hard page break, **WP 131**, WP 132
Hard return, **WP 10**
Headers, **WP 134**–136, 137
  suppressing, WP 136
Headwords, **WP 162**
Help function (F3), **WP 9**
Home key
  arrow keys and, WP 36–38, 40–42
  moving to end of document, **WP 17**
Indent key (F4), **WP 78**
  codes, WP 79
  ending, WP 80
  margin settings and, WP 78–81
Input device, keyboard as, WP 3
Inserting
  blank line, WP 11
  changes in text, WP 100–102
  text, **WP 75**, WP 156
Insert key, as toggle, WP 77
Invoking macros, WP 141–142

Justification, and print formatting, WP 111

Keyboard, as input device, **WP 3**
Keystrokes, and macros, WP 141

Leader dots, WP 117–118
Left Arrow key, **WP 5**
Left margin, symbol for, WP 12
Left/Right Indent key (Shift-F4), **WP 83**
Line(s), keeping together, WP 133–134
Line format key (Shift-F8), **WP 104**
  changing margins with, WP 104–106
  line spacing and, WP 108–110
  tab settings and, WP 107–108
Line length, and margins, WP 103
Line spacing, WP 108–110
Lines per inch, setting, WP 114
List macros, WP 142
List files function, **WP 125**
  exiting menu, WP 127
  use of, WP 125–128
Ln (line), status line, WP 18
Loading WordPerfect, WP 7–9, 28
Look function, and file management, WP 128
Look-up function, in speller, WP 167
Lowercase letters, WP 4
  searching and, WP 154

Macro, **WP 140**-141
  invoking, WP 141–142
  keystrokes and, WP 141
  listing, WP 142
Main word list, in speller, WP 165
Margins
  changing with line formatting, WP 104–106
  cursor movement and, WP 41
  default, WP 28
  deleting codes, WP 106
  indent key and, WP 78–81
  Left/Right Indent key and, WP 83
  left and right, WP 102–103
  line length and, WP 103
  temporary, WP 78–81
  top and bottom, WP 103
Menus
  Date Format, WP 139–140
  Files, WP 128